OUTDOOR LIFE
DEER
HUNTER'S
YEARBOOK
1986

Outdoor Life Books, New York

Stackpole Books, Harrisburg, Pennsylvania

Cover photo credit: Tom Brakefield

Copyright © 1985 by Times Mirror Magazines, Inc.

Published by

Outdoor Life Books
Times Mirror Magazines, Inc.
380 Madison Avenue
New York, NY 10017

Distributed to the trade by

Stackpole Books
Cameron and Kelker Streets
P.O. Box 1831
Harrisburg, PA 17105

ISSN 0734-2918

ISBN 0-943822-60-2

Second Printing, 1986

Manufactured in the United States of America

Contents

Preface

"Why do you hunt?" One hunter seldom asks another that question. The answers seem so obvious to most sportsmen that they never think about them, much less try to put them into words. Most of us are reduced to such fumbling answers as: "My dad took me hunting when I was a boy," "I enjoy getting out into the woods during the fall," or "I like it." If you are forced to answer on an unsophisticated level, the last answer may be best, but the questioner then asks, *Why do you like it?*" Trying to answer that is like trying to respond to the Army psychologist's questions about your attitude toward young ladies.

In the leading article for this edition of *Deer Hunter's Yearbook*, "Why We Should Hunt," reprinted from OUTDOOR LIFE, Stephen J. Bodio, the well-known writer, hunter, and conservationist, answers searching questions about hunting. Some of his responses will surprise you and give you a lot to think about. His words may also greatly increase your pleasure when you go afield, gun in hand. If you are ever asked these seemingly simple questions by a non-hunter, Bodio's remarks may be very helpful. If the questioner is sincere in his or her curiosity, it pays to answer with clarity and equal sincerity.

The 1986 Yearbook includes many stories on deer and deer hunting reprinted from OUTDOOR LIFE magazine. Several other stories originated with the two annual publications, *Hunting Guns* and *Deer and Big Game,* both of which are edited by the OUTDOOR LIFE staff.

This Yearbook follows the tradition of past editions, but there is a new departure. Because OUT-DOOR LIFE does not have a regular archery column, it has not recently published a major article on selecting archery gear for deer hunting. To fill this need, Rich LaRocco, the Western field editor of the magazine, wrote the article titled, "The Best Bow and Arrow For You," for this volume. Another previ-ously unpublished article has been included. This is "Blacktails and How to Hunt Them," by Dwight Schuh. It was written especially for the Yearbook because it was felt that readers throughout the country are especially curious about this fine game animal, which is confined to a narrow range in the far West.

The two original articles are new. You'll also find a very old one, "The Man Behind the Gun," by the late Jack O'Connor, who was OUTDOOR LIFE's Shooting Editor for many years before Jim Carmichel joined the staff. Jack O'Connor wrote the article many years ago but, for some reason, the magazine never published it. It finally appeared in the February 1984 issue of the magazine and is reprinted here. The message in the story is just as important as it ever was, and reprinting it in the Yearbook gives younger readers a chance to sample Jack O'Connor's writing. We are sure they will be just as pleased as the generations of hunters who grew up reading Cactus Jack's fine stories.

The remaining articles consist of hunting narratives and "how-to" stories on deer hunting and firearms plus a few stories that were included for their humor and color. They are just plain fun to read, and we couldn't omit them.

The stories in this edition of the Yearbook provide a good sampling of the best material published recently in OUTDOOR LIFE, *Hunting Guns,* and *Deer and Big Game.* Because they were drawn from three different publications, the variety is remarkable. We hope you find a lot of useful information in these pages, and we also hope that you are entertained and amused.

George H. Haas
Senior Editor
OUTDOOR LIFE **Magazine**

Why We Should Hunt

By Stephen J. Bodio

Photograph by Ed Dutch

No apologies, for years now hunters have been telling us why they should be allowed to hunt. In this time—"in our time, which is a rather stupid time," as Ortega y Gasset said—it appears that we must justify everything that gives us pleasure. While the "apology-for-hunting" school of literature has given us some fine writing, notably John Mitchell's *The Hunt,* I am tired of justifying my existence. I'm here to tell you that good hunting is morally, ecologically and, above all, esthetically superior to any other outdoor activity.

Television has made this the century of the observer. People who have never been closer to any animal other than a park pigeon or a neurotic dog, drool over luciously photographed panoramas of the Serengeti while some Hollywood-coifed, addlepated narrator invites comparison of the bond between the mothers and the offspring of the wildebeest to that of the viewer. Once, after a seven-course game dinner, we settled down to watch one of these nature extravaganzas. I had provided the game, and my partner, an utterly civilized but open-minded restaurant critic, had taken charge of the menu. We called the production "Bodio kills it, Nadeau cooks it."

Our host's wife, Ginny, knew the source of the food but, despite this, she grew distressed as the cheetah eyeballed the cute antelope. As it burst from its stalk with its incredible supercharged acceleration, she averted her eyes. Oblivious to her, when the

Photograph by Dwight Schuh

cheetah "turned" the gazelle, we raised a sponta-neous cheer. As the dust settled and the narrative resumed Ginny was gone.

"She had to leave; she hates killing. You know." This was said tolerantly by her husband, but with the sort of amazement usually reserved for someone well loved but odd who, for instance, eats with her bare hands in a restaurant. "You're the only people we know who cheer the bad guys on the nature shows."

I do have some arguments with vegetarians on evolutionary, psychological, nutritional and, again, esthetic grounds, but what really drives me up the wall is the meat-eater observer who acquiesces in the killing that provides his fast-food hamburger or even his plastic chicken while all the time decrying the brutes who kill the animals, saying loudly "I just can't take the idea of killing."

If I am to eat meat, I cannot be passive—I want to know what it's all about. If this century has taught us anything, it should be that we cannot let others get their hands bloody for us.

Animal liberation? It seems to be self-evident that all animals are equal in some essential way to you and me—at least for those of us whose doorway into hunting was an all-encompassing fascination with animals. But does this make it immoral to eat them? If so, exactly what or who is immoral? The shark? The peregrine falcon? The Amazonian tribesman? The vanished and revered horse cultures of the American West? How about the literature urbanite or the vegetarian whose dog eats cow parts from cattle whose culture makes the West into an arid, monocultural desert?

Hunters do not set themselves off from the rest of creation as though there could be a glass wall be-tween them and the universe. They acknowledge the

inevitable and molecular pathways between the sun and their flesh, and also the peculiarly human evo-lutionary heritage that has made them into *Homo sapiens* rather than range-munching cows. It is no accident that there are more similarities between our social structure and that of wolves than ours and that of wildebeests or even monkeys. If we weren't supposed to eat meat, we *couldn't*. Try feeding ven-ison to a cow.

Cruelty is another issue. Most predators kill cleanly because they must. A prolonged struggle with their prey may well result in damage that will also rapidly kill the predator. Some very powerful or efficient predators—African hunting dogs and great horned owls come to mind—may begin eating at once, even before the prey's death, because they have nothing to fear. No one, however, has ever ac-cused even the worst of human hunters of that. For reasons of efficiency, esthetics, and because we have evolved a superior capacity for empathy and com-passion, we tend to kill cleanly or at least try to do so.

Beyond that, we should consider the quality of an animal's life, as well as that of its death. Any animal raised under modern factory farming conditions lives an almost unimaginably unnatural existence. It is confined in artificial light, fed chemicals, and de-beaked and deballed until it reaches an end no more nor less painful than that of its wild counterpart. The wild animal lives in freedom, as far as the coded pathways of its inherited behavior allows and, if it subsists on plants, it usually falls to a predator in the end, whether the predator is wolf, hawk, or hu-man. I don't know about you, but I know which I'd prefer. Even a threatened animal's terror-stricken flight, which so horrifies a numb TV spectator, is natural and accepted. That scene will happen many times during the animal's life. After the escape, the gazelle begins to graze, the pigeon to preen—with no recriminations—even as the leopard feeds and the falcon plucks. Maybe we should take our empathy one step further. Maybe our modern judgment of the hunter as a "bad guy" is a fear of death itself, now that dying is so remote from most of our lives.

Animal rights advocates, in pursuit of an impossible ideal of individual worth that could only occur to a person alienated from the system of life and death and eat and be eaten, may be dooming wildlife in the real world to man-made, unnaturally lingering deaths. Right now, they are fighting burro and wild horse removal on desert sheep range that can just barely support the native sheep and can easily be damaged to the extent that it supports nothing. They argue that non-native creatures have rights, too.

These people at least have some philosophical consistency. What of those who harass wildlife in order to "save" it? In New England, they have advocated making loud noises, blowing horns, and even exploding firecrackers in the woods during deer season, as well as hanging scarecrows and unpleasant-smelling objects in trees. In England, sonic devices have been placed in streams and rocks have been pitched into waters to frustrate anglers by driving away fish. Considering wildlife's need for territory and at least intermittent sanctuary, these severely misguided do-gooders probably kill more wildlife more unnaturally than any hunters.

All this, however, is argument, if not apology. Let us proceed to celebrate some of the good things about hunting, even if, in the process, we *really* manage to irk the antis, on the grounds that, as some 18th century wit put it, that which offends the Puritans is not so much the suffering of the animals as the pleasure of the sportsman.

My hunting, and that of any other decent hunter, is a positive good rather than something to be excused by the opposition's generosity. When I hunt, I drift through the woods with all senses sharpened, using my body as well as my eyes to fit myself into this most fascinating puzzle. When it works, it does so with an almost audible click.

Good hunting is a reward to your senses and your sensitivity. Classifications of the word hunting such as fishing, subsistence, sport, and trophy are artificial. Some so-called subsistence hunting today is mechanized slaughter by participants who drive snowmobiles, use high-powered modern rifles, and keep only the choicest cuts of meat. Some "trophy" hunters are conscientious naturalists who plan their stalk through a year of reading and scouting, use primitive weapons, and carefully eat or use every scrap of their quarry's body below the coveted horns. Though I might characterize myself as a sport, recreational, or ceremonial hunter because I neither desperately need the meat nor care very much about antlers, I both subsist largely on game for my meat ration in the fall and will keep and admire any durable relic of my kill.

In some science-fiction future, perhaps the only people left who eat meat or understand and talk to animals will be underground and illegal hunters—romantic poachers. In his wonderful fantasy novel *Beasts*, John Crowley envisioned a group of people, a sort of city-sized commune, who withdrew from all interference with the earth into a monolithic "arcology" called Candy's Mountain, surrounded by thousands of square miles of preserve.

" 'None shall ever pass through it forever and ever; they shall name it No Kingdom There, and its princes shall be nothing.' Withdraw . . . you have done enough damage to the earth and to yourselves. . ."

Such a message of withdrawal can have only one logical end—elimination of our species. Somehow that doesn't seem as healthy to me as immersing ourselves again in the wild. Vanishing from the earth is more like a kind of ultimate crime against man and nature, a denial second in enormity only to an atomic war where we would take many other species with us.

Unless you hold with philosopher/ornithologist Alexander Skutch that all predation is ultimately evil (and then what must you think of nature? Of, well, God?) then we are a part of the earth and to withdraw from it is wrong. What better way back to our evolutionary beginnings than at least an occasional sacramental hunt? Last year, writer Rick Bass provided the only good argument that I saw for opening the Alaska national parks to hunting, making them "park preserves." If people can hunt in the parks, then "there will be more people falling in love with Alaska. There will be more people protecting Alaska."

Hunting, done well, breeds involvement a lot better than looking at nature pictures does. My Audubon Society activities are more driven, my knowledge of threatened creatures and places is made more intimate by my hunting and fishing.

You know the expression "hands on?" My feeling for the prairie, my dislike of erosion and monocultural crops are intense because I have put my hands on a lesser prairie chicken, a strange, long-winged grouse with a Plains Indian headdress. I fear and hate acid rain because I have caught five-inch native brook trout with flanks like starry skies and insect-nourished coral flesh, relics of populations that invaded my native Massachusetts hills right after the glacier left, and I know that they are vulnerable. I oppose the unending condo-ization of my home town because I hunted ruffed grouse through those second-growth woodlands every year from my childhood until I left New England. I gave up one summer to live in a tent on the back of a mountain so I could attempt to stock peregrine falcons in a place where they had lived before DDT. If I had never seen a trained peregrine stoop out of the sun to knock a pheasant from the sky, would I have cared that much?

If you hunt, you know that you must preserve the wild; the wild becomes a part of you and you discover that you have always been a part of it. 🦌

PART 1

THE QUARRY

Can Science Produce A Race Of Super Bucks?

By Kathy Etling

Item: Dawn was just breaking when the hunter noticed movement behind a sprawling mesquite bush. He froze when, moments later, a gigantic whitetail buck stepped out in the open. He raised his gun and fired once. The buck stumbled and ran only 25 yards before collapsing in a heap. The hunter walked over to the trophy and checked for signs of life. When he found none he started to field-dress the animal, but first he used his knife to sever the buck's testicles from the body. Then he took a small container out of his daypack and placed the testicles inside. Packed in a chemical solution, they would survive the ride to a major southwestern university. Here, they would be quick-frozen for future use in experimental research dedicated to the development of a line of "super bucks."

Item: There were 20 does captured and bred to REX II last year. But only Doe No. 14 had produced a fantastic-looking yearling buck. The ranch foreman watched as a tranquilizer dart found its mark deep within Doe No. 14's flank. Several burly cowboys carried her now-limp body into a nearby Quonset hut where a veterinarian was waiting. Doe No. 14 had earlier been injected with a drug to make her superovulate, or produce a large quantity of eggs at once. Now, she had been stripped of these eggs— much like a spawning salmon in a hatchery. These

For the present, a whitetail that's big enough to make the record book can't be bought.

eggs would now be inseminated in a small glass dish in the laboratory. The semen was from REX II, the buck with the largest rack on the ranch. Within days, these fertilized eggs—now embryos—could be separated, with 90 percent accuracy, into buck and doe embryos. The doe embryos would be discarded and the buck embryos would be implanted in surrogate doe mothers. Six months from now, a crop of potential super bucks would fill the enclosure outside. And they would all be full brothers.

Item: The hunter walked to his garage and looked at the three whitetail racks hanging on the walls. As he stood there, a plan formed in his mind. Quickly, he got a ladder and pulled the racks off their hangers. He went inside and returned with a saw, some fiberglass, and a file. A feverish night of activity followed while he cut and fit the antlers together until he had a reasonable facsimile of a new world record. He sanded the composite rack down, stained it, and stepped back to admire his handiwork. The next morning, he called several local outdoor writers. A short while later, he was proudly showing them the

"new world record." The writers were impressed. Pads and pencils in hand, they interviewed the hunter and took pictures of him with the giant rack. The hunter finally had enough of a good joke and told the writers that they'd been fooled. After a few sheepish grins, they left.

All this may sound unbelievable but it really isn't. Persons in search of the new super buck have done, are now doing, or will be doing all of these things in the near future. The science of tomorrow is now here. Biogeneticists are not only working for man but also for man's quest for the super buck. One of the few questions left is not if man has the scientific knowledge to accomplish all this, but how long it will be before anyone with enough money can drive to an enclosure and, for a price, shoot a buck bigger than anything now gracing Boone and Crockett's *Records of North American Big Game.*

Item 1 is nearly a reality right now. A container such as the one described is being designed and should be ready soon. Item 2 is also feasible using methods currently practiced in cattle production.

Item 3 actually happened and shows how intense the interest is in trophy whitetail racks.

Quality whitetail hunting is a high-stakes game. Any game of chance has its high rollers—the heavy gamblers. These gamblers range from breed-them-by-the-book conservatives to reckless anything-goes adherents, and includes every type in between.

Most big buck research currently is being done in the South. Texas, for example, has universities that are involved in several different facets of research, corporations that provide funding for the research, and individuals—both ranchers and managers—who are interested in improving the quality of deer on their land. All are different segments of the hunting fraternity, and all are keenly interested in the phenomenon that is the super buck whitetail.

Much of this interest was generated from the recent discovery of a new world-record non-typical whitetail found dead near St. Louis. The print was barely dry on this story when yet another monster non-typical was unearthed. The second deer had been dead for 40 years but was only recently publicized. Stories of monster whitetails are running at

Genetic research is an important part of breeding the new class of super bucks, but herd management, too, must be considered.

Photograph by Gary Knepp

fever pitch. Even now, the hunt is on for a giant typical buck that, it is rumored, was killed illegally many years ago and now has supposedly been sold to a collector.

Even before all this publicity, super bucks had caught the hunting public's fancy. Any whitetail will stir the average hunter's imagination. When that whitetail possesses a superior set of headgear, he becomes something so special and so unique that hunters would give their eye-teeth for even a glimpse of the animal. A chance for a shot at such a deer is the stuff that dreams are made of: It's an opportunity for a place in the record book.

Of all the animals hunted, the whitetail is the most elusive, yet most attainable trophy for the ordinary person. The chance of shooting one belongs to everyone, regardless of wealth or stature. For the present, a whitetail that's big enough to make the book can't be bought—at least not on the hoof.

There's a lot being done in the quest for the super buck. While there's more going on than can be reported on in an article of this length, there are several types of research being done that are of interest to anyone who enjoys hunting the wily whitetail and who longs for a chance at an outstanding buck.

Texas A&M University in College Station, Texas, is the place most often mentioned when the super bucks are discussed. The university's research ranges from habitat management to the most daring studies being done at the present time. It is the latter research that makes the program so controversial. Numerous experts, each qualified to deal with his or her own specific field of study, are on the Texas team.

Dr. Dwayne Kraemer of Texas A&M has been instrumental in the design of the container mentioned at the beginning of this article. The final design hasn't been perfected, but it will probably use freezer cold packs containing dry ice or liquid nitrogen.

Researchers at the university have already started perfecting artificial insemination procedures. Super-ovulation techniques will probably be in use in less than a year. Surrogate mothers will be used so that scientists won't have to wait six years in order to compare six brother bucks. Geneological traits can be studied much quicker when surrogates are used.

Dr. Kraemer emphasized that, while super buck configuration interests many people right now, big antlers are not the only thing that researchers are concerned with at the university.

"Superior antlers are important," Kraemer said, "but we're also looking for deer that can best utilize their food or that are the most adaptable to their surroundings. It's highly improbable that an outstanding set of antlers can be developed with consistency without any consideration being given to other factors.

"For example, if someone was to breed a line of deer too intensively—in order to concentrate a su-perantler gene—the result would be a severely inbred animal. With inbreeding comes the chance that birth defects may result, including reproductive problems. What good would super antlers be if the ability to pass them on was impaired?

"People are going to get involved in super buck breeding whether or not they have guidelines to follow," he continued. "Right now, the management and the hunting of whitetail deer is a big industry in Texas. We're interested in supporting this with education—especially in the reproductive area. It's going to happen. We want to be sure that some thought accompanies any action taken. This will benefit hunting everywhere."

Texas A&M's research program is funded by a number of organizations, including Exxon, the American Deer Research Fund, which is affiliated with the American Trophy Hunters of San Antonio, and the Houston Safari Club. How fast the scientists can proceed with their research is entirely dependent on their resources.

Dr. Jack Inglis, a professor of wildlife management at Texas A&M, is also concerned with super buck development. He approaches it, though, from the standpoint of habitat.

"There's no good way to manipulate genetics," he said. "What if, after all this research has been done, the deer are back out on the range and a hunter shoots a scrawny-looking buck with an inferior rack because he thinks it's obviously poor stock. Maybe that was the super buck and, because of a severe drought, he wasn't up to his potential. That's what habitat management is all about. Make the most of what you've got. You can probably make it produce good quality animals with a little work."

Dr. James Kroll, a professor of forestry at Stephen F. Austin State University in Nacogdoches, Texas, explained why some ranches' big buck programs fail to produce outstanding trophies.

"You must understand the basics of population genetics for effective trophy management. Let's say you have 1,000 people and you measure all of their index fingers. The majority would have normal-length fingers while some would have long fingers and others would have short ones. If we wanted only people with the longest index fingers, we'd have to remove every person from the group with fingers shorter than a certain length. But what if we removed only those people with the longest and the shortest index fingers? That's right, the *average* would be favored. And that's what a lot of managers are doing down here with their trophy programs: shooting trophies (long fingers) and spikes (short fingers).

"A good trophy management program must be under the control of a single individual who makes the decision whether each buck lives or dies," Dr. Kroll continued. "Many ranches don't want one person to have that kind of authority and so their programs suffer."

Texas is especially vulnerable to private big-buck management programs because such a large amount of land is privately owned and can be effectively fenced to contain deer. Dr. Kroll explained more problems that can occur with such operations.

"It's sort of sad but, right now, some game farms are involved in 'hit-or-miss' super-buck programs. They either buy or corral a big buck and turn him loose with their does. And that's where it stops. No one researches the does' backgrounds, and a doe contributes as much or more than a buck to a deer's traits. While bucks contribute points and shape, we believe does contribute mass and spread. And no one knows what kind of stock a buck like this comes from. Maybe he won't pass on his antlers.

"These breeders overlook the traits that make a big whitetail so superior. Things such as cunning, daring, and sense of survival are ignored in the search for bigger racks.

"Currently, I'd guess that more than 50 ranches are involved in super-buck development programs," Dr. Kroll told me. "And interest is increasing all the time. The only thing holding many of them back is the high cost involved. Recently, one program released a bunch of 'bred' bucks and later discovered that 50 percent had died. That doubled the cost for every survivor."

Dr. Kroll posed a very thought-provoking question: "A long time ago, there lived a relative of our whitetail that is known today as the Irish elk. What made this deer so unique was his incredible antlers—up to 12 feet in spread and 90 pounds in weight—all on a five-pound skull. Why did they develop these outsize antlers? No one knows. But it's believed that they contributed to the eventual extinction of the Irish elk. Could we be moving in the same direction with our beloved whitetail? It's a question worth pondering.

"Some breeders are losing sight of why so many people hunt," he added. "Bred whitetails hold no meaning for most people and they hold no meaning for me. Someday, you may be able to walk into a place, pay the price, and walk out with a Boone and Crockett-caliber buck. But a wild trophy will always make my heart beat a little faster just by being the incredibly unique animal that he is—a chance combination of those qualities that make him so special coming together in nature to produce a trophy worthy of the name. No amount of dollars can buy what's made like that."

Dr. Harry Jacobson, who's involved in genetic research at Mississippi State University, is probably the pioneer of big buck research. Jacobson and his team were the first to extract semen from a dead buck, perfect a freezing technique that wouldn't render it useless, and then successfully inseminate a doe. He works with captive, known-line deer, looking for the reasons that they develop the types of antlers that they do.

"There are places where there's room for genetic improvement in the wild population," Jacobson said, "but they're probably few and far between. Many places have tried harvesting spikes in an attempt to upgrade their herd. But what if the spike gene was inherited from the mother? How would you go about eliminating those does carrying the spike-antler genetic code and not the ones with the heavy-rack code potential? Almost impossible. What you'd have to do is cull the does severely while you're eliminating spikes so that the remaining does would almost certainly have been fathered by a fork-antlered or better buck. But a program like this is time-consuming and it takes years before you can see results.

"I've known landowners who just couldn't wait to get their hands on one of those big Michigan bucks to release as breeding stock to upgrade their herds, but they don't consider the risks involved: First, natural selection chooses animals suited to their environment. Big body size plus dark color absorb sunlight and conserve heat for northern deer. Small body size and light coloration does just the opposite—it helps dissipate heat in desert surroundings. Selective resistance to local disease is also a factor. A manager could still lose if his imported super buck was a poor breeder. Some of my captive deer, the ones with the most outstanding antlers, are not the dominant animals. Other, inferior animals do the bulk of the breeding.

"Don't misunderstand—genetics are important," Jacobson continued, "but they should be the very

Hunting at a ranch that practices good herd management should not detract from going after a super buck in the wild.

last step in a management program. More important is maintaining proper herd densities, desirable age and sex structure, and improving habitat. While genetic improvements for livestock have been accomplished through artificial insemination and other programs, it's a completely different game with wildlife. Domestic animal breeders can control all facets of their programs—including the selective removal of individuals with undesirable traits. This isn't feasible in the wild.

"We've progressed to a point where a few people have a little knowledge about whitetail genetics," he added. "But a little knowledge can be a dangerous thing."

Two ranchers who obviously agree with Jacobson are the persons who run the H.B. Zachry Ranch in south Texas and the Y.O. Ranch, perhaps the most famous of all Texas spreads. They both use escape-proof fencing, but they also practice sound management principles for livestock and wildlife, and adhere to a strict harvest schedule—one that takes both antlered and antlerless deer. Both also enjoy excellent success as producers of quality whitetail deer.

As Al Brothers, manager of the H.B. Zachry Ranch said of those managers who are looking for instant solutions, "It's kind of like a cattle breeder who buys an expensive bull that's supposed to produce calves with more weight at weaning time—but then gives no thought to what that calf is going to eat. Some whitetail breeders are skipping the basics of good nutrition and trying to get right to the end result. It just can't be done."

The Boone and Crockett Club is watching all of these happenings with more than a casual interest.

Wm. Harold Nesbitt, administrative director of the club, said, "I think research is far enough along to make genetically engineered super bucks possible sometime soon—but I'll cross that bridge when I come to it."

Boone and Crockett has already tried to eliminate those deer not "naturally" bred by revising the Fair Chase Statement. The definition of "unfair chase" has been expanded to include "hunting game confined by artificial barriers, including escapeproof fencing, or hunting game transplanted solely for the purpose of commercial shooting."

What keeps hunters honest? Besides the fact that no game farm managers are at the point where they are currently breeding Boone and Crockett-caliber bucks, not much. A notarized statement signed by the hunter and attesting to the fair chase must be submitted with any contending entry to the record book. Other than that, there's very little that can be done to authenticate such entries. It's up to hunters not to lose sight of the wondrous occurrence of a *wild* super buck. We should remember that, although hunting at a ranch that practices good game management is undoubtedly a great experience, it should not detract from going after the result of random mating between a buck and a doe: A super deer that could live in your woodlot or mine.

Deer Talk

By John Weiss

Illustrations by Leon Parsons

The bottom had just about dropped out of my deer hunting. After diligently scouting an area in southeastern Ohio where there was plenty of fresh sign and after patiently sitting on stand for five days, I had seen exactly zip. It was the final day of the season and the last minutes of daylight were rapidly fading when a big doe came loping in my direction and my remaining spark of hope suddenly turned into a glowing ember. Very slowly, I raised my slug-loaded shotgun and began settling the crosshairs on the deer's lung region. There would be no antlers, I thought, but I'd get my winter's supply of venison.

Then I noticed that the doe was holding her tail off to one side at a sharp angle. I knew what that meant and took my finger off the trigger. The doe went on and vanished in a latticework of brush and honeysuckle.

My insight paid off. Several minutes later, a handsome buck came down the very same trail. I raised my gun a second time and, in addition to collecting my deer meat, received a fine eight-point rack as a bonus.

Even though I had done my scouting well and had spent close to 50 hours sitting in a tree. I got that buck only because I could interpret whitetail body language. Otherwise, I'd have settled for the doe without remotely suspecting that a buck was following her.

If you learn to interpret the body language of whitetails and the sounds they make, you'll be a better hunter. In this particular case, the doe was holding her tail cocked off to one side in the universal signal female deer use to tell bucks that they're in estrus and receptive to being bred. If you ever see a doe exhibiting this type of body language, freeze! Within the next several minutes, you'll almost surely get a shot at an amorous buck so preoccupied by a doe that he'll have no idea you're there.

Bucks communicate with their tails, too. In prime habitat, several bucks may have overlapping home ranges. They share the turf. The largest, dominant

buck commonly saunters around with his head held high and his tail slightly lifted and extended straight back. This is a threatening posture which proclaims to lesser bucks that he's mucho hombre and that they had better not mess with him. Subordinate bucks with lower rankings in the pecking order acknowledge the status of the superior deer by walking timidly in a stiff-legged gait with their tails tucked between their legs.

The value of knowing this comes into play when a hunter is patiently watching a major deer runway. If a six-pointer comes along with his tail tightly clamped against his hindquarters, an enterprising hunter might elect to let the deer go about his business. Although the six-pointer may be quite acceptable, his tail is telling all the world that he's quite low on the totem pole and that there's a much larger buck on the prowl nearby.

At the other end of a whitetail's anatomy, head-holding mannerisms can be equally revealing. A whitetail employs head-bobbing when it senses

danger and wants to drum up some further activity to sort out its suspicions. The deer begins to lower its head toward the ground as if to feed but then quickly jerks its head back up. This sudden, unexpected movement can cause a predator or hunter to flinch and reveal his presence. If you fall for this, you'll probably be left, at best, with a difficult shot at a departing animal.

If, on the other hand, the deer lowers its head almost to the ground and begins to nibble the greenery, you can go ahead and slowly raise your rifle. The deer is mistakenly sure that all is right with the world.

The head-bob is a body movement during which a deer uses its eyes to detect danger. Other head movements are geared to the use of other senses. For example, when a whitetail holds its head high and tilted back and the upper lip is curled back so that the gums show, the animal is smelling something and would like to find the source of the scent. Biologists refer to this as the "Flehman posture." It

is named after the scientist who first interpreted the behavior. The Flehman posture is most commonly displayed when a rutting buck catches a whiff of a doe in heat. However, does and bucks also assume the Flehman posture as a favorable reaction to many other odors. These include any number of commercial deer scents used by hunters.

Conversely, when a deer lowers its head to about knee-level and its tongue protrudes out of the side of its mouth, the animal has smelled something that has triggered alarm. Most often, human scent elicits this universal fear response but it can also be triggered by a commercial deer scent that is not appropriate. This could be a rutting scent used during the non-mating season or an apple scent used in country where there are no apple trees.

Insightful hunters can use this knowledge to fine tune the placement of stands and to determine which scents are best for the particular region or the time of year. When whitetail body language tells you that deer smell something that is alarming, note the wind

direction and relocate your stand or blind if you suspect that the animals are catching your body odor. It may also be your chosen deer scent that is causing the animals to panic, and you should experiment with other potions.

When a deer is alerted by a sound, it cups both ears and points them in the direction from which the sound came, hoping for follow-up sounds that will tell it what made the initial noise. Many times I've seen deer do this, and then turn and bolt for no apparent reason. Five or 10 minutes later, some other hunter usually comes poking along.

Just as often, deer swivel their ears in different directions. They can point one ear forward and the other directly to the rear. This is nature's way of allowing them to monitor their bailiwicks simultaneously in different directions. When a hunter observes this kind of body language, he should know that there's something else making noises that interest the deer. That something may be another hunter or several hunters participating in a drive.

In other instances, particularly if the deer is a doe, watching the animal's ear movements can help to put antlers on the wall. If a doe has one ear cupped forward and the other pointed backward as she minces along, she's checking for anything that might be up ahead along her intended route or behind on her backtrail. Early in the hunting season, she's probably keeping track of twin fawns following somewhat behind but, during the months of November and December, a rutting buck is probably following her. Don't alert the doe. Let her pass unaware of your presence and rivet your attention on her backtrail.

If a deer suddenly lays its ears back, the jig is up. You've blown your cover and the deer knows you're there. The insides of a whitetail's ears are very sensitive and the animals fold them back just before fleeing so they won't be stung when they bound through brush. When you see this behavior, it's often wise to take the best available shot because the deer will be gone in seconds.

This body language provides the hunter with vital information that can tilt the odds in his favor. Whitetails are gregarious and maintain a community awareness. They use body language consciously and unconsciously to keep tabs on each other and on other creatures. An astute onlooker can determine a deer's state of mind and what the animal will usually do next by interpreting its body language.

Most hunters are well aware that spooked deer usually run with their tails held high and waving from side to side. Actually, this behavior is more characteristic of does than of bucks. Because the brown coloration of deer blends well with their surroundings, it would be easy for a mature doe in flight to quickly lose her offspring, making them vulnerable to predators. The doe's waving white flag is like a neon sign to young fawns. It guides the fawns when they follow the doe through dense and dark cover as she quickly dodges left or right or bounds over obstacles. This sometimes has disastrous results, however, and explains why fences, especially those made of barbed wire, are hazardous to deer. Every year, many fawns and yearlings are entangled in wire fences and die a slow and gruesome death. The mother jumps the fence and, seeing the jump signal of her tail, the young ones follow suit. But since they are usually trailing several yards behind the mother, they often jump a bit prematurely. Instead of clearing the fence, which they are easily capable of doing, they come down on top of it so that their forelegs or hind legs are caught between the strands.

Since bucks do not take any responsibility for rearing their offspring, they do not instinctively "flag" when running. When they do raise and wave their tails, it is merely a happenstance. There's valuable insight here for hunters. When several deer are routed from their beds and are bounding away, it's often quite difficult for a hunter to pick out a buck. Try to focus your attention on the animal that has *not* lofted a waving white flag and then look for antlers. In many cases, your sights will settle on the only buck in the group.

When deer are not fleeing but are going about their everyday business, the ways in which they hold their tails can tell you many other things. For instance, hunters on stand often conclude that they have been spotted when a deer stares at them. Thereupon, the hunter begins raising his rifle and the motion does indeed reveal the hunter's presence, causing the deer to bound away. If the hunter had remained motionless and had watched the deer's tail, he might have filled his tag. Scientific studies have shown that deer are quite adept at spotting the slightest movement. Yet, if a hunter remains as still as a statue, a deer usually cannot distinguish him from a stump or a tree trunk.

On countless occasions, deer have looked straight at me from as close as 20 yards, craning their heads from side to side to change perspective. Yet they did not really see me. Provided there is no revealing scent or sound to arouse other senses, the deer eventually decide that whatever I am, I pose no threat, and they very shortly return to unalarmed behavior. Moments later, when the head is turned away or their view of me is blocked by screening cover, I'm able to raise my rifle or bow.

Pulling this off depends on how the deer is holding its tail. If the tail remains down and, perhaps, occasionally swishes from side to side, you can be confident that the deer is not suspicious of danger and doesn't know you for what you are. It's smart to play the waiting game for however long it takes. On the other hand, if the deer raises its tail so that it is horizontal and pointing straight to the rear, you might as well take the best shot you can make. The animal is spooked and will almost always make a quick exit. Yet you must temper such interpretations with good judgment and react according to the circumstances. I've often seen deer coming toward me, holding their tails straight back. The deer were actually moving away from the other hunters or fleeing from them. The animals did not know that I was

there. Remember, too, that bucks commonly extend their tails straight back to intimidate subordinate bucks.

Whitetails also use a wide repertoire of vocal noises and hunters should learn to interpret these, as well. Fawns commonly make mewing sounds when they are temporarily separated from their mothers. If you hear them, a doe is almost always nearby. Few people would knowingly shoot a doe with fawns, but that's not the point. If you know she is there, you'll want to make every effort not to cough, reposition your feet, or make any other sound or movement. To do so would alert the doe and would probably cause her to flee in panic, thus alarming any bucks in the area.

The most common vocalization made by whitetails is a deep, raspy snort created when the animal suddenly exhales a large volume of air. It's a universal fear response, most often elicited when the deer smells something that alarms it. These snorts can be triggered by visual and auditory cues, as well.

Of course, if a deer has pegged your location and snorts as it bounds away, there's not much hope of shooting the animal that day. But if you're sitting on stand or still-hunting, be alert for deer snorts coming from some distance. Likely as not, the deer is hastily retreating from another hunter. By listening to the intermittent snorts the animal makes as it moves, you can often get a "fix" on the deer's route. This allows you to get your gun up and pointed in the right direction.

Several years ago, I used deer snorts to tag one of the biggest bucks I've ever taken. I was hunting from a tree stand in the Sumter National Forest in South Carolina. I heard a deer snort several hundred yards to my left. Because the deer snorted every few seconds, I could tell where it was going. The distance was so great and the cover so thick that it was unlikely I'd spot the animal from the stand.

On nothing more than a gamble. I quickly abandoned my stand and jogged about 300 yards to my right toward a 10-acre clearcut. I had scarcely positioned myself behind a gum tree when the buck stepped out of the dark forest and tried to cross the opening. His impressive headgear now hangs on my office wall.

There is yet another kind of deer talk. It's a low, guttural, grunting noise and it's made when bucks in rut are following the scent trails of does in estrus. The sound is quite reminiscent of the euphoric noises a hog makes when it is rooting around in a full feeding trough. If you hear this sound while sitting on stand, don't even blink! Momentarily, you'll probably spot a buck zigzagging along very rapidly with his nose tight to the ground like a bird dog working a scent. He's trying to catch up with a ready doe. The buck's mind is fully occupied and the shot is usually an easy one.

We know that a human being's body language and tone of voice often speak more clearly than mere words. Much the same applies to whitetails, but you must be able to interpret.

Where America's Super Deer Are

By Erwin A. Bauer

Exactly 35 years ago, my old friend Steve Reid shot a 10-point whitetail buck of truly bragging size in Ashtabula County, Ohio. Steve had the head mounted and hung it in his living room, where many of his friends admired it. On a blustery, snowy morning two years after he shot that buck, Steve got another 10-pointer that had the same shape and dimensions. He had that head mounted, too, and placed it over the fireplace beside the first one. The resemblance between the two was so uncanny, so obvious to any deer hunter, that more than one visitor thought he had double vision—or one bourbon and branch water too many.

"And would you believe," Steve would invariably ask, "that I shot the second buck in the same beech woods, less than 400 yards from where I got the first?"

On the basis of those splendid twin trophies, my late hunting buddy began to develop the Reid Theory about whitetail deer. He was convinced that the biggest bucks live in only a few isolated places. When I last saw him, I believed his duplicate deer were only a remarkable coincidence. But now, years later, I know—or think I know—better. I also have a theory that's very similar to Steve Reid's for finding and collecting a super whitetail deer.

My formula is as simple as any can be. Go back, I mean *right* back to *exactly* the same spot where a trophy was shot before, and hunt there—the same area, the very same woods, the same swamp, the same edge of a grainfield, or whatever. If possible, concentrate all your hunting in that immediate environment. You can't go wrong.

I firmly believe that the same set of circumstances that yielded one big buck will produce another—maybe more. Let me give an example or two.

For several years running, I spent most of the long hunting seasons in south Texas on a ranch in top whitetail country. Some of this time was devoted to hunting, because that ranch contained many good deer. But once the hunting season was finished, I spent most of my time crouched behind a camera. One elevated blind soon became my favorite location. The site, on a low ridge, was picturesque. It overlooked a *sendero*—a wide, cleared swath through mesquite brush—that led toward an ancient, rusting windmill and a water tank. More important, male deer just seemed to gravitate to the site.

It is important to mention another fact here. The first, second, and fourth-largest bucks taken on this 12,000-acre ranch during the past 25 years had been shot from the same blind from which I took my photographs.

At daybreak one slate-colored morning, I had barely settled into a swivel stool to set up a tripod when a deer emerged from the thicket just west of the sendero, presenting a fairly easy rifle shot. Even in the dim light, I could see that its rack was massive. Right away, my pulse began to pound. It wasn't nearly light enough yet to take any photographs, and I knew in my heart that the deer would retreat into dark cover before sunup. As I figured, the buck van-

Photograph by Edwin A. Bauer

My theory for collecting super bucks can be applied to monster muleys, as well.

Photograph by Jeanne Brakefield

I firmly believe the same set of circumstances that yielded one big buck will produce another—maybe more.

ished after only a few minutes of browsing in the open.

I guess my attention wandered after that disappointment. Next thing I knew, the buck emerged from the opposite side of the sendero to browse. Somehow I'd missed seeing it cross over. The old pulse was suddenly pounding again when I realized that I was looking at not one, but two almost identical whitetails. Each carried antlers of the sort that any hunter would be lucky to glimpse just once in a lifetime of hunting.

During the next few mornings, those two—plus a third deer almost as handsome—appeared near my blind and ventured closer to me. I was getting some good photos. Late one sunny afternoon, one of the bucks came within 40 or 50 feet. It would be difficult to believe my own experience without the photographic evidence. One of the bucks was the largest I have ever seen alive and on the hoof.

Now let me summarize. Here was one spot where three of the four largest deer on 20 square miles had been taken. The odds against this are almost astronomical. In addition, in the same area I had pho-

tographed two bucks that almost certainly would qualify for the Boone and Crockett Club record book. Obviously, this is more than a coincidence.

So I submit that the combination of terrain, excellent habitat, high-quality and nutritious browse, plus superior genes, has been producing bigger, healthier whitetails in that one spot than in the surrounding areas. In addition, light hunting pressure allowed the males to reach their maximum size— and their peak antler growth—before they were shot.

No matter whether it is Texas, the Adirondacks, Georgia, or Minnesota, some areas simply produce bigger whitetail bucks year after year. Likewise, some smaller, more restricted spots within these general areas provide the finest trophies of all. The best advice for a serious trophy hunter to follow is to focus on one place, on one specific 100-acre area, say, where a top trophy has been taken before, preferably within the past two seasons. The same holds true for blacktails and muleys. Hunt where the bloodlines are good.

In many states, particularly in the densely populated East and Midwest, the annual road kill of deer is unfortunately very high. Deer mortality on highways may even come close to matching the legal deer harvest by hunters. Wherever it is carefully tabulated, the road kill can be an accurate index of deer abundance in any locality; the higher the road-kill toll, the higher the whitetail population. When working for the Ohio Division of Wildlife years ago, I learned something else from deer deaths along the highways.

North of Delaware, Ohio, a busy highway bisected farmlands not considered good deer country. Road kills occurred only infrequently, indicating few deer. Along one particular short stretch of that highway, however, at least one unusually large buck was struck by a vehicle late every autumn during the rut. In three years, three bucks that would have made splendid trophies were killed on that 150-yard stretch of road as it crossed a stream bordered by a woodland. One of these bucks, retrieved by the game warden, had antlers huge enough to be photographed and reproduced in outdoor columns throughout the state.

That deer would not have scored as high as the 16-point non-typical buck taken by Wyatt Brown a year later. When he dragged his deer out of the field to the nearest highway access point, he emerged beside a yellow "Deer Crossing" sign erected on the site of the earlier road kills. It couldn't have been mere coincidence. Unfortunately, no deer of any kind are being hunted in that vicinity today. A subdivision of homes and a small shopping center stand where the super bucks were once produced.

Most big buck spots are not guaranteed to survive very long anywhere. Habitats naturally change or are changed by man. Swamps and wetlands are too likely to be drained. Some dense thickets with much deer browse eventually grow up into woodlots where favorite deer foods become scarce. During recent decades, whitetails have been adapting to life

Photograph by Tom Brakefield

Timing is very important for a trophy hunter. Look for super deer where one turned up last fall or the year before.

along the edges of agriculture and, in St. Louis County, Missouri, in 1981, the largest non-typical whitetail rack ever measured was discovered on such land. But farming patterns also constantly change. What was a trophy buck locale can be eliminated overnight, while a new one might be created nearby as old grainfields are left uncultivated or as they revert to brush.

So timing is very important for a trophy hunter. Look for super deer where one turned up last fall or the year before. The fact that a record head was taken in a certain location five or 10 years ago is not quite as significant, although it is never a bad sign.

Areas with high deer populations, generally speaking, are not the best ones in which to find super bucks. For one thing, the abundance invariably attracts hunters, maybe too many hunters, and open seasons are established wisely by state game agencies to assure a large harvest. In addition, the heavier the hunting pressure on a herd, the more likely it is that most of its bucks will be taken before they reach trophy size. During 50 years of whitetail hunting,

the biggest bucks I have seen, without exception, have been where the deer population tends to be low, where the buck-to-doe ratio is high, and where hunting pressure is light.

I may have grown somewhat prejudiced. I simply do not enjoy hunting where the woods are swarming with red coats. I prefer to wander quietly and alone where deer are not constantly in wild flight and where I have some reason to believe that a big old buster is living. Large numbers mean nothing to me. The older I've grown, the more I am thrilled by seeing one large buck, rather than herds of deer, in the wild. For a buck to grow big antlers, though, he must survive at least five hunting seasons and winters—difficult if not impossible in areas out West. A buck must also have the capability, genetically, to grow big antlers. Sometimes such bucks turn up in the strangest places.

Several years ago, I was hunting antelope on my friend Cal Hanson's ranch in eastern Montana, not far from where the Yellowstone River flows into the Missouri. One day, after a lunch during which the conversation was mostly about hunting and wildlife, Cal led me to an outbuilding where he stored tools, saddles, and tacking.

"Now take a look at this," he said, handing me a set of magnificent whitetail antlers.

The 11-point rack had extremely heavy, wide-spread beams attached to a whitened skull.

"I picked it up off a carcass this spring," Cal continued, "in a strip of willows along the river. Couldn't tell how the deer died, but it probably was very old, and we did have deeper than normal snow for a long time last winter.

"I've been wondering," he added, as he lifted the antlers, "if there could be another one like it living down there right now. Almost nobody hunts down there."

"I wouldn't be surprised," I answered.

As it happens, there was at least one fine deer on Hanson's place. One of the most neglected outdoor resources in America today is the whitetail hunting available in several Western states where the species is gradually expanding its range. The river bottomlands in eastern Montana are a good example. Whitetails are seldom hunted too hard wherever the larger mule deer are also available. But Cal, his son Cal Jr., and I were out in the field well before daylight on opening morning.

It seemed strange to be hunting whitetails with a scent of sagebrush in the air and with Vs of Canada geese passing and honking overhead. I selected a stand where a dead cottonwood had been toppled by the wind. Its trunk formed a natural blind at the base of a standing cottonwood. I sat behind the trunk. From this spot on a low bluff, I could overlook a vast area of bottomland brown with autumn. The silver ribbon of the Yellowstone was just visible in the distance.

At first light, two does appeared and were soon joined by a third about 350 yards away. But, until sunrise, no other deer appeared. Then, I noticed the does staring intently toward a brushy draw. Turning to look the same way, I watched a buck slowly walking parallel to the draw, never coming completely into the open. He was about 500 yards away and much too far for me to try a shot. But through my rifle scope, I could tell he was a better-than-average buck with a very wide spread. After he disappeared into a screen of willows, I never saw him again, although I spent four days looking.

Cal Jr. was luckier; he saw either that buck or a carbon copy. Just before dusk that opening day, a buck appeared from a willow stand 200 yards from where Cal watched. He made a clean, one-shot kill. The animal was a fine 10-pointer. Its antler configuration convinced us that he was a relative of the winter-killed deer his father had found.

Similar incidents have happened far too often for me to regard them any longer as just coincidence. A few years ago, my wife, Peggy, and I were hunting in the Texas Trans Pecos country—a wild, dry, rugged region slashed with deep canyons that borders the Rio Grande River. Mule deer and whitetails share

the lonely landscape, and I have often seen both species browsing at the same time on the same rim.

The mule deer do not grow as large or carry antlers as heavy as those on muleys of the Rocky Mountains. The whitetails are small and quite plentiful. A fully grown buck may not exceed 100 or 110 pounds in live weight, and an eight-pointer is certainly something to brag about.

The year before our hunt, an unusually large whitetail buck had been taken on a thin, high ridge isolated by steep canyon walls on three sides. It was by far the finest whitetail collected in that vicinity since anyone locally could remember. The evening after we arrived in camp, Peggy decided that she would hunt on that same ridge.

"After all," she told me, "lightning does strike more than once in the same spot."

There was one trouble with her plan. I pointed out that the ridge was almost impossible to approach without being seen, and that a deer could easily drop down into a draw the instant it spotted a hunter approaching. There also was very little cover anywhere on the landscape.

"It's a perfect spot for a smart old buck to be," she answered, "and I'll be out there before daylight, before he can possibly see me coming."

My wife may hunt whitetails the rest of her life and never have another hunt work out so perfectly. Awake hours before daylight, she made her way alone, following faint game trails and stark landmarks silhouetted against a clear night sky. Once on the ridge, she was able to watch daylight slowly materialize as she sat with her back against a rock. Time passed in slow motion. The sound of hooves scraping hard ground turned out to be a doe and fawn passing barely 20 feet away. Suddenly catching Peggy's scent, the doe snorted, and both deer bounded away. Now Peggy worried that she might spook any buck standing unseen in dark shadows nearby. She confesses to having had some doubts about a buck being anywhere nearby at all.

Suddenly, there it was, standing about 100 yards away, where it probably had been bedded. The running doe had alerted the buck and it was looking in the direction in which the two had disappeared. Peggy has seen more than her share of bucks through the viewfinder of a camera and through a rifle scope. She knew that this buck was at least a very good one. Carefully, she shifted her rifle onto a solid rest and squeezed off a shot. Then, she remembers having a terrible attack of buck fever.

The deer had a perfectly symmetrical 10-point rack and would have counted as a good buck no matter where in America it had been taken. But, for a Trans Pecos whitetail, it was absolutely outstanding.

Maybe taking two trophy deer in two seasons on one dry windswept Texas ridge is only a coincidence. After all, any such hard-to-reach spot is an ideal refuge where a whitetail buck can grow old. But long experience tells me otherwise. When I go deer hunting this year, it will be exactly where a trophy fell last fall.

Big Bucks Are Different

By John H. Williams

It was October 1, years ago, and a high-school buddy and I were partridge hunting. We were in a very dense swale, northeast of Gladwin, in the northern part of Michigan's Lower Peninsula. All of a sudden, there was a commotion among the limbs of a windfall beside me. Believing, momentarily, that it was a partridge trying to explode from cover, I swung my 20-gauge pump in that direction.

What came out of that windfall was not a partridge, but the largest whitetail buck I'd ever seen. He broke cover, took about 10 paces, stopped, and stared at me. For what seemed an eternity, that buck just stood there in all his magnificent glory, staring at me.

If there is one thing that ignited in me an inextinguishable desire for big whitetail bucks, it had to be that moment. I'll never forget it. Even today, in my mind's eye, all whitetails are compared to my image of that long-ago buck.

As a kid who had yet to tag his first deer, I was awed by that buck. More than anything else, I wanted to hunt bucks like that one. "But how?" I wondered. I didn't even know anyone who had taken a whitetail like that. But now, after more than 25 years of deer hunting experience, I believe I've gained some insight into that question and into some of the riddles of big bucks.

The key to successfully hunting *any* animal is to understand the creature, and this is especially true of trophy whitetails.

It is important to make the distinction between whitetails and trophy whitetails. Trophy whitetails are, by all accounts, among the rarest of big-game animals. There are an estimated 13 million whitetail deer in the continental United States. Roughly 60 percent of these are does, so that leaves five million bucks. Only four or five out of every million bucks would qualify for listing in the Boone and Crockett Club record books. If we'd say that even 10 times this number would qualify as "big" for our purposes here, we're still only talking about 250 animals spread across all of the United States. That comes out to one animal for every 14,400 square miles!

Big Bucks Are Different

As a biologist, I'm intrigued with the question of whether big bucks are different because they've lived longer—and hence are wiser—or whether they start out different and so live longer. The jury is still out on that one. As a hunter, I'm satisfied just to know that they *are* different and that, in order to pursue them intelligently, I must understand those differences and know how they translate into characteristic behaviors.

Big Bucks Are Loners

Whitetail deer are, for the most part, gregarious animals, living in a principally matriarchal society. They live in small family units of three or more individuals. These units generally consist of a mature

17

doe, her offspring of the previous spring, and some-times her offspring from the year before. Two or more of these family units often come together and form larger groups. Small bucks, 1½ or 2½ years old, will generally be found within, or at least associated with, these groups. The bucks, especially the 2½-year-olds, have a more casual association with these groups than the does, but they will be found with them nonetheless.

Older, therefore bigger, bucks are seldom seen among the does; in fact, they actively avoid being with does for most of the year. When large bucks are found in close association with other deer, it's generally with other large bucks. It's not uncommon for two, three, or even four big bucks to live together in an all-male unit. These groups are quite permanent, except during the rut, when the bucks drift apart for a time.

Big Bucks Avoid Exposing Themselves

If your aim is simply to shoot a whitetail, hunt the fringe or edges of cover. Hunt openings in heavy cover; hunt fields in farm areas; and hunt runways leading from feeding areas to heavily used bedding areas. Hunt areas that show a lot of deer sign and a high incidence of deer usage. If, however, you want to shoot a trophy whitetail, avoid such areas.

Big bucks, if they use openings at all, do so only when they're forced to or when they have the complete cover of darkness. Two years ago, I hunted on a farm in southern Michigan. On the fourth day of the season, I shot a superb eight-pointer with a 23-inch spread and 29-inch main beams. As I sat admiring him, the farmer's 22-year-old son came along a nearby creek, checking his rat traps. For several seconds after he caught sight of my trophy, he stood there with his mouth open.

"Man, I've been watching the deer around here all my life," he said. "I've never seen one that big. I never dreamed one like that lived here!"

Long before the first rays of daylight, big bucks will abandon crop fields, orchards, and open wood-lots, and head for dense or isolated cover, which is their natural haunt. They won't leave this cover again

Photograph by Tom Brakefield

until long after nightfall. Because of such behavioral traits, big bucks can live practically under your nose without you ever knowing they are there. This fact cannot be overemphasized, and it's for this reason that a high percentage of whitetail bucks that live 4½ years or longer die of natural causes.

I'd be willing to bet that, within 10 miles of the area I normally hunt in southern Michigan, at least three, and perhaps as many as five bucks die of old age each year. I believe that there are two major reasons for this: lack of hunting pressure, and hunting tactics that are ineffective for taking mature bucks.

On opening day a few years ago, I thought—rather naïvely—that I might actually catch a big buck in the open. There were two dense tangles of cover in my hunting area, separated by an opening roughly 100 yards wide. From the sign present, I had every reason to believe that a big buck was using both areas to hole up in during the day. I thought that, if I covered the opening, perhaps I'd catch him pussyfooting between the two.

Shortly after daybreak, I heard a deer moving to my left and in front of me, approaching the opening. Moments later, a doe stepped cautiously out and slowly followed the runway that cut between the two pockets of cover. Shortly after that, I heard another deer approaching, just as the first one had. Once more, a doe nervously broke cover, slowly following the run. A couple of hours passed and nothing moved. I had seen no other hunters and had heard only a couple of shots far in the distance. Just before 11 a.m., I again heard a deer approaching.

The cover was so thick that I hadn't been able to see either of the does until they had stepped out. This time, it was the same. The deer approached the opening, just as the others had done, and stopped. This time, however, the deer bolted across the opening in a flat-out run. From the instant it hit the open until it disappeared on the other side, it never broke stride, never slowed down. I can still see the sunlight glinting off his massive rack. Big bucks are smart, and that fellow was nobody's fool. He wasn't about to get waylaid in the open. I left that night feeling pretty foolish. I should have known better.

Big Bucks Move In Slow Motion

This is not a contradiction of the incident above. When exposed, a big buck will get back into cover as quickly and as directly as he possibly can. The thing to remember is that he'll seldom expose himself.

Move through good deer country and you'll see deer scattering in front of you, running off in all directions as you approach them. Watch deer feed: They're nervous, anxious and, at the first detection of danger, they'll bound off, flags flying. Big bucks are skulkers and much craftier than other deer at avoiding detection. They prefer to walk away from danger or, even better, to let danger walk away from them. Because they're seldom caught in the open, this is often possible. They frequently lie right where they are and let danger—you—pass them by.

Big bucks are far less apt than most deer to retreat at the first hint of danger. Even when they are disturbed enough to exit, big bucks generally try to do so slowly, remaining unnoticed. Seldom will they flush and run—more likely, they'll sneak off.

The seasoned hunter takes advantage of this trait by hunting in slow motion. He uses his eyes and ears instead of his feet.

The Significance Of The Rut

The latest research on the rut holds real significance for hunters in Northern states. During late October and early November, the creation and maintenance of scrapes reaches its peak, yet the prime time for breeding is still two weeks away. The significance of scrapes then seems to be the identification by other deer—both bucks and does—of the most dominant bucks in the area. It is not, as previously thought, the place where the dominant buck actually meets the estrous doe. It is, of course, the dominant buck in any given area that makes the majority of the scrapes.

Research shows that all deer within the area will visit and investigate scrapes, but the dominant buck will, in all probability, visit and renew them after dark. Bucks actually shot over scrapes, therefore, are most likely to be smaller than the bucks that made them. How then do we get to the real big boys, the truly dominant males we desire? The answer to this question involves a lot of hard work and a thorough knowledge of the deer in your hunting area.

A buck makes scrapes to identify himself to the local herd as a dominant animal. He accomplishes this communication by rubbing overhanging tree limbs with his scent glands and by urinating on the scrapes. This lets all the deer in the area know who he is and it tells the does that, when they're ready, he'll be available. When the does are ready to breed, they will seek him out. During the 24 to 36 hours that a doe is in heat, she is as much as 28 times more active than usual. This heightened activity level

Big bucks are far less apt than most deer to retreat at the first hint of danger. Even when they are disturbed enough to exit, do so slowly, remaining unnoticed.

Photograph by Leonard Lee Rue III

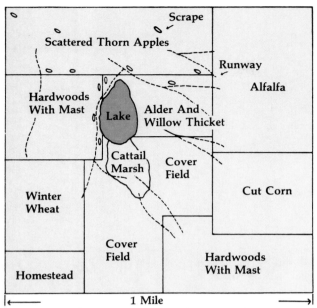

Sketch of typical farm country. Look for big woods near areas of heavy deer use.

practically guarantees that she will encounter a suitable buck.

Because the buck wants all the deer to get the message that he is ready and willing to serve, he makes his scrapes in the area of highest deer usage. Your job, then, in terms of scouting, is to find out where that area is. Specific questions that must be answered are: Where are the deer feeding? Where are the majority of them bedding? Where is the densest convenient cover available for the dominant buck?

The accompanying sketch is specific for farm country in Michigan's Upper Peninsula, but analogous layouts could be made for any area. The most remote corner of this big-woods terrain is going to have a pocket of suitable cover somewhere near the area most deer are using, and that's the place to look for signs of Mr. Big. Look for particularly large scrapes that are three feet or more in diameter (bigger bucks, generally speaking, make bigger scrapes). Look for outsize tracks sunk deeply into the earth, indicating extreme weight. Look for the oversize droppings typical of big bucks, too.

Effective Hunting Strategies

If you hunt in a group and are willing to share your opportunities for a trophy, you may find drives very effective—but only when they are done correctly. Very often, the dense cover that a big buck retreats to is isolated and, unless he is absolutely forced to do so, the buck will not leave it. The best approach involves only two hunters. With one of you on stand, the other can slowly, and *as quietly as possible*, move through the area. The driver stands almost no chance at all of a shot; those monstrous racks don't grow over peasize brains. But, if the driver is persistent enough, he will eventually get

his chance. Of course, the hunters should switch roles at agreed-upon intervals.

The only other effective methods for hunting really big bucks is to take a stand and stay put. Big bucks will not forsake their havens during daylight hours, but they will move about within their confines and will do so quite freely. To be most effective, the hunter should be on his post a half-hour before daylight and he should not leave until the dark—period. Once the buck senses your presence—and he will if you move about during the day—the jig is up and you might as well move on.

It has been my experience that the middle portion of the day is best for hunting really big bucks. I've seen more big bucks between 11 a.m. and 3 p.m. than during any other time period. I believe that, by midday, these big boys are hungry, stiff, and perhaps cold. They get up off their beds, wander about *within cover* for an hour or so, then lie down again. They'll only do that, however, if they believe that they're alone. That's why it's critical to get into the cover early and stay put.

Look again at the diagram. Most deer are feeding most actively in the alfalfa field in the upper right corner and on the mast in the hardwoods to the left. They are bedding among the thorn apples along the upper boundary. The most dominant buck in the area has created a line of scrapes along the broken edge extending from the hardwoods to the corner of the alder/willow tangle just to the right of the lake. The scrapes serve to identify him to the herd and allow the does to know he's willing to service their needs. He beds within the alder/willow thicket, where he has access to all his needs and yet has his required solitude and protection.

Where a hunter might position himself for such a hunt would depend upon several factors. Early-season bowhunters, in an area with little hunting pressure, might choose a stand where the lake, thorn apples, and willow thicket meet. If there's little or no human intrusion, a big buck might well wander to the edge of the thicket before dark or perhaps might linger near the edge even after daybreak.

A midseason rifle hunter had better find an avenue leading into the interior of the thicket and plan to remain there the whole season, if need be, because by then, the buck he's after will have seen and heard enough hunting action to know he wants no part of it. This hunter's best location would be between a major runway (such as the one leading from the thorn apples) and the lake, or between the runway and a favorite bedding area.

A late-season muzzleloader should concentrate on southerly exposures within the dense cover. On particularly sunny yet cold days, he should take a stand along the boundary area between the willow thicket and the cover field, or perhaps along the edge of the cattail marsh. Here, the buck can garner the warmth of the sun and still have an easy and rapid retreat to cover. Remember, cover is always the critical component to any hunting strategy designed to tag a big whitetail buck.

PART 2

HUNTING WHITETAIL DEER

Psych Up A Buck

By John Weiss

The successful pursuit of whitetail bucks hinges upon many things. Hunters must have a working knowledge of how the species lives and moves and feeds which, in turn, allows them to be in the right place at the right time. At the moment of the actual encounter, the hunter must then call upon a high level of proficiency with his chosen sporting equipment, be it rifle, shotgun, bow, or muzzleloader.

Yet one thing a vast majority of hunters fail to consider is the mental aspect of their undertakings and, curiously, it is this little-understood phenomenon that may actually be the most important ingredient of all.

Athletes have long known that, when they're "psyched up," they can draw upon mysterious inner resources that can give them a distinct edge over their opponents and, conversely, if they become "psyched out," they might as well head for the showers. As a result, they mentally strain themselves to the limit to achieve a level of unparalleled concentration and, subsequently, performance. The drama that predictably unfolds during Olympic competition is a prime example of how mind over matter is one of the most crucial elements in bringing home the gold.

"We're just beginning to understand the wealth of vast, untapped mental energy that we all possess," champion weight lifter Paul Kukonen once noted after pressing a barbell he'd earlier said he was

Photograph by Ralph F. Quinn

physically incapable of lifting. "But just like muscles, we need to develop and continually exercise these latent mental powers if they are to be of value in achieving new goals."

There are many ways in which all of this finds its way into deer hunting camps every year. Think back upon your own camps and you'll probably recall certain hunters who seem to always get their bucks. Before opening morning arrives, they seem to already *know* that they're going to succeed, whereupon they then merely head afield to carry out their appointed tasks. Call it confidence or positive conditioning but, whatever the case, it has so cemented itself into the very fiber of their thought processes that they simply take it for granted that they'll score.

Yet, in the same camp, you probably also are aware of certain other hunters who always seem defeated before the season has even opened. They've convinced themselves that they won't see any deer; that if they do see deer, there will never be a big buck in the group; and that even if there is, they will probably miss him anyway.

As unbelievable as it sounds, I know one hunter—who lives in Pennsylvania, no less—who has gone 17 consecutive years without taking home venison. Consciously, he desperately wants to take a buck, and he's even had shooting opportunities. But he has so negatively programmed himself, over the years, that his subconscious simply will not allow him to score.

Other hunters have personalities that are exactly the opposite. For them, there's always a pot of gold at the end of the rainbow, and they're always happily and enthusiastically on their way to retrieve it. Last year, for example, my neighbor took three splendid bucks during the course of outings in Wyoming, Kentucky, and Ohio.

"I'm riding such a natural high," he said smugly.

23

"I feel like I could go out right now and take a fourth buck with a slingshot."

Clearly, deer hunting is similar to many of life's other undertakings in that success feeds upon itself but, unfortunately, so does failure.

The obvious question that arises is: How does a hunter generate a positive mental outlook so that his annual deer hunting forays are guaranteed to result in success?

One way is by launching a personal campaign to learn as much as possible about whitetails and every aspect of hunting the species, no matter how diverse or irrelevant some things may seem to your own current needs or interests. It is incredible how many hunters venture afield every year who couldn't identify a scrape if they accidentally stepped in one, don't have the foggiest notion of what "midrange trajectory" means, and think a Baker stand must probably be some type of camp cooking equipment.

These hunters are sorely in need of intensive deer hunting education. The more knowledge they acquire, the more their confidence will grow. *If you know exactly what you're doing and why you're doing it, and are secure in the knowledge that your skills have been honed to the best of your ability, a positive mental outlook is certain to follow.*

Experiencing some degree of immediate success is also crucial. Parents commonly adhere to this philosophy in trying to interest their young children in fishing. Do they take their kids dry-fly fishing for brown trout? Heck no, they take them worm fishing for bluegills. Why, then, should a hunter in search of his first deer feel compelled to take nothing but a trophy buck?

The truth of the matter is, legitimate trophy whitetails are few and far between, and being willing to settle for nothing less virtually dooms your prospects for success right from the beginning. Besides, there is no correlation whatsoever between antler dimensions and successful, satisfying outings. Of the 45 bucks that I've taken in the last 12 years. I can honestly say that several small six-pointers actually proved to be more challenging and, therefore, more rewarding when I finally collected them, than several others that were twice as large.

If I were to offer a prescription, then, for someone wanting to launch upon a long and memorable career of successful deer hunting, I'd have to recommend this: Begin by pursuing the species in a particular region where the whitetail population is very high, and be willing to take the first legal animal that comes along, even if it's only a spike or a doe. What you desperately need right now is confidence, and the only way that you can get it is through experience. Since any hunter's "first" deer is always the most difficult hurdle, get that animal on the ground as quickly as possible. Look at it as a foundation upon which many following building blocks will soon fall into place. Look at that first deer as the seed of your positive mental outlook that you want to immediately germinate and begin growing. The so-called "trophies" will wait.

Photography by Gary Knepp

Legitimate trophy whitetails are few and far between. For the new hunter, it is better to be willing to take the first legal animal that comes along. This will help build confidence.

There are other mental gymnastics that you can perform to dramatically increase your chances of scoring. Moreover, they can be used, not only by beginning hunters, but may prove invaluable to veteran hunters, as well.

Take the matter of trying to patiently sit on stand for long periods of time. With each additional hour of seeing nothing, a negatively programmed hunter is sure to become more and more discouraged.

Yet other hunters with positive outlooks train themselves to view the same situation from an entirely different perspective. In fact, the longer they maintain their vigils, the more fired up they become and the more expectant of success. They know about and believe in the philosophy of "reverse geometric progression." What I mean is, assuming that you've done your scouting well and are situated in an area of high deer traffic, the longer you go without seeing anything, the *better*, not worse, your chances of success become!

Continually strive to force-feed this attitude into

your mental framework and it will easily enable you to tough it out still another hour on stand, and yet another hour after that. Sooner or later, your buck *will* come along. Yes he will! He has to, for it's his trail and his sign indicates regular use. Since he's not chained to a post somewhere, he may be about to step into view any moment.

The greatest detriment to maintaining this level of patience on stand is continually hearing shots in the distance. It sometimes gives even the most expert hunter the disconcerting suspicion that, in this supposed oasis of deer country, he alone has made the mistake of situating his stand out in the desert. This invariably gives birth to the growing temptation to abandon the stand and begin prowling around elsewhere. In the final analysis, it is this decision that does indeed significantly reduce your chances of scoring.

Again, mental conditioning can see you through these inevitable periods of anguish if you can maintain the highest level of confidence in your *own* abilities, skills, and knowledge. Forget about the other hunters in the woods. Tell yourself over and over again that most of them are boobs who are just now, for the first time, checking their rifle sights by shooting at targets behind camp. Rest secure in the knowledge that *less than 1 percent* of the shots you hear are big bucks meeting their makers.

This point was driven home one time in southern Ohio. I was sitting on stand and hadn't seen even a chipmunk in hours. Then shots began popping away about one mile down a nearby hollow. The intermittent gunfire lasted so long that I finally convinced myself that all the deer in the township were down in that hollow, and that the hunters there were having a heyday filling their tags. So I left my stand in hopes of getting in on the action. Eventually, I came upon the two hunters who had been doing all the shooting. They hadn't seen a single deer all morning and, when they came upon an old dump, they decided to amuse themselves by shooting the rats!

It should go without saying that I was totally disgusted with myself for losing confidence in my own abilities. After unloading my gun, I literally ran back to my stand and, two hours later, collected the splendid eight-pointer whose routine I had pegged weeks earlier.

There are still other mental arenas pertaining to deer hunting and matching wits with whitetails that have been little explored, understood, and written about because they fully fall into the twilight-zone world of our mysterious subconscious abilities.

For example, many in the medical and veterinary professions firmly belive that both humans and animals have "sixth senses" in which they unknowingly, from time to time, radiate and receive certain types of brain waves.

The particular mental energies presently under greatest study by behavioral scientists are *precognition* (knowing in advance that something is about to happen), *clairvoyance* (being able to discern things not recognized by the other senses), and *telepathy* (being able to mentally transmit to another creature assorted thoughts, motives, and emotions).

In deer hunting situations, an illustration of precognition might be sitting on stand and suddenly feeling an eerie, tingling sensation of anticipation and, only moments later, having a buck materialize before you, even though you were not forewarned by your other senses (such as hearing or sight). An example of clairvoyance might be an overwhelming gut feeling or hunch that you'll get your buck on a certain day of the season, or the chilling sensation of somehow knowing in advance what his rack configuration will look like, even though you've never actually seen the animal before. And an illustration of telepathy would be a situation in which you see a buck in the distance and, although he's headed another way, you're able to somehow "will" him into changing directions and coming toward your stand.

Don't laugh, because any seasoned hunter who has logged thousands of hours in pursuit of whitetails will admit (secretly, perhaps) that he has experienced one or more of these weird phenomena at least once. The fact that hunters don't experience them more often probably can be attributed to a combination of things. As individuals, some of us simply possess greater psychic powers than others and, as a species, our evolution toward a more civilized, urbanized lifestyle has gradually witnessed the dulling of all of our senses.

One of the most bizarre deer hunting experiences I know of happened to Gene Wensel of Hamilton, Montana. Wensel, a nationally known hunting authority, has bagged numerous monster bucks, including many of record-book class (most by bowhunting). He is the author of the classic book, *Hunting Rutting Whitetails,* in which he described the event like this.

"It was November 1972, and I'd just finished studying a treatise on positive thinking and mental attitude. I decided to put the book to the test by 'concepting' a buck to come to my stand at a specific time, 9 a.m. After climbing into my tree stand at the crack of dawn, I began drawing upon my mental resources to program myself for the happening.

"I concentrated so hard that my whole body hurt. My brain was as tight as a piano wire about to snap as I sent out telepathic messages for three solid hours. The pain of such intense concentration is unbelievable. Then, suddenly, at one minute before 9 a.m., I began getting a tingling feeling that something was about to happen and I stood up. Moments later, a toy buck [Wensel's way of describing a six-pointer or smaller] came running straight in my direction! I decided not to shoot at him and finally he saw me, wheeled around, and evaporated into the distance. Then another movement caught my eye and here came a coyote, again running straight toward me! Again I heard sounds, and a second buck, this one a dandy trophy, came dashing toward me and, when he was in range, I put an arrow into his chest. By this time, my head was like jelly. To say I was flabbergasted would be an understatement and that's why I haven't told this story to very many people. Most wouldn't believe a word of it, and I swear it's true. All three of those animals came from three different directions, they were the only animals I saw that morning, they were all running straight toward my stand, and they all appeared between 9 a.m. and 9:02 a.m.!''

The probability of this event being coincidental is too remote, for the odds of such happenings being attributed to mere "chance" are simply infinitesimal. Interestingly, it's also worth noting that, when the spooky episode was all over, Wensel said he had an intense desire to go to sleep. Since then, he's tried to pull off this stunt again, but every time he begins his telepathy routine, his body begins aching so much within only 10 or 12 minutes that he has to give it up.

"I think maybe I cooked my brain too much back there in 1972," Wensel said, "but, nevertheless, even though I can't explain it all, I am a believer."

On several occassions I've tried, unsuccessfully, to duplicate Gene Wensel's epic performance and can testify to the pain such intense concentration generates.

I have had numerous thought-transmission experiences with deer, however, that are similar to the experiences many claim to have had with other animal species. There is documented evidence, for example, that dogs and horses in particular are quite adept at "sensing" fear in man. They also seem to somehow know when man intends harm to them, even though there initially may be no outward display of hostility.

I've seen virtually the same thing occur with whitetails in both hunting and nonhunting contexts. When armed only with a camera, for example, I'm consistently able to get much, much closer to deer (and other animals) than when I'm carrying a bow or a gun.

Could it be that when I'm intent upon shooting only photos, I subconsciously send out some type of non-predatory mental signals or brain waves that the animals receive and classify as harmless? Could it be that, when I have a bow or a gun in my hands, my intentions are of such a predatory nature that the animals receive those telepathic signals and react accordingly by taking evasive action?

How many times have you been sitting on stand, completely relaxed as you patiently maintained your vigil, perhaps not even thinking about deer, but rather about your job, your family, or the Christmas shopping list you have to begin compiling. Suddenly a buck appears in the distance, heading straight for your stand. Immediately, your body tenses! Your thought processes are now riveted upon one thing and one thing only: hoping desperately that you'll be able to kill that animal. Then, in an instant, the deer slams to a halt, just as though he's run into a solid wall of "something." Then he about-faces and

disappears. You know positively that he did not see you, hear you, or smell you. What, then, *was* it that mysteriously told him that he was in peril and that he'd better get out of there fast?

I don't know.

I do know this, however. These strange occurrences seem to happen to bowhunters far more frequently than to gun hunters. Since bowhunters typically have much closer encounters with their quarry, we can surmise that mentally matching wits with whitetails is a relatively close-range affair. Perhaps the mental energies we possess have, over time, become so dulled through lack of use that their "ranges" of effectiveness have appreciably lessened.

Regarding the predatory mental signals that a hunter may suddenly begin radiating when he spots an approching buck, what to do? Well, obviously few of us have such control over our faculties that we can avoid becoming tense when a big deer is coming in.

But no matter whether I'm bowhunting or gun hunting, one axiom that I've long accepted, particularly when a deer is in close, is to avoid direct eye contact, at all costs, whenever the animal happens to randomly look my way. Biologists claim that eye contact, among all creatures, plays a crucial role in their interactions. And psychologists who study animal and human telepathy claim that brain waves trying to escape from the skull emanate primarily throught the eye sockets. They theorize that this is why a majority of telephatic experiences are unidirectional—that is, they move in one direction only.

Admittedly, all of this may seem quite far-fetched (in fact, just thinking about it makes me shiver), but I do know for a fact that my chances of scoring are better if I never look a deer straight in the eye. Instead, I concentrate upon the aiming point where I want to place my bullet or arrow. It's almost as though I entirely block out of consciousness the rest of the deer and "see" only the lung region. Sometimes, I can't even later recall looking through my scope or bowsight but, instead, as crazy as it sounds, I remember trying to intensely "will" my slug or arrow into a certain spot. Curiously, major league baseball pitchers throwing for the strike zone, professional golfers attempting to sink putts, and pro basketball players frequently admit to being oblivious to everything going on around them as they focus every ounce of their mental energy on their "aiming" points.

All of this is very "heavy" material, to be sure. And, too, some of it may fall into the category of nothing more than preposterous gibberish.

On the other hand, some of the country's most proficient hunters believe that matching wits with whitetails involves far more than simply squeezing the trigger or releasing a bowstring. They believe that we're on the threshold of a whole new dimension of deer hunting. They're the same hunters who, 20 years ago, were branded as lunatics when they suggested that we climb trees to hunt deer.

Three-In-One Deer

By Robert H. Marlowe

I have hunted whitetails for 12 seasons and, like most hunters, I've acquired some deer-hunting savvy. I have taken many deer and some people say that I am an expert. Expert? Well, what do *they* know?

I was 45 minutes into my first hunt and I was disgusted because there were more hunters in the woods than there were wild animals. I decided to return to my car. Halfway back to the car, I came upon a buck that didn't expect to see me anymore than I expected to see him. My friends thought I planned it that way. My luck has continued in that fashion, and that's how I became an "expert."

The Monday after Thanksgiving, Ohio's shotgun-slug deer season begins. The gun season lasts for one week only, and I usually take the entire week off from work. This season would be different, however, because I was starting a new job and could only take off the first two days. If I didn't get a deer, I planned to return on Saturday and make one last attempt. My 12-year-old son Scott would also join me for his second deer hunt. Ohio has a random drawing for doe permits and, because we all had received permits, we felt confident that we would not come home empty-handed.

Our hunting party consisted of Skeet Parsons, a long-time friend of mine from Columbus; his son Rocky, who is also my brother-in-law; my son Scott; and, of course, myself.

Skeet and Rocky came to my house on the Sunday before opening day. We had already filled the camper's propane bottle, crammed six months worth of food and clothing into it, and were ready to go. Hoping that nothing was forgotten, I kissed the remaining kids, gave the dog a pat on the head, and we started out for the rolling hills of southern Ohio and Vinton County.

The drive to our campsite took about 1½ hours, and we had plenty of time to think about the events to come. Would we collect that monster buck? Had we really picked the best stands? Who had to cook first? Worse—could we eat whatever they cooked? All of these thoughts ran through our minds while we made our way to the camp.

At the campsite, we put the camper in place and did some last-minute scouting. In the evening, we returned to the camper and ate our first camp meal. Skeet cooked it and it wasn't bad. We sat around and talked about hunting, of course.

The year before, Scott had taken his first deer, a

movement to the left of his stand. He slowly raised his scoped, 20-gauge Ithaca and brought the crosshairs to rest on the neck of a large buck about 35 yards away. The buck was sneaking along the hedgerow toward him. Scott is an excellent shot and squeezed the trigger slowly. The buck fell in his tracks. Overcome with excitement, he forgot to count the buck's points—all 11 of them! He couldn't budge the 200-pound deer, so he signaled Skeet for help. Because Scott needed help, Skeet passed up a shot at a spike buck. Instead, he dragged Scott's deer back to camp while Scott carried the guns. (Scott weighs only 60 pounds.)

Although Skeet had misgivings about using Scott's stand, having just field-dressed Scott's deer nearby, he decided to give it a try. Within minutes, four does passed behind him. Then two does and two fawns approached the gut pile in front of the stand. They stopped, stepped around it, and then went into the thicket. Drivers from another camp had started moving through the thicket and Skeet heard brush moving and cracking. Suddenly, a beautiful eight-point buck stepped into view. With his scoped, 870 Remington, he put one shot through the base of the buck's neck. The buck dropped instantly.

I had just returned to camp for lunch and I heard Skeet shoot. I went to help him drag out his buck. Who would have guessed that two nice bucks would

fat doe. He was in a ground blind next to a big elm tree near a multiflora rose hedgerow surrounded by 350 acres of dense bottomland thicket. For the 1982 season, we installed a stand in the elm so Scott would have a good view on both sides of the hedgerow. Skeet would be up in a tree about 300 yards away along the same hedgerow. They would be able to see each other because there were no trees between them. Rocky and I planned to drive the car about a mile and hunt in some tall timber, then return to camp at 11 a.m. Meanwhile, Scott and Skeet would remain on their stands all day.

We had only one thing left to do. Sportsmen, as we all know, have little superstitions—lucky socks or sweaters, or doing certain things in a way that is supposed to bring luck. Well, the previous year we had found *our* luck. Everyone has to dance for his deer. The dance is a cross between a hula and Indian rain dance. The longer you dance, the larger the deer. The previous year, I told Scott I would dance for him. I also danced for a four-point buck for myself. The next morning, we both collected our deer. Mine was a four-point buck! The dance was scheduled for sure for that evening. We all humiliated ourselves with this crazy dance. Scott danced for a six-point, Skeet for an eight-point, and I danced for a 10-point (no need to be greedy). Rocky danced but, heaven forbid, he confessed that he did not believe in the dance.

The following morning, Scott reached his stand about 7 a.m. He put buck lure on cotton balls and placed them around the tree. About 7:30, he noticed

Illustrations by Leon Parsons

be taken from one stand in the same day?

Back at camp, Skeet and Scott encouraged me to take Scott's stand that afternoon, while Rocky took Skeet's early-morning stand. After debating the dos and don'ts I convinced them that there was too much human scent around Scott's stand, as well as two gut piles in front of it. But who could argue with another hunter's success? And, after all, I had danced!

Scott accompanied me to his stand to give me moral support. We were on the stand by 12:30. We waited for 2½ hours and didn't see or hear anything. I was thinking of Scott and Skeet and how happy I was that they had gotten their deer. Seeing the glow on my son's face after he took his first deer the year before was something I'll never forget.

In the midst of my reverie, Scott and I heard a twig snap. We leaned forward slowly and looked to the left. The buck was coming from the same direction that Skeet's and Scott's deer had come. He was heading along the hedgerow toward the gut piles. It was 3 p.m. I eased up my 20-gauge Ithaca and held the scope's crosshairs on his shoulder. The hedgerow partially blocked a clear shot. The buck was coming right to me, and his rack looked huge. I fought the urge to continue looking at his rack. Instead, I held the crosshairs on his shoulder till he passed a thin spot in the hedgerow. At 40 yards, I squeezed the trigger. The heavy-antlered buck took two leaps and disappeared back into the thicket.

Scott was shaking and he asked if I had hit the big buck. I said I knew the crosshairs were on his shoulder when I fired. We heard brush crashing for a moment. We waited two, maybe three minutes and then climbed down and went to the spot where the big buck had entered the brush. There was a heavy blood trail, and a line of broken saplings and brush. Fifty yards from his exit, we found the biggest buck I had ever seen. Never did I think I would take a deer like that. When the rack was measured, it scored 190⅛ Boone and Crockett points, and qualified for the Buckeye Big Bucks Club.

My one shot had pierced his lungs. Although he had only 13 points, his rack was heavy and wide with a 28-inch outside spread. His antlers were six inches around at the base and he had one point 10 inches long pointing down on his right side. He was a truly magnificent animal.

We had taken three bucks from one stand on the first day of the season. Scott, Skeet, and I believe in the dance, but Rocky did not believe and he did not get a deer. Maybe next year he, too, will dance and believe in it.

If you happen to be in Vinton County, Ohio, next deer season, and you happen by a small camper that is bouncing up and down, pay no mind. It is just four happy idiots inside dancing for deer. All deer hunters are not as crazy as we are, but not all hunters have a stand like Scott's. More importantly, not all of them know how to dance for their deer.

The Spell

By Don Wright

At 2 a.m. the alarm went off. It sounded like somebody beating on a wash tub with a sledge hammer—we slept right through it.

At 9:30 the Cadillac broke down. (My brother Joe is the only person I know who drives a Cadillac to go hunting.) By the time we got the car repaired and stepped into our Uncle Hacker's woods, there were only two hours of daylight left. Nothing had gone right but my brother assured me that things had to get better.

"Are we going to hunt the hills, same as last year?" I said, drawing on my mittens for it was fast turning cold.

"I'd like to try the bottoms," Joe said, slinging his .308 over his shoulder. "There was a good-size herd down on Caney Creek last week."

Having hunted with Joe for enough years to know that he wouldn't be satisfied until he had at least checked out that area, I shouldn't have argued but I did.

"That was at least a week ago, man. The deer might have left the country by now."

"They're still down there," he insisted, moving to the logging road that led to the lowlands.

When we reached the turnoff to the Caney bottoms, we agreed to meet at the old sawmill on Rough River at sundown. I stepped up my pace, anxious to get over the ridge and down to Rough River to quickly find a tree that would prove adequate for a stand. The anxiety, plus the fact that my head was in the wrong place, caused me not to see the buck

standing in the road until he spun and leaped toward the brush.

It was an easy shot but, even as I pulled the trigger, I knew I had missed. I cursed myself as I reloaded my .54 flintlock. Although I knew it was a waste of time, I checked for blood.

Joe, meanwhile, huffed and puffed over the ridge. "Where's the buck?" he asked.

I flung my hand angrily toward the woods.

"You haven't hit a deer in three years," Joe said unblinkingly.

"I know it! I think I've lost confidence in my rifle."

"Maybe you had better change guns before it

Illustration by Ken Laager and Paul Di Campli

completely ruins you.''

I shouldn't have resented Joe's irritation for he had come running at the sound of my rifle several times in the past three years, during my spell of bad luck, only to hear the same story: ''I missed again.''

We separated again and I continued toward the river. About 20 yards ahead of me I spotted a spike buck darting into a patch of briers. I could see his ears and horns through the underbrush and, with a surge of confidence, I decided to shoot him in the head.

How a man who has taken 35 deer in less than 16 years of hunting could miss something the size of a deer's head is beyond me but I never did know where that deer went! Thankfully, the sound of the shot didn't carry over the ridge, so Joe was unaware that I had fired again.

At the mill I found a well-used deer trail with one set of tracks standing out significantly from the rest. They were big, as big as I had ever seen. And they were deep, a depth gained by heavy weight.

I chose a tree close to the trail and climbed to a fork 15 feet above the ground. I blew out my breath and watched the vapor drift slowly up the hill—the wind was in my favor. As the sun disappeared, the temperature plummeted below freezing and, of course, my nose began to run. Absentmindedly, I wiped it with the back of a cocklebur-covered mitten. (Fortunately, Joe does not come running to the sound of a scream.)

Leaves rustled, causing me to momentarily forget my close encounter with a cocklebur . . . squirrel. But then brush broke to the sound of a heavy animal and, like a great gray ghost, the deer materialized right before my eyes. I was stunned by the size of the animal and I knew again the heart-pounding pressure (or pain) of buck fever. He stood perfectly still for a full minute, Almost invisible in the shadows of a sun already set. I held my breath.

Soon he was moving again—a ground-covering trot that angled him closer to me with each powerful stride. I slowly cocked my rifle, fired, then fanned the cloud of engulfing smoke like a madman in hopes of finding the deer neatly laid out and awaiting my skinning knife.

My heart stopped. The buck was running now, alert and seemingly untouched. As he disappeared into the brush, I stared hard, sure that my eyes were playing tricks on me. His movements had become erratic—he was hit.

Shaking from delayed nervous tension, I slid down the tree trunk and moved to the point where I had last seen him. I immediately spotted blood.

"Did you get him?" Joe asked.

I did one of those "twinkle toes" numbers, leaping into the air and spinning about. "I've told you a thousand times not to sneak up on me like that," I shouted.

Joe chuckled.

"I got a ball in him," I continued more calmly.

"What was it?" Joe asked.

"The biggest deer I've ever seen! Weighed 300 on the hoof, maybe more."

Joe looked toward the river. "Did he cross?"

"I didn't hear him hit the water. I don't think so."

Joe mentally gauged the distance to the water. "I bet he did."

"I would have heard him," I snapped, "close as the river is."

"Maybe, maybe not."

Joe moved toward the river, studying the underbrush.

"Be no trouble to trail," he said. "He broke limbs with every step he took."

We followed the limbs to the riverbank.

"There it is!" I whispered, staring across the river at the deer standing broadside to us.

"Where?" Joe was searching our side of the river.

"Over there, where you said he'd be!" I used the muzzle of my rifle as a pointer.

"Where?"

"Over there, darn it," I cried excitedly, expecting the deer to bolt at any moment. "Go ahead and shoot him. My gun's not loaded."

Joe raised his rifle, sighted, then lowered the gun. "I can't find him in the scope."

The thought raced through my mind that, regard-less of the obscure lighting that was keeping Joe from locating the deer, I could always blame him if we came home emptyhanded.

"Give me the gun," I said.

"No."

"Then shoot him and quit messing around about it."

Joe slowly raised the rifle. I took a long deep breath. The shot echoed across the river bottoms and—if you haven't guessed it by now—yes, the buck took one might leap and landed right square in the river. We stared at the water in dumbfounded astonishment.

"Son of a gun," Joe said.

We could see a light spot a foot or so under the water and, even as we watched, the spot began to move, picking up speed as it drifted into the main channel. In helpless frustration we watched the glow beneath the surface move downstream.

Joe looked at me with a blank expression and said, "He's getting away."

"Like heck he is," I said as I stripped to my shorts in what seemed like less than one second's time.

I needed that deer. He was proof that I had broken the spell that cost me six bucks in three years.

Oblivious to the penetrating cold I sprinted 50 yards downstream, slid part way down the 15-foot incline and hit the river in a long shallow dive. The icy water took my breath and I gasped several times, swallowing more river water than I like to think about.

It was a battle just to cross the 30 yards of water. Thirty yards doesn't sound like much of a river but, when you add the fact that it is almost as deep as it is wide and as swift as a mountain stream, it becomes a considerable distance.

"Where is he?" I called, treading water that was over my head, even though I was no more than three feet from the farthest bank.

"Ahead of you, maybe five feet farther out," Joe answered.

I did a breaststroke into the mainstream.

"He's right in front of you, about a foot under the water," Joe called.

I felt the deer bumps against me. He was bobbing along with his rump up so, naturally, I grabbed his tail. That was a mistake. No sooner had I gotten a good hold on the tail than the antlers entwined around my foot and ankle.

"Darn," I sputtered as the deer pulled me under, "they'll be dragging the river for both of us."

I did one of those Tarzan wrestling the wild beast numbers and, when I surfaced, I had the antlers in a death grip and the head completely out of the water.

Although I was already in midstream, the bank where Joe waited looked to be 100 yards away. Holding the deer close to my chest as I had been taught to do in a junior life-saving course, I did a sidestroke toward the other shore.

We swept downstream at an alarming speed and, as we passed an old stump that stuck above the water, I wrapped my arm about it, intending to rest a bit before continuing on the few remaining feet to the bank.

The stump disintegrated at my touch and again I found myself fighting the current—and the deer—just to get my head above water.

Using the last of my strength, I grasped a root at the water's edge and pulled myself ashore. The freezing air caused my teeth to chatter and my body to shake so hard that my bones rattled. Bracing my foot against the root, I tried to drag the deer up the bank. Perhaps I was too spent from all that had gone before or maybe the deer was just too heavy but, whatever the reason, I couldn't budge the animal. Too cold and exhausted to make another attempt, I wedged the antlers firmly between the roots.

"Swim over and float the deer with you," Joe hollered.

I looked at the black swirling water. "I'd never make it," I said. "I'm not even sure I can made it *without* the deer."

"What's the matter with you?" he countered.

"I'm just about done in." I was so cold I could hardly breathe.

"You can make it," he said positively. "The water's warm, isn't it?"

I couldn't believe I heard him right. "What?" I hollered.

"The way you dove into the river it looked like it might be warm," he said with a laugh.

"About as warm as an ice cube," I answered sourly between shivers.

"Well, just in case," he said, "I'll pull off my clothes and come down to the water. If you get into trouble, I'll come in and get you."

"Thanks a lot," I muttered.

Joe stripped to his Levi's, moved downstream until he located a washed-out area that formed a small mud-covered beach perhaps 20 feet in length and slid down the bank to the water's edge.

"If you need me, I'll be here," he said.

I took a ragged breath and slid into the river, leaving the buck behind. I was completely numb by the time I staggered out of the water and slipped into my clothes.

"You OK?" Joe asked as I slumped into a sitting position, feeling more like 63 than 43.

"I'm all right," I answered. "Just give me a minute or two to rest."

When we reached the house, Joe explained that we had a deer down on the other side of Rough River and asked Hacker what he would if it was his?

"Why, I'd swim the river!" he laughed.

"Don's already done that," Joe said.

"Did you swim naked?" asked my aunt.

"Almost as naked as a jaybird," I answered.

We borrowed Carroll Jones' flat-bottomed boat and our Cousin Kent's truck and headed for the bottom. With Joe in the bow holding the light, I paddled across the fastmoving stream toward the deer. Joe slipped a rope over the

buck's head and we started back, towing our trophy proudly behind us.

In midstream the paddle snapped. Can you believe that—it just snapped off! I made a desperate lunge for the bottom half, almost capsizing the boat.

"What the hell are you doing?" Joe asked as the boat began racing downstream.

"I'm not doing anything," I said. The boat swept past our landing point and Kent's voice came out of the darkness, adding insult to injury. "Where you boys going?"

"You'd better do something, Donald," Joe said, shining the light in my eyes and almost blinding me.

"I'm doing all I can, darn it!" I said, holding up the flat for Joe to see.

"What happened to the paddle?"

"I broke it."

Joe gave me one of those mean penetrating looks.

I wore that stub of a paddle out and got both Joe and me wet, but we finally managed to get close to the bank to catch an overhead branch.

We were a long way from our designated landing point so, leaving the boat and with Joe holding the light, Kent and I took turns towing the deer up the edge of the river. We worked the animal around roots, snags and trees until at last we were back at the mud beach where we started.

"Its a big one," was all Kent said as we dragged the deer out of the water.

After retrieving the boat and hauling it up the bank to the truck, we tied the rope that held the deer to the bumper, intending to hoist the buck up the incline. But when Kent tried to start the truck—you may have guessed it—the battery was dead. There we were, two miles from the house with a truck that wouldn't run, a boat without a paddle and the deer still on the riverbank!

After a bit of a "discussion" we struck out walking. Joe and I dragged far behind so Kent went on without us. When we finally reached the house, Kent was sitting by the heater, grinning widely.

"You boys must be getting old," he chided.

Before I could utter a remark of my own, Carroll arrived in an ancient Volkswagen and, for the third time, we found ourselves headed for the river.

This time it was finally over. The buck dressed-out at just under 250 pounds, sported an 11-point rack measuring 22½ inches up the main beam, 22½ across the beam spread, and five inches around the base. The tines were 11 inches long and he was just under nine feet long from the tip of his nose to the point of his hind hooves.

A little after 1 a.m. we wearily trouped back into the house. The hunt had taken 10 hours—most of which were in darkness—and we had walked a total of 12 miles, used three vehicles and a boat, and swam the river *both* ways.

As Joe and I crawled into bed I thought about Kent's statement: "You boys must be getting old." And I wondered . . . you know, he just might be right! 🦌

Spring Scouting For Whitetails

By Glenn Helgeland

It might seem that the spring of the year and scouting for whitetail deer are mutually exclusive. In some areas of the country, that may be true, but certainly not in the snowbelt. Spring scouting there may be the key to more and bigger bucks for you.

I first noticed the value of spring scouting for whitetails several years ago when my wife, Judy, and I were looking for hunting land to buy. We wanted land badly, so we started looking as soon as the snow melted.

"By fall, maybe we'll find something we like and can afford," we told ourselves.

One particular plot of oak brush, hazelbrush, and hardwood ridges, with cornfields intermittently spaced on two sides and low oak ridges on a third, caught our attention. I am sure you understand why.

Deer trails had been pounded into the earth. Leaves in the trails were pulverized and deer pellets dotted the trails. Yet the deer didn't winter there.

"Half the deer in the county come through here at one time or another," we thought.

More looking confirmed our belief that it was a good area and we bought it. That land eventually proved every bit as good as we had hoped, but we worried some when we checked it a month or so after buying it. Deer sign wasn't nearly as common.

Bob Fratzke of Winona, Minnesota, a deer hunting friend and one of the best whitetail hunters I know, pinned it down for me.

"When you checked it early in the spring," he said, "you were looking at sign put down the fall before, most likely during the rut, but definitely just before snow fell or when it was first falling. That's the beauty of a blanket of snow. It puts everything on hold until you have time to check for sign thoroughly next spring."

In snow country, the first week or two right after the snow melts is prime scouting time. The soil is moist. Trails, tracks, and scrapes show clearly. In fact, trails and tracks often look freshly made at first glance, but a closer look shows that they are not. If conditions remain unchanged, and generally they do, these same locations will be prime for deer hunting the following fall.

The cover in spring is wide open. Snow-packed weeds and leaves are flattened and the trees and bushes are naked. Every nuance of the terrain is visible—the dips and small rises that will be concealed once the vegetation greens up and the understory becomes dense. This is important whether or not you live in snow country. The more terrain details you can see, the better the scouting potential. The relationships of various kinds of terrain and cover to deer movement patterns are very noticeable.

In the spring, when the snow is gone and the leaves are off the brush, you will sometimes run across shed antlers. Finding them tells you that the buck that carried them survived both the hunting season and the winter.

Illustrations by David Taylor

In snow country, the first week or two right after the snow melts is prime scouting time. The soil is moist. Trails, tracks, and scrapes show clearly. If conditions remain unchanged, these same locations will be prime for deer the following fall.

When I began serious spring scouting, one of the first things that surfaced was the reason why I had sometimes been slightly out of position for buck sightings and shooting when bowhunting. Deer use slight dips in the terrain—shallow little draws, swales, low rises—to conceal their movements much more than I had realized. Bucks are particularly good at this. They also tend to drift through cover instead of following an established trail. As a result, good areas may have little sign of deer passage.

These slight variations in the terrain also require less vegetation to hide the deer; the land itself covers part or all of their bodies. How many times have you heard someone say, "All I could see were his antlers?" On this kind of terrain, what looks like an open area may not be. I look for places such as this on the downwind side of thickets. One jump and a deer can be into thick cover—unless I see the animal first.

Every good place has one best spot to set up, on

Deer use slight dips in the terrain to conceal their movements much more than people realize. By scouting in spring, before foliage comes in, the terrain is easier to see, and such dips can be noted for fall hunting.

the ground or in a tree. "Almost" isn't quite good enough, especially in bowhunting where the range is usually short and the speed of the arrow isn't enough to overcome a mistake in choosing a site for a stand.

"You can be 50 yards or less from an excellent location and not realize it until you take a clear-eyed look at it when the leaves are gone," Fratzke told me.

Scouting at any time is nothing more than trying to solve a puzzle.

"I don't believe that deer do anything just because they did it," Fratzke remarked. "There are reasons for everything, even though we often can't figure out what they are. Anyone can roughly pattern big buck movements and it can be done, to a degree, in the fall, but only if you have found the right general area first, and that is best done in the spring."

This is especially true when scouting unfamiliar territory. The main reasons we usually get by with only autumn pre-season scouting is that we're most often scouting familiar territory to confirm things that we learned during previous seasons. We can do this with a minimum of movement and without alarming the deer too much. Too much pre-season scouting,

however, can push deer out of their existing movement patterns.

Scouting in the spring is the best way to concentrate solely on scouting. We all scout during hunting season, but the problem is to separate scouting from hunting. Scouting an area may spoil it for hunting and, if we don't have other hunting areas ready, the problem may be amplified. Deer usually move farther than we realize they do, simply because we think of them as having "homes." Because of this self-limiting human tendency, we often don't range far enough afield in our scouting to learn what conditions exist a few ridges, woodlots, or fields away from our main area. Therefore, many hunters aren't prepared to switch to another area when it's necessary. We aren't sure where the deer have gone.

"Over the course of a year, I spend 90 percent of my time outdoors scouting and 10 percent hunting," Fratzke told me. "When I go to a stand, I want to *know* that something is likely to happen there. Just hoping that a good deer will come past isn't enough. Sometimes things go as planned; sometimes they don't. But I find that the more time I spend scouting, the 'luckier' I get when I'm hunting.

"It's easy to fall into the trap of spending a lot of

time honing your shooting skills and far too little in the woods figuring things out. That's putting the cart before the horse."

Fratzke knows what he's talking about. The walls of his den are adorned with the mounted heads of 16 whitetail bucks. They aren't basket racks, either; they're big eight-point or better bucks and all were taken with bow and arrow. And yet he doesn't rattle deer and uses no masking scent, although he does use sex lure sparingly during the peak of the rut. He keeps himself and his clothes extremely clean, wears rubber boots, notes wind direction carefully, and always has so many carefully selected stands ready that there is always at least one good fresh one available at any site in case the wind direction changes.

"It's impossible to have too many good stand sites," he says. "The more I have, the better my chances. I always want exactly the right stand under changing conditions and at any time during the hunting season. Scouting like that takes time, and that's the reason I spend so many hours in the woods during the off season."

Another valuable aspect of spring scouting is that stand sites can be cleared out and prepared for the following fall. Each stand looks as it will when the foliage has dropped. You can see if you will be well hidden or not and you can clip branches that would make it impossible to shoot or move silently. Clearing out in the spring means that your scent and movement will be long gone come hunting season, and the trimming will have been accepted by the deer.

A compass is just as important on spring jaunts as it is during fall hunts. It's just as easy to forget directions when looking at trails and other sign as it is when you're trailing a wounded buck. The compass also helps check prevailing winds. This enables anyone to position a stand better in relation to deer trails or general movement patterns. After you've made a shot, you'll also have an easier tracking job if you know the terrain well. When you have a good idea of where the animal will go after it is hit, your chances of recovering the animal improve.

In any patch of woods, the hunter should ask himself why deer do this or that and, when that puzzle is solved, he should find out when they do it. Knowing the answers makes a hunter more confident and, when you are confident, it is easier to sit quietly on stand or move in just the right way at the right times.

"Even though I scout year-round, spring scouting is the real beginning," Fratzke said, "I want to see how the deer came through the winter. My winter scouting told me where they were bedding and feeding at that time, but spring scouting tells me how to tie together last fall, wintering areas, and the next season."

The toughest part of all of this may be to remember to scout with an open mind and open eyes so that you can see what's lying in front of you, not just what memory and past experience tell you is there. Since we all have preferences in hunting areas and styles, our biggest downfall is to see only what we want to see.

Another problem to avoid is scouting only the areas that you think will be good. Because hunters often do this, they are sometimes surprised by the big buck that comes from an unexpected direction. This is also why a novice sometimes gets a trophy buck. He didn't know enough *not* to do a certain thing or *not* to go into a certain area. He wasn't hampered by narrow thinking.

Fratzke summed it all up when he said, "I analyze the sign, the terrain, and the cover. When I put it all together, I know where to go and when. With added fine-tuning during the summer, I keep it all up to date and, when the season comes, I'm in the right place at the right time."

Scouting in the spring is the best way to concentrate solely on scouting. We all scout during hunting season, but the problem is to separate scouting from hunting. Scouting an area may spoil it for hunting and, if we don't have other hunting areas ready, the problem may be amplified. According to Bob Fratzke, "It's easy to fall into the trap of spending lots of time honing your shooting skills and far too little in the woods figuring things out." He knows what he's talking about—the walls of his den are hung with the mounted heads of 16 whitetail bucks, all taken with bow and arrow.

The Rung Way To Hunt Deer

By Robert L. Bryant

For those unfamiliar with ladder stands and their uses in deer hunting, it is just what the name implies—a ladder with some form of seat or platform at the top. Like other elevated stands, ladder stands improve the hunter's vision by getting him up above the brush and above the line of sight of a deer. It also gets human scent up and out of the deer's nostrils.

While manufactured stands run from $50 to $150 or higher, a good ladder stand can be made for less. Ladder stands can usually be made from materials such as wood scraps that are available around the house. But even if you had to buy the lumber and so on, the cost would run about half that of the less expensive manufactured stands.

One of the main advantages of a ladder stand is versatility. Because the ladder supports virtually all of the hunter's weight, ladder stands can be used on smaller trees. Climbing stands often cannot. Likewise, most climbing stands are not designed for unusually large trees. Again, this does not affect hunter using ladder stands.

Affordability, portability, comfort, ease of use, and ease of construction make ladder stands a virtual must for serious deer hunters.

Ladder stands can be built to any specifications. Some hunters, for example, think that if you don't get 12 to 15 feet up, you're wasting your time. Others commonly use tree stands as low as six feet off the ground and still have deer walk almost directly under

When adorned with a simple bench seat, ladder stands can put comfort into deer hunting.

Photographs by the author

them. Ladder stands can accommodate hunters with any height preference.

The largest one I have ever built was 14 feet off the ground and was made from 4 × 4-inch posts with a 3 × 2-foot piece of metal catwalk used as the platform. I use it as a permanent stand. Most of my permanent ladder stands vary from eight to 10 feet in height.

My portable ladder stand is eight feet three inches high and is made from western (fir) cedar, for the lighter weight. The ladder legs are 20 inches apart and the platform is made of three-quarter-inch plywood measuring 22 × 20 inches. I notch a V in the side of the platform so it can be secured to the tree. The portable ladder stand has five steps made from 2 × 4s and two supports, each two feet long and also made from 2 × 4s, to buttress the platform against the ladder.

I painted the stand a dull green and use a small cotton rope for securing it to a tree. The stand weighs about 28 pounds. Balanced over my shoulder, I can carry it a long way and have, on many occasions.

When moving from one location to another, the stand fits conveniently in the back of my truck. With the platform next to the cab and the legs resting on the tailgate, it sticks out just 1½ feet. The stand rides perfectly in this position and equipment can easily be stored under it. When I'm ready to hunt, all I have to do is pick it up and start walking.

Ladder stands do not have to be made from wood. One hunter I know took half of a 16-foot aluminum extension ladder and placed a folding metal chair seat on top of it. This is a very lightweight stand and, at the end of the season, he simply unbolts the seat and puts the ladder back together again.

If you can find a damaged aluminum extension ladder that is only damaged on one section, latch on to it. You can put a metal seat on the undamaged portion or, better yet, place a plywood platform at the top. This stand is sturdy, lightweight, and completely portable. Perhaps the only disadvantage of aluminum is excess noise. Keep in mind, too, that you'll have to camouflage the reflective aluminum surface.

Another material worth considering is thin-wall conduit. These stands are strong and surprisingly lightweight. I have also seen ladder stands made from water pipes. While these are very strong, they are also very heavy, although they make a fine permanent ladder stand.

Some hunters use chains and chain boomers to fasten their ladders to trees. I've never liked chains on portable stands for a couple of reasons. They are, again, very noisy and increase the weight. I've always preferred a small stout rope to any chain. The exception would be if you plan on leaving your stand in the woods over a period of time. If the woods you are hunting sees a lot of traffic, you may want to consider using a chain and lock.

On my portable ladder, I secure my rope about 6½ feet up, slightly above head high. It's easy to tie

This variation of the wooden ladder stand is made from pipe and is both lightweight and strong.

All of these ladder stands were inexpensive and relatively simple to build.

at this height and it holds the stand very well. Some hunters place two ropes on their ladders, one about four or five feet up and the other at the top of the platform. If the ladder is narrow—under, say, 20 inches wide—I would recommend two ropes. Anything 20 or more inches wide should give enough stability.

The weight of the stand should not be a major consideration—unless you'll be carrying the stand into the woods on your own. Consider the 14-foot monster I mentioned earlier. After building the ladder at home, I was able to get my four-wheel-drive truck to within 100 yards of the location in which I planned on setting up the stand—thanks to an old logging road. With the aid of a friend, it took three trips from my truck to get all the material to the location. Once there, we placed the ladder on two concrete blocks, securing it to the tree with four 2 × 4 supports, two at the top and two halfway down. Then, we placed the 3 × 2-foot metal catwalk at the top.

Really, though, a stand like this is a little far out, but we had the material, time and, most important, a good location. Usually, a stand this high would be a handicap. In this case, though, the particular area we hunted was a thicket of mature hardwoods. Once off the ground, you could see a long way.

Most of my permanent stands are slightly higher than my portable stand. As I've already stated, they run about eight to 10 feet off the ground. They also have larger platforms, usually about 2½ to three feet

square, and are made of three-quarter-inch exterior plywood. The ladders are usually 24 inches wide and built out of treated pine 2 × 4s.

Some ladder stands are placed directly on the ground while others are set on bricks or blocks. On two stands, I bolted a three-foot section of creosote-treated fence post—one on each leg—letting them protrude past the 2 × 4s about one foot. Both stands are used in farm areas, therefore the creosote smell is something the deer are familiar with.

Another advantage of ladder stands is that they give you the ability to secure the stand without using nails. A ladder stand that is lashed down properly is sturdy, safe and, best of all, movable. If you hunt private land, make sure you have permission from the landowner to place a ladder stand on his or her property. If you feel safer using nails, first be sure that it is legal in your state, then ask the landowner for permission to do so.

I don't know of any timber companies that welcome nails in trees so, if you hunt on timber company or public land, you'd better use a rope for holding your ladder stand to a tree. You may want to chain and lock your stand, but do this only if you plan on removing it at the end of the season. It could get in the way of timber operations.

Every stand hunter should have at least one ladder stand, be it a portable or a permanent. They're easy to make and you won't be disappointed. In fact, you may be like me. You won't be able to stop with just one.

Pick A Red-Hot Deer Stand

By Tom Huggler

It doesn't surprise me that my friend Bill's wife balances their family checkbook. After all, Bill isn't the sharpest guy I know. You wouldn't think to look at him that he'd be much of a deer hunter, either. He's in terrible shape. A quarter-mile hike in the woods leaves him gasping and, on a quiet morning, you can hear his smoker's hack 100 yards away. I'd bet my last broadhead, though, that he will tag a prime buck this season. Despite his appearance, Bill is one heck of a deer hunter.

You probably know fellows like him—unassuming types who uncannily bring home venison year after year. That ability involves far more than luck. Years of experience have taught them many things about deer hunting, and possibly the most important part of their expertise is knowing how to pick an effective blind or stand. It makes sense: Find the right spot to kill a buck one season, and the odds are that you'll get more deer there in later years, barring great changes in habitat or deer populations. Deer are creatures of habit; so are the best deer hunters.

Unless you are superskilled at tracking or still-hunting big game, stand hunting is probably the best way to get your buck. Deer populations are booming in many parts of the country, and so is the number of hunters. Increased hunting pressure has sharpened the wits of already-smart bucks to a razor's edge, but it also keeps them moving—with luck, right past your carefully chosen blind or stand. Consider these 10 points when making your stand selection, and if you can give a thumbs-up to at least

Once the leaves drop from the trees, a hunter using this tree stand becomes skylighted.

The most effective stands blend into the surroundings. This stand could be used early and late in the season.

seven of them, you'll improve your odds at tagging a buck.

Pick Multiple Stands

When you consider all the factors that go into choosing a great ambush site, you will see that relying on a single location makes little sense. A whole lot of variables conspire in fall to change the deer's feeding, bedding, and traveling habits. For example, those abundant food sources that make for good stand spots in early fall—grain crops, alfalfa fields, and hardwood mast—may be in a railroad car or under three feet of snow by season end. Bitter weather sends mule deer and elk from the high country, and it can force forest whitetails to yard in lowland cover. Deer become more mobile, if snow depths allow, as available food shrinks. The rut also alters their habits. Bucks, for instance, are then more interested in does than food. Hunting pressure is yet another factor that changes deer patterns.

One key to successful stand-hunting is to be flexible. A site that looks redhot in September may be barren of deer in November. My friend Larry Hartwick has shot 23 whitetails throughout Michigan, most of them in the farm country near his Cass City home. He hunts nearly every night during the split bow season, the two-week firearms season, and the special muzzleloader season. In recent years he has used about 50 stands that vary in effectiveness due to weather, wind direction, and time of season. He relies on both natural and constructed ground blinds, and his tree stands are located on public as well as private land where they must be removed at the end of the season.

"I don't use them all in any one year," Hartwick explains, "but I know they're there if I need them. No way could I hunt effectively if I had only a couple of spots to choose from."

Once you've decided to select multiple stands, you need to know where to locate them.

Pick Areas With Deer Sign

Most hunters can identify deer tracks, droppings, bed depressions, trails, and pawings in the ground under nutbearing trees. Some deer sign, however, is a lot more subtle. A tuft of hair on a fence might be a clue to a solitary buck's regular crossing area. Buds nipped off bushes and saplings, even low-hanging trees, are often signs of browsing deer. If undisturbed, deer will meander along, taking their time and feeding selectively.

Pre-season scouting for sign can help you determine why deer are using a particular area. A trail, for instance, may indicate a crossing spot. Beds denote a resting area, especially if old and new depressions are evident. Scuffed leaves under hardwoods with mast could mean that deer feed there. The signs might also be from foraging wild turkeys or squirrels, so check for tracks and droppings to be sure.

Although I keep an eye open for deer activity year-round, I get serious about scouting two weeks before the bowhunting opener in my home state of Michigan October 1. By then bucks are usually trying to rid their antlers of velvet by rubbing up against staghorn sumac and young trees. Rubs are easy to find. In one study I've seen, researchers claim that a single buck may rub as many as 150 trees. Some experts say that bucks practice rubbing and pushing on trees to build up neck muscles and to show off their macho stuff as well. Scrapes are yet another sign of bucks—they warn the competition about trespassing and let receptive does know that the maker is standing at stud.

A hunter who locates active deer sign close to the season opener will be a trump up on finding the best stand location.

Pick The Right Habitat

Knowing why deer use a particular area can help you ambush one. A feeding area, for instance, is best hunted at first light and again late in the day. In heavy cover—deep woods, scrub oak, and sloughs—midmorning to midafternoon is best. Deer are likely to be loitering or resting in such safety zones then. Even so, one of the hottest places to locate your stand is in a natural crossing area, a piece of cover that deer move through en route to feeding or resting habitat.

Such spots are often found along the edges where two types of habitat meet. Not surprisingly, edge cover usually follows the natural contour of the land. High-country scrub oak gives way to mature timber farther down the mountain. Tag alders in a low area that merge with aspens or hardwoods higher up make for an edge. Some edges are obvious—an alfalfa field next to an oak woodlot, or a cattail marsh between a lake and mature woods. Deer like to move through edge cover, and that is why these spots are excellent for stand-hunting. If conditions allow, choose your stand on the thicker side of edge cover.

Crossing areas can also include fingers of cover that reach into fields or open woods. Brush-stuffed fence rows, or such natural bottlenecks as sections of woods in an hourglass shape, are examples. In farm country, irrigation and drainage ditches provide corridors for sneaking bucks with trophy headgear pulled low. They are best hunted when they are on the move. That is likely to be in early morning or from late afternoon until dark. Crossing areas are good places to post, too, in a drive. Deer use these same covers as escape routes.

Posting a typical crossing area paid off big last fall for hunter John Vieau, who was hunting farmland near his downstate Michigan home. He had seen a boss buck twice while bow-hunting earlier in the area, and chose a crossing spot to post on opening day of the firearm season. At 7:15 a.m., other hunters drove the huge buck and a doe past him. Vieau shot

Territorial boundary scrapes are usually made by bucks in open areas and aren't considered prime sites for stands.

Photograph by Leonard Lee Rue III

These hunters scouted the area before building their stands, and the extra effort paid off.

Photograph by Tom Huggler

the 22-pointer with a slug through the shoulder at a distance of 20 feet. The deer sported a 23-inch inside spread and scored 188⅞ Boone and Crockett points.

Pick Tough Cover In Late Season

If deer in your area get intense pressure, or if your state allows a late season, consider taking a stand in the thickest, nastiest cover you can hike into. Surviving bucks, haggard and nervous from the rigors of the rut, and of eluding hunters for weeks, usually seek a desolate area where they will be left alone. Deep-wood swamps, farmland sloughs, river-bottom timber tangles, and thick stands of cattails are likely places. Big bucks don't normally show up in feeding areas with other deer, and if they do appear, it is usually after dark when all is safe. To tag a year-end trophy buck, you'll have to waylay him on his own turf.

Larry Hartwick has located a few of these out-of-the-way places, and if he has not yet taken the buck of his choice by late December, he turns to them. One place in particular, two miles from roads and across a river, has provided him with three late-season bucks.

"It's a Michigan jungle area," Hartwick admits. "In fact, you wouldn't think so many blowdowns and such thick cover could be found in one place." He hides in an immense pine stump and waits for deer en route to cornfields more than a mile away. You, too, can locate remote areas and choose stands before season to use later as an ace in the hole.

Pick Stands Off Trails And Scrapes

Active breeding scrapes usually differ from boundary scrapes in both size and location. Breeding scrapes are likely to be two to four feet in diameter, and normally are found in heavy cover areas under overhanging brush or limbs. They usually are muddied with deer tracks and urine. Territorial boundary scrapes, on the other hand, may be smaller and usually are made in more open areas, such as alfalfa field edges and corners of woods.

Breeding scrapes are better than territorial scrapes for placing a stand over if you're careful not to contaminate the area and if you set up some distance away. I know one hunter who won't get within 50 yards of active scrapes, believing that the smartest bucks hang back from them and circle cautiously. The same idea helps when you're hunting a runway. Two seasons ago, while posting a worn deer trail, I saw 24 does and yearling deer in three days. A lone buck, maybe a six or eight-pointer, slipped through heavy woods parallel to the trail and about 40 yards from it. Just as a hunter might scout a distant area with binoculars, that buck was trolling for does in heat. To cut the risk of exposure, he used his nose from a safe distance. A stand off the main trail might have paid off for me.

Pick A Stand For Favorable Wind

If you have little time for scouting and even less for securing tree stands and building blinds, at least consider a couple of alternate sites for playing the wind game. Many hunters don't realize how keen a deer's nose is. I have known deer to spook 200 yards away when they caught my scent. A smart whitetail or muley buck's nose never fails him. Send him a whiff of human scent, and you can kiss any hope of a kill goodbye.

A partner and I each tagged a black bear two years ago, partly because we had all the wind variables covered with back-up blinds and stands. And although thermal currents are usually discussed in terms of Western big-game hunting, you should know that morning air generally rises and evening air usually settles back to earth, and not just in the mountains. One windless fall afternoon last year in Michigan, I watched a black bear glide down a game trail toward my tree stand. I had a nocked broadhead at half-draw when he suddenly grew cautious and stopped, 10 feet from where I was aiming. He melted away, and then, as night's chill came on, began to circle my stand. Twenty minutes later, catching my scent under the tree, he charged away. That experience makes me wonder if ground blinds might be better suited to evening hunting and tree stands for mornings.

Pick Stands In Natural Surroundings

The most effective stands are those that blend into the area naturally. Choose blowdowns or huge stumps for natural ground blinds, or consider low-profile blinds at the base of thick trees or in depressions. Use available materials such as rotted logs, boughs from a dead conifer, cattail stalks, or weeds. If you're going to construct board blinds or other elaborate structures, do it well before the season so that deer will become familiar with them. Just like a fussy housekeeper who notices when even an ashtray is moved, a buck may detect changes in his home range.

When choosing trees for stands, select those with ample canopy above to avoid skylighting your profile. A friend of mine once spent 30 evenings in a tree stand and never pulled his bow. Only after another friend told him he had walked up and seen the hunter etched against the dropping sun did my friend understand the problem. A spruce or pine tree can make an ideal stand if you cut away only enough boughs to allow an unimpeded shot. If conifers aren't suitable, locate your stand in a clump of trees, instead of a tree standing alone, to help break up your profile and to conceal movement. You should be as high as you can go and still feel confident of a killing shot. Some bowhunters I know apply what they call the 20/20 rule: At least 20 feet up and no shots more than 20 yards.

Pick A Stand For Visibility

Try to predict where bucks will show and then be certain that you have a clear shot to that spot. Whenever I decide on a new stand, I picture myself taking shots in all directions. In addition to trimming away those branches that might get in the way, consider cutting shooting lanes if you're hunting in heavy cover, and when bowhunting take a couple of daily practice shots with field arrows. Obviously,

you can't tailor the locale to suit your needs completely, but it is surprising what opportunities a little forethought can reveal.

A few years ago, I built a small ground blind of stumps and pine branches and then cut out shooting lanes in three directions, figuring that a buck wouldn't dare come through the same woods I had walked. But at 8:30 opening morning, that's exactly what happened. Spotting movement from an eye corner, I screwed my head around in time to catch the sun glinting off a white antler. The buck ambled away through the woods right where I should have cleared a shooting lane. I never saw him again except in my sleep.

Locate morning and afternoon stands so that the sun will not be in your eyes. You'll gain extra minutes of shooting time.

Pick A Comfortable Stand

You will be able to hunt longer and with more enthusiasm if you are comfortable in your stand. In ground blinds, that might mean having a tree to lean against and toting along a cushion. For tree stands, bring a safety rope. Consider making or buying a tree stand with a built-in seat. Rain gear, extra gloves, and warm boots and clothing can help extend hunting time.

One warm October afternoon while I was on a tree stand, the sun suddenly hid behind clouds and the wind came up. Soon it began to snow. It was an ideal time to be hunting, but I was shivering so badly in my uninsulated coveralls that I couldn't steady my drawn bow. While climbing down I spooked a small buck coming my way.

Pick A Stand For Proper Access

Choosing a stand correctly includes planning how to get to it. Pick a route that will not take you through an area likely to hold deer. For example, walking through a hay field or orchard in early morning makes as little sense as cutting through a bedding area in afternoon. Many hunters overlook this important point, perhaps figuring that spooked deer eventually will return. That may be true of yearlings and does, but seldom with often-hunted bucks. When possible, enter your stand with the wind in your face.

Considering proper access paid dividends last fall for archer Don Sharp and one of his friends. They had opening-day bow permits for Shiawassee National Wildlife Refuge near Saginaw, Michigan. Scouting was not permitted, but the hunters consulted a refuge map, and figured that a canoe could get them deep into the tract and behind other hunters who might move deer toward them. The strategy paid off. At dawn, they carefully chose tree stands. At 10:30, Sharp killed a 13-pointer, which weighed 220 pounds when dressed. His partner followed up half an hour later with a seven-pointer.

You, too, can take a stand for deer this fall. Considering each of the 10 points will increase your chances of scoring.

Twelve Ways To Find Your Buck

By John Phillips

Tagging a deer is easy. All you have to do is get a deer in your sights, squeeze the trigger, and let your bullet do the rest.

But finding a whitetail deer can be difficult. Thousands of outdoorsmen spend days attempting to take a deer in areas the animals rarely frequent. Many hunters sit in a tree stand or a ground blind day after day waiting for a deer to appear because they have seen a few tracks. Other sportsmen waste their time on stand because they have found a few droppings. Some hunters set up their ambushes close to a tree where a buck has rubbed his antlers. Although all of these outdoorsmen are hunting over deer sign, there is no guarantee that the hunters are in a good place to take a deer.

Effective hunters locate bucks in many different ways because they know that four driving forces—food, water, fear, and sex—motivate deer and determine their behavior. These outdoorsmen also understand that whitetails are creatures of habit and use the same trails and perform the same routines day in and day out, except when changes in the weather or food supply, the intrusion of hunters, or something else disrupts their set routines. These hunters are also aware of the deer's acute senses: good hearing, a keen sense of smell, and sharp eyes that can detect the slightest movement.

Here are 12 routes that you could follow to venison this fall.

No. 1

Determine which of the buck's major needs is in the shortest supply and set up an ambush close to the location of that essential.

Photograph by Leonard Lee Rue III

46

"One of the ways to find deer concentrated in a particular area is to locate a place where food, water, or ready does are available and where the demand is intense," said Dr. Ross Shelton, extension wildlife specialist with the Mississippi Cooperative Extension Service. "If there is a drought, the deer will be traveling to water. If there is a shortage of food, they will concentrate where food is still to be found. During the rut, you will find bucks in places where they are most likely to meet does."

No. 2

Contact the wildlife biologist, conservation officer, and landowner to determine the preferred terrain and food, and the deer's greatest current need. Terrain and cover vary, and the route to successful deer hunting varies, too. For this reason, the best information to be had in a particular region where you

Photograph by Leonard Lee Rue III

The white flag's up (above) and the buck is moving out but, if you know his preferred escape route, you can be on stand where he's headed after having a friend push him out. In the absence of abundant wild food, deer invade grainfields and pastures to feed (left). If you know the food situation, you can be in the right place to score.

hunt will come from that state's deer specialists. The landowner usually knows the land, the deer, and their habits, and can also tell you where he has seen the most deer. The county's conservation officer sees deer almost every day and will be able to advise you about the best places to find your deer.

No. 3

You should hunt the most productive terrain for your area, though the direct route to your destination may be through unfamiliar land.

"Terrain is a key factor in locating deer," according to Nate Dickinson, big-game unit leader for New York's Department of Environmental Conservation. "In many parts of New York State, most of the nut-producing trees grow on southern slopes. Since these trees produce some of the most favored food for deer, sportsmen in our region often concentrate on southern slopes, but they also look for other food-rich areas such as abandoned apple orchards. Current topographical maps are an immense help."

According to Ron Fowler, game staff specialist in South Dakota, "Shelterbelts (windbreaks) provide both food and cover for whitetails on the edge of agricultural croplands in South Dakota, so shelterbelts are very good places to hunt."

In the Deep South, the edges of soybean fields and river-bottom swamps are good places for deer hunting.

Horace Gore, whitetail deer program leader for Texas Parks and Wildlife, suggests: "Breaks in the terrain such as the cleared lanes on either side of fences often lead hunters to deer."

No. 4

You can often determine the deer's preferred food source in a specific place, and take a stand close to that food source. The whitetail needs 10 to 12 pounds of food per day.

"Even deer within one state have different preferred food sources," said Dr. Shelton. "That preference is often determined by the time of year and the availability of that preferred food. For instance, in my area of the South, the deer seem to prefer persimmons, crab apples, and sloes (a type of wild plum) in the early fall during bow season. But later on, deer favor white oak acorns.

"In parts of the state where no wild fruits grow, the deer's favorite food may be something entirely different. The hunter should find out what the preferred foods are in the area he plans to hunt during the time he wants to hunt."

Dale Sheffer, chief of the division of game management for the Pennsylvania Game Commission, told me that "Hunters can look at small trees such as red maple, black cherry, or young oaks in our region and determine whether or not deer are feeding on this type of browse. Look to see if the twigs of trees and shrubs have been chewed off. Rabbits often utilize the same food source as deer, but rabbits cut twigs off squarely as though they had been cut with scissors. When a deer feeds on twigs, he chews and tears the ends. A deer has no upper front teeth and cannot cut a twig cleanly.

"If acorns and nuts are the preferred food, a hunter has to know how to distinguish between squirrels and deer feeding on the nuts. Sometimes, squirrels chip the shell of the nut away to get to the kernel, but deer most often pop the nut in half to squeeze the meat out of the shell."

In some places, deer feed on agricultural crops rather than on wild food. For instance, abandoned apple orchards in New York may be excellent places to find concentrations of deer while, in the West, grainfields are invaded by deer in the winter and, in the South, soybeans draw large numbers of whitetails.

No. 5

Deer often overcome many obstacles to feed on their favorite foods.

Empty white oak and water oak acorn shells directed Allen O'Dell to a hardwood bottom in a Southern river swamp last season. O'Dell knew the deer were feeding on the acorns in this particular bottom because he had found many tracks, droppings, and cracked acorns during pre-season scoutings, but heavy rain fell before O'Dell could hunt. The flats where the deer ordinarily fed were under three to eight feet of water. Most of the ridges were very narrow and there was little food on them, but the ridges were the only places where the deer could have gone.

As he started to wade across a slough toward a ridge, O'Dell saw some movement in the water out of the corner of his eye. At first, he thought it was caused by ducks, but he stood motionless. Then he saw a doe standing chest deep in the slough 20 yards from the bank. The doe was feeding on floating acorns.

"Apparently, when the water came into the bottom, fallen acorns had floated up and formed a ring about 20 yards from dry ground," O'Dell told me. "The deer stuck her nose into the water, picked up floating acorns, and then let the water run out of her mouth before popping the shells."

For the next two weeks, O'Dell hunted the slough and, though he saw many deer, he didn't get a shot.

"I would see as many as 20 to 30 deer in a drove moving through the slough," he told me. "They were eating the acorns out in the water, but bedding on the ridges."

Normally, hunters do not expect to find deer in water but, because of the flooding, these deer went after their preferred food until they exhausted the supply.

No. 6

You can often find the trails whitetails travel to their main food source, and O'Dell did so.

"There were three places where the deer crossed the bottom," he told me. "After some investigation, I found three crossings where they forded the slough in comparatively shallow water. The deer could cross on these fords and only be in three or four feet of water. In two weeks of hunting, I shot three bucks and saw between 150 to 200 animals by taking stands near the fords."

The trail the deer utilize to go to a favored food source is often the best place for a sportsman to take his stand. Sometimes, there are several trails leading to a particular food source, and many hunters try to guess which trail is used most.

"One of the best methods I have found to determine whether or not deer are using a trail is to check the place where the trail goes under a fence," Dr. Shelton explained. "There will be deer hair in the barbs of the fence if the deer are using the trail. Remove the hair each day. Then check daily to see if new hair is stuck on the wire."

A heavily used trail will have many deer tracks on it and you will find a large amount of fresh deer droppings. The freshness of the droppings can be determined by squeezing a few between your thumb and index finger. A fresh dropping is soft, but an old dropping is hard and dry unless there's been rain recently.

No. 7

You can often funnel the animals to your stand if the deer are using several trails to go to feeding areas from their bedding grounds.

"When there are three or four possible trails the deer can use to get to a food source." Dr. Shelton told me, "I build natural barriers with limbs and branches across all the trails except the one I want to hunt. This tactic is especially useful for the bowhunter who has to bring the deer in close for a shot. I do this four or five days before I use the stand."

Generally, a whitetail will not attempt to leap these barriers, although a deer can clear a very high barrier from a standing start when it is frightened.

No. 8

It's best to hunt a preferred food source at the right time of day.

Since deer are primarily nocturnal feeders, the best time to hunt a preferred food source is either in the morning, when the deer are leaving feeding areas, or in the late afternoon when the animals are returning to their feeding area.

"If a hunter moves into a feeding area before daylight or at daylight to take a stand, chances are extremely good that he will spook the deer that are already feeding," Shelton told me. "The morning hunter will do better if he takes a stand near the trail running from the feeding area to the bedding area."

Many afternoon hunters hunt over green fields or agricultural crops. These sportsmen sit on the edges of the fields and wait for the deer to come out of heavy cover to feed in the fields. However, outdoorsmen who want to hunt in the afternoon should consider the advice of Ron Fowler.

"The hunter who finds a deer trail that runs from bedding cover to a field should take a stand on the trail 50 to 100 yards from the field," Fowler said.

In watery or flooded areas, deer habitually use shallow areas to ford creeks, streams, and sloughs. Find the favored crossings and wait them out.

Photograph by Tom Brakefield

"This works better than sitting on an edge and depending on the deer to come out into the field. The larger bucks often stay 20 to 30 yards back in the woods and wait until nightfall before they come into the fields."

The hunter who meets his buck on the trail leading to the field may kill a bigger and better buck than he would have if he had waited for the deer to step into the field.

No. 9

You can stage a deer drive if you can find escape routes leading away from bedding areas.

Many hunters disregard bedding sites as likely places to shoot a buck. The chances of taking an undisturbed deer in its bed are remote. However, if you find the escape trails whitetails use when they are spooked from their beds, you can often bag a buck. Deer beds can be distinguished by locating areas where leaves or grass are packed down in the outline of a deer's body. In snow, there is a depression with dry leaves on the bottom where the deer has scraped the snow away.

By midmorning, the deer have bedded down after feeding. Deer can eat their fill in an hour, and then bed down in a safe place and regurgitate the partially chewed food and chew it again before finally swallowing it. One hunter takes a stand along a deer's escape route from the bedding site. The second hunter walks boldly into the bedding cover from the opposite side to spook the deer and drive it down the escape trail and into the sights of the first hunter.

I remember a buck I hunted in a soybean field a few seasons ago. As I approached the field, I saw his high rack and large body, but he was always out of range. Each time I approached, the buck left the field by an escape trail—no matter how carefully I stalked him. Every time I spooked the deer from the field, he ran along the escape route.

I got a friend to help me. We crawled up to the edge of the field and saw the white antlers above the beans.

"Give me 30 minutes," I whispered. "Then stand up and walk toward the deer."

I circled the field, and positioned myself on the escape trail 50 yards from the field and 30 yards from

Where the buck-to-doe ratio is high, preferably one-to-one, bucks must actively seek out does. With all that movement, taking a stand where there is a lot of sign is often the best way to go.

Photograph by Leonard Lee Rue III

the trail. Then I heard the beans swishing and saw the buck on the run. Twenty yards from the field, he slowed his gait and began to walk down the escape trail and right into the center of my scope. I squeezed the trigger, and the fat beanfield buck dropped.

That was a simple two-man drive. In some areas, notably Pennsylvania, big drives with several standers and drivers are common.

No. 10

It's often possible to locate a buck's line of scrapes and to take a stand near the line or between the scrapes and the feeding area.

Many articles have been written on hunting deer during the rut, and many of them discuss scrape hunting. Scrapes are bare, pawed-up places with a strong smell of deer urine. Hooked, splintered twigs and crushed leaves over the scrape act as a stop sign for does ready to breed. A doe is in heat for 30 hours and then comes back into heat 28 days later. Bucks make scrapes and frequent them in order to meet willing does.

The bucks return periodically to freshen their scrapes. One of the best ways to determine if a scrape is fresh is to pick up a handful of the pawed-up earth and smell it. A strong urine smell indicates a fresh scrape because a buck urinates in the scrape each time he comes back to it.

Dr. Shelton, however, believes that scrapes are not always sure bets.

"Suppose a buck has a line of six scrapes," he told me, "and the hunter takes a stand close to scrape No. 3. If the buck comes to check for a doe, he may find a female at scrape No. 6. The buck may spend a lot of time with that doe, walking with her and waiting for her to stop so he can service her. The buck may stay with her until the third day, hoping she will permit him to breed her again. Meanwhile, the hunter doesn't see anything for three days. On the fourth day, the buck may work his scrapes again, but he may stop at scrape No. 1 first and find a doe. Hunting scrapes is not always a sure way to take a buck."

No. 11

Sometimes it is possible to let a doe lead you to a buck. Although scrape hunting can be productive, Bit McCarty, a good friend of mine, has found another productive way to hunt during the rut.

"I look for does," McCarty told me. "During the rut, the buck looks for does to breed. When he finds does, none of them may be ready to receive him. The buck often stays near those does for a long while. I have located plenty of bucks by moving through the woods close enough to a group of does to see them but far enough away so they do not see me.

"If the buck is not with the does, he will often be standing 20 to 30 yards behind or to the side of them. Sometimes I see does feeding in a field or a hardwood flat and catch a glimpse of horn in a fallen treetop or a patch of thick cover. The buck is waiting nearby so he can watch his harem. Then, it's a matter of making a stalk or waiting for him to make a move."

No. 12

Bucks travel around a lot in search of ready does only where the buck-to-doe ratio is high, one-to-one, if possible. The state's deer biologists can usually tell a hunter where this ratio is favorable. In areas where there are many does for every available buck, males can simply bide their time and wait for does to come to them. In such places, few scrapes are made, and scrape hunting is impossible or not productive.

Backtrack Your Buck

By Jeff Murray

Photograph by Gary Knepp

Sometimes, while pursuing the elusive whitetail deer, a "hopeless" situation can become the spark for a brilliant discovery. Like a meteor out of the dark, something hits you, leaving a lasting impression on how you view things. The discovery of this sort that tops my list occurred several seasons ago. Nothing else I've ever learned about hunting whitetails has proven as helpful in bagging bucks. It started with an unexpected snow squall one November afternoon.

Snowflakes were falling like goose feathers, almost touching one another, and I could see no farther than the tip of my nocked arrow. Snow worked its way from my hunched shoulders onto my neck. But it would have taken a bulldozer to get me off that stand; it was a deer hunter's dream. Four wellworn trails—two on each side of the three where I was stationed—formed a neat, tic-tac-toe grid. Even though I had spent three fruitless days there, I was confident that I would eventually get a deer.

Now for the hopeless situation. I was shivering uncontrollably, my teeth chattering like castanets. It seemed to be snowing sideways as I slid down the old poplar tree. I hadn't gone 100 yards, quartering into the wind, when I jumped a big deer that romped into a tag alder thicket. I didn't notice whether or not it had a rack.

Halfheartedly, I circled the alders in hopes of intercepting the deer on the other side. I easily picked up the tracks in the fresh snow, and followed them until they doubled back into the thicket. For some reason, I decided to follow them back to see where the deer had come from instead of where it might be going. This led to my discovery. First, I found a large bed, then another. When I found a line of fresh scrapes, the full impact of what I was onto finally hit me. Here, in 20 minutes of scouting, I had located a buck's hangout! These were fresh beds and scrapes, being used *during the day, during the hunting season!* I wasted no time putting my portable tree stand between the beds and scrapes. Then I got out of there.

Like clockwork, the thick-necked eight-pointer sauntered by my stand the very next day. When he turned broadside, 12 yards away, I drove my broad-head into his heart. The buck dropped at the edge of the alder thicket, not more than 50 yards away. So my discovery paid off. What's even more intriguing is how that spot has continued to yield a buck each year since. Even though it doesn't look nearly as promising as the popple stand with the tic-tac-toe deer trails, that's where the bucks always seem to be during the day, during the hunting season. And it was no fluke. Other hunters have used my "backtracking" method to achieve similar results.

Backtracking is not a replacement for pre-season scouting nor is it a shortcut to a freezer full of venison. It does, however, answer the questions that

Photograph by Leonard Lee Rue III

most field reconnaissance trips only begin to raise: Which scrapes are active and which ones are dormant? Which ones are worked during the day? Which trails are used during the day? In the morning? In the afternoon? Where do bucks bed during the day? Where do they feed?

Indeed, backtracking is much like target sighting a scoped rifle after it has been bore-sighted. It works especially well for the deep-woods deer hunter who is often beset with the nettlesome task of untangling whitetail patterns where there is no discernible difference between bedding and feeding areas. In northern Minnesota, where I hunt, deer feed, bed, and breed all in the same cover. It does me little good just to find bedding and feeding areas. I need to pinpoint a buck's daytime whereabouts. Backtracking is the key.

Some hunters certainly will ask, "Why give up a day or two of hunting, especially during the rut?" I have three, short answers to that question. One, you could bump into another buck traveling through the territory. (I once filled my tag this way by shooting a fat forkhorn on the last day of the season.) Two, you could run into the buck you're backtracking as he completes his circuit. (This happened to me last year and I was as surprised as the buck was. Now I'm more on the lookout.) Three, you'll be in the woods, and, whenever you're in the woods during the rut, almost anything can happen.

Backtracking often turns out to be a learning experience from the ground up because most hunters rarely track deer nowadays, and those who do are usually banking on finding where a deer is going, not where it has been.

The first order of business is finding a buck's fresh track. How will you know a buck's track from that of a large doe? Apart from sighting the buck, there is no single, reliable method. Here are some clues that should raise your success rate to 85 percent.

- Start with the largest set of tracks. Although a big doe could have bigger hooves than a small buck, big bucks usually leave good-size prints.
- Any splayed print, emphasized by the imprint of dewclaws, is readily attributed to a buck. A running deer, however, puts more weight into its leaps, coming down much harder than a walking deer; the result, quite often, is a dewclawed, sprawling toe mark. Dewclaws are noteworthy only in prints left by a walking deer. This could indicate a buck.
- Does walk like women in high heels; they pick up their feet within a pigeon-toed line of travel. Bucks, on the other hand, tend to drag their feet and cast them outward as they travel.
- Does leave trails that appear to meander. Bucks seem to travel in a more direct route, as if they had a purpose and a destination in mind (perhaps a doe in heat).
- A buck with a swollen neck and a massive rack carries more weight off the front shoulder than a doe or a younger back. Therefore, a print with

a deep impress from the tips of the toes of the *front* feet is likely to belong to a buck.
- A single set of tracks is likely to indicate a buck. A mature buck is a solitary animal during the hunting season. Does are more gregarious, traveling with other does, yearlings, and fawns.
- A doe urinates in her tracks with a wide, irregular spray that enters the snow at an oblique angle. A buck's urine perforates the snow in a more precise manner, directly below the animal. Red-stained urine probably indicates a doe in heat.
- A buck with a fairly wide rack will walk around a section of close-growing vegetation rather than negotiate his antlers through it. If you're on a track that has been sticking to game trails until it crosses one of these thickets, you could be onto a buck.
- The largest set of tracks leading to and from a scrape or a fresh rub is likely to belong to a buck.

Easiest of all to track and age is a fresh set of prints in three to four inches of snow. A brand-new track is letter-perfect with a crisp, sharp outline, noticeable even between each hoof mark. As time passes, the edges become less distinct; the track will acquire a feathered look, and ice particles will begin to fall into the depression. In spite of these rudimentary rules of thumb, I used to have great difficulty in determining how fresh a track really was. Just when I'd decide, someone would disagree, causing me to second-guess myself. Not anymore. Now, I can spot a truly fresh track nine out of 10 times. You can, too.

All you have to do is get hold of a deer's leg, with hoof attached, of course. Try your bowhunting buddies, a butcher, or a local conservation officer (be sure to tell him what you're up to). Wait for snow. Now depress the hoof with about 40 or 50 pounds of pressure (check on the bathroom scale to see how this "feels") in the snow. Observe. Do it again, and again, and again. Soon, you can have a friend make a number of tracks to test you on finding the freshest ones.

Backtracking to a guaranteed kill can only be accomplished during the rut. Finding out where a buck has been doesn't tell you that he's going to be there today or tomorrow—unless a mighty strong force causes him to continue in his ways. That's why scrapes are so vitally linked with backtracking. I would never set up over a scrape—no matter how big and fresh and pungent—unless I knew a buck was in the immediate vicinity, guarding that scrape during the day.

Most hunters know when rutting activity peaks in their area. Hunting seasons often coincide, so the hunters are probably in the woods at the best backtracking time. But there is a better time—the "second rut." Does that were not successfully bred will come into heat again in another four weeks or so. Throughout much of the nation, this occurs in December, after the last rifle has been fired at a deer. It's an ideal time to pattern bucks unaffected by hunter pressure. December scouting also invariably

When backtracking, think backwards. To find a daytime bedding area, locate tracks made in the afternoon.

offers good snow cover for tracking in areas that might have been bare during November.

Aging a track is nearly as important as determining the sex of its maker. You could end up wasting a lot of energy if you follow tracks made at the wrong time of day. Here's what happened to a friend of mine.

Gary had just completed his tracking, certain he was set up over some hot scrapes. He had determined that the buck would enter his scrapes from the south when that was the downwind position; otherwise, the buck would enter these particular scrapes from the west, where a large spruce bog buttressed the knoll his calling cards were laid out on. For three days, Gary saw nothing but blue jays and squirrels. One night, after dinner in camp, he decided to switch areas, so he took a flashlight and went back to retrieve his portable stand. A huge 10-pointer bolted from underneath the tree stand when he was no more than an arm's length away.

Back at camp, we analyzed the situation. Why was the buck using the scrapes at night and not during the day? It appeared that we were back to square one.

"Are you sure it wasn't a different buck from the one you were tracking?" I asked.

"Can't be," he said. "Those tracks are a perfect match."

"Are you sure they were fresh tracks?" I asked. "Maybe they were from the night before."

"Yeah, they were fresh, all right," he said. "I cut the tracks first thing in the morning, right after the snow ended. . ."

We looked at each other in astonishment as the revelation hit us simultaneously. Gary, indeed, had been backtracking a buck's fresh tracks. But the more he tracked them, the farther into the previous night they took him. He recalled that it had taken at least two miles of tracking for him to find the scrapes. We had simply forgotten to think backwards. From this lesson, we know well that the only track to backtrack, if you want to know what a buck is doing during the day, is one made in the afternoon or toward dusk.

If there is a trick to aging a track, it starts with understanding gravity. After a deer's hoofprint disturbs objects from their natural position, the tracks will look "fresh" to the discerning eye only until the disturbed objects settle. How long does this take? On bare earth, about five hours. In the snow, 10 minutes to an hour. If you get on all fours and scrutinize tracks with a small flashlight, you will be amazed at how simple and constant this principle is.

Unfortunately, many hunters become intimidated by the notion of tracking a deer without snow. In fact, anyone with enough patience to sit on a deer stand for a day can learn to do it.

Most of us have seen deer tracks along river bottoms and creek beds. Whitetails are bottomland creatures. The simplest procedure upon finding such a trail is to smooth out all the tracks at midmorning, then come back during the afternoon and observe. If there are fresh tracks coming directly from high ground, where big bucks are most apt to make their scrapes, try backtracking. If you find any beds along the way, that may also be a good area to fine tune for a stand.

In just a few seasons of backtracking, I've learned more about whitetail patterns than I could from 50 years of deer hunting. A day spent backtracking is worth at least five seasons in the woods.

A topographical map is an invaluable asset in plotting your strategy. But even the best maps available are far too minuscule for me, so I take the particular map section I'm interested in to a printer and have it enlarged to the size of a full page. Then, I mark deer sign as well as travel routes, benchmarks, and helpful hints to keep things in perspective. An aerial photo, enlarged to the same scale, is also helpful.

If you've been coming up short after doing all that you can to find bucks in your area, try backtracking. You won't be disappointed.

Photograph by Erwin A. Bauer

Antler Rattling

By Ray Sasser

Bill Carter's seat wasn't exactly ringside, but the fight was the best heavyweight confrontation Carter had ever witnessed. The duo of south-Texas bucks that were using one another for punching bags definitely constituted "the main event." Even from 500 yards away, the Houston sporting-goods dealer knew the deer were trophy bucks.

"I got out my spotting scope, poured myself a cup of tea, and enjoyed the show," Carter recalls. "I'd seen a real wide buck in that area but he was only an eight-pointer. Other hunters on the ranch had told me about a buck with much larger antlers. When the two deer separated, I realized I was looking at both those deer."

The deer with the biggest antlers got the worst end of the fight. Having used up a lot of energy in an intense rut, the big buck found himself pushed around by the contender.

Carter, a veteran, worldwide hunter, knew exactly what to do. He snatched up his rifle and his rattling horns and closed the distance between himself and the fight scene. After scouting the area carefully, he climbed into the low branches of a mesquite tree, settled himself as comfortably as possible into the junction of two limbs, and clashed a pair of antlers together.

He twisted the deer antlers to simulate the sound of bucks going at it. He raked the antlers against the trunk of the tree. His sound effects produced instant action. Several small bucks came on a dead run.

Carter had to be careful not to spook the curious juvenile deer. He rattled off and on for 35 minutes before the big deer showed. Carter heard a nearby wire fence *twang* when the buck jumped it.

He got a glimpse of the deer moving to get the wind in his favor. It was a big buck, all right, but was it the one Carter was after? The deer turned its head, giving Carter a view of an enormous spread of antlers. Clinging precariously to a limb with one hand, shooting with the other, Carter executed the difficult 150-yard shot.

"I don't mind telling you I was excited when I walked up to that buck," Carter told me. "He had fallen in tall grass. All I could see as I walked up was one side of the antlers sticking up above the grass."

Carter's deer had 13 points and an incredible 30½-inch inside spread. A broken brow tine, possibly suffered in the battle Carter had witnessed, kept the big deer out of the record book, but it was still one of the most impressive bucks killed in Texas in 1982.

Rattling a giant buck in south Texas on the last day of the hunting season doesn't really surprise anyone who is familiar with Texas hunting. That vast expanse of brush is the capital of horn rattling. In southern Texas, the big bucks are deep in the rut late in the open season. But this cussed and discussed technique called horn rattling, despite common opinion to the contrary, will attract deer in places other than Texas.

About 1,500 miles northeast of Bill Carter's ranch, Noel Feather Jr. sat perched in a tree stand on Thanksgiving Day, 1982. Feather was hunting near a whitetail scrape not far from his home in Sterling, Illinois. About 15 minutes after daylight, Feather clashed his rattling antlers together and twisted them to and fro in a sequence that lasted 2½ minutes. He quietly laid the horns aside, picked up his bow, and

A big buck may appear out of thin air in response to rattling, and many a hunter has missed because of buck fever.

took up a silent vigil. Nothing happened. After 45 minutes, Feather again took up his horns and went through another rattling sequence. This time, a deer came in from behind his stand.

"I heard the deer walking in leaves and I was afraid to look that way," the bowhunter recalls. "I'd been spotted in that stand before, so I just sat still. The deer circled around the stand and came in from my left. The first thing I saw from the corner of my eye was half the rack sticking out from behind a tree. My heart jumped at the sight of those antlers!

"The buck stepped out in a perfect spot—a little opening—and I put an arrow through his lungs. He took about three jumps and then walked to the top of a knoll about 75 yards away. He looked back the way he'd come and then his back legs buckled. When my heart finally got back to normal, I got down out of the stand."

The deer Feather rattled and arrowed was a monstrous non-typical whitetail that scored 220⅛ Boone and Crockett points, a record-book deer. It was the third Boone and Crockett buck Feather had killed in Illinois! All three racks have been measured by an official Boone and Crockett measurer, but they have not yet been officially accepted for listing in the book. The three bucks were all suckers for the clashing antlers. Feather has also rattled up bucks in Minnesota and Wisconsin.

Far from Illinois, deer hunting guide Jim Crumley was telling Tink Nathan about a giant whitetail that lived in a residential area near Crumley's lodge on Chesapeake Bay. The big buck was record-book material and, apparently, was the Einstein of whitetails. The deer knew its home territory so well that it successfully evaded hunters.

Nathan, who markets a variety of deer hunting scents under his Safariland Hunting Corporation label, put his son, Jeff, then 16, in a tree stand bordering a narrow spit of woods where the buck had been seen.

"I climbed another tree and rattled horns. This big buck, the buck that never made mistakes, came to the sound. He came within 50 yards, a little too far for a bow shot. He was a record-book deer, all right. As far as I know, no hunter ever killed that deer."

Nathan has rattled up many other bucks in Virginia, West Virginia, and Maryland. Carefully selecting the conditions under which he rattles, he figures the odds are about 66 percent that deer will come.

So horn rattling is not just another Texas brag. It works in other states, as well. Bob Ramsey thinks the technique will attract whitetail deer, under optimum conditions, anywhere the animals are found. Ramsey, who is a Lone Star horn-rattling guru, also believes there's a lot more rattling going on in other states that you hear about.

"Getting people in other states to talk about horn rattling is kinda ticklish," admits the homespun central-Texas rancher who gives seminars and has produced a number of films that show bucks coming to the horns.

"I know hunters in Iowa and New Hampshire who've rattled up bucks, but they don't like to talk about it. I believe they want to keep the technique a secret. If everybody in the woods has a set of rattling horns, you can bet the bucks will get educated real fast.

"In Texas, horn rattling is a tradition. Most of the Texas hunting takes place on private property. Hunters here can talk about rattling up bucks and not worry about other hunters doing the same thing in their favorite spot."

The clashing together of deer antlers, thumping the horns on the ground, raking bushes and trees, is obviously designed to fake the sound effects of two bucks in a duel. Other deer—does as well as bucks—come to the sound. Just why they come is a matter of speculation, but three logical reasons include sex drive, territorial protection, and plain, old curiosity.

"There's only one reason two bucks will lock up in a serious fight," says Texas Parks and Wildlife biologist Horace Gore.

Gore, who is head of the state's whitetail program, oversees the nation's largest deer herd.

"Deer almost never have a serious fight unless it's over the sexual favors of a doe," he says. "When an old buck hears the sound of a fight, he knows there's a doe in heat.

Dr. James Kroll, a whitetail management specialist with Stephen F. Austin University in east Texas, favors the theory of pecking order and territoriality.

"Based on what little we know about the social order of whitetails, I believe bucks come to a fight hoping to get in on the action," Kroll told me. "If a buck gets badly whipped, all the other bucks will jump on him. They'll kick him while he's down."

Kroll thinks that deer living in overlapping territories establish their pecking order early. Whitetail battles are most apt to occur later, during the rut, when bucks travel out of their home ranges.

Then there's the curiosity aspect of horn rattling. Noted Texas wildlife photographer Ed Dutch was hunting a south-Texas ranch when he heard what had to be two bucks engaged in a knock-down drag-out dispute.

"As I started getting nearer the fight, I began jumping deer everywhere," Ed remembers. "There were some does there, but most of the deer were bucks. I saw seven or eight good bucks in the immediate area of the fight sounds. They must have been watching the fight just like people in at ringside."

Enthralled by all the deer, Dutch spooked the combatants before he could fire a shot. One thing he learned from the sounds the battlers made is that hunters can't possibly make too much noise when they rattle.

"When two big deer fight, it's a fierce struggle," he says. "To approximate the sounds, you would really need about three guys—one to clash antlers, one to roll around on the ground and crash into bushes and trees, and another to thump the ground with another set of antlers."

Such an elaborate production would undoubtedly attract bucks, but few would be shot. When a deer comes to the horns, it knows almost exactly where the sound is coming from. Unlike a deer that's just going about his business in typical fashion, a rattled buck usually comes in hyperalert and knowing where to look. The slightest motion immediately attracts his attention.

Ed Dutch, while guiding hunters and taking photographs, rattles up between 100 and 200 whitetails a year. He notes that it's not just the bucks that are rattled.

"Few of the deer I've rattled in have been shot," he recalls. "Most of the time, the buck comes in and leaves without the hunter ever seeing it. And, in the best of circumstances, it's pretty unsettling when a big buck jumps out of the brush and stands at close range, looking you in the eye. Some hunters get so excited that they don't shoot."

Bob Ramsey agrees. Ramsey has rattled up more than 1,000 Texas deer, many of them for other hunters. The most unsettling experiences occur when bucks come at a dead run. The rattling pro has watched hunters forget to raise their rifles. On two occasions, the hunters pumped cartridges through their firearms without ever pulling the trigger.

"With a good buck standing there looking at us," he remembers, "one fellow pumped all his shells out on the ground. Then looked at me and asked, 'Bob, can you see where I'm hitting'?

"I just nodded and pointed to the shells lying around his feet. He couldn't believe he hadn't fired a shot."

For deer rattling to work, the experts agree that two critical criteria must be met. The deer must be actively rutting. In fact, rattling probably works best toward the end of the rut when most of the does have been bred and the bucks are frantically moving around, trying to locate remaining, unbred females during their brief estrus period.

The whitetail rut remains something of a mystery. In some states, particularly those with a short hunting season, the rut does not coincide with the legal hunting season. An occasional deer might come to the clash of antlers out of curiosity, but the technique is hardly worth trying in those states.

Texas hunters have determined that the second critical condition required for good horn rattling action is a balanced deer herd. In a situation where does greatly outnumbr bucks, the technique doesn't work very well. That's true in Texas as well as in other states. The greatest rattling success occurs where there's a good population of mature bucks and a buck-to-doe ratio approaching one-to-one. Ramsey thinks you should try rattling if there is a buck-to-doe ratio of one-to-three or better.

RATTLIN' HORNS

When wildlife biologist Charles Allen of Lufkin, Texas, got interested in horn rattling, he was interested in a big way.

"I saw a huge 10-pointer rattled up to within 20 yards of the horns, and I was converted," Allen says. "I set out to find a pair of rattling horns that were just perfect, and I finally found a set with just the right curvature."

Allen used his Stradivarius antlers to bring between 30 and 40 bucks within range of himself and his hunting friends. Every hunter who saw the horns work tried to talk Allen into selling them.

"I realized that a good set of rattling antlers is hard to find. Those with the proper curvature are usually antlers from a mature trophy deer, and not many people are willing to saw up a trophy."

Allen started experimenting with artificial antlers made by forcing synthetic materials into an injection mold. He couldn't get the sound right until he analyzed the specific gravity of whitetail antlers in a physics lab. He then mixed minerals with his synthetic materials to duplicate the real McCoy. The result is Rattlin' Horns, synthetic antlers that sound like the real thing, remain stable during changes in the weather, and never lose their "live" sound.

After extensive field testing, Allen is now marketing Rattlin' Horns (patent pending) in two colors—fluorescent orange and natural brown. They're available for $29.95 postpaid from Rattlin' Horns, Box 1035, Lufkin, TX 75901.

The timing of your rattling efforts and the place where you rattle have a lot more to do with success than any "secret."

"I know hunters who have rattled up bucks by clacking a pocket knife on a rifle stock, by clashing two dead limbs together, or by scuffling the bark with their boots when they climbed a tree," says Ramsey, who has simultaneously rattled as many as nine bucks on three different occasions.

"The trick is rattling near a buck that's in the right frame of mind. A fellow I know in south Texas was using a stick to rake limbs from the grill of a bulldozer when a buck jumped out of the brush, every hair standing on end, spoiling for a fight. The auxiliary engine on that bulldozer was running at the time. Being in the right place at the right time is definitely more important than any rattling technique."

The right time, as we've already established, is during the rut. The right place is an area with a good buck-to-doe ratio. A state game agency can tell you when deer normally rut in your hunting area and they should be able to provide buck-to-doe statistics. The date when the rut starts varies somewhat from region to region within many states.

Specifically, the right place to rattle is where a buck can hear the clashing of the antlers. The pros like to rattle where they've repeatedly seen a good buck and feel confident that the animal is close by. In an unfamiliar area, fresh buck rubs and scrapes are the best indications of a buck's presence.

Because sound carries better on a still day, a frosty,

windless morning is prime rattling time. In open country, deer have been known to home in on rattling horns from as far away as half a mile. Thick woods tend to muffle the sounds, as does the wind.

In Texas, possession of good rattling horns confers undeniable status. Hunters have been known to saw a trophy rack apart just to make impressive rattling tools. A sizable set of antlers produces a louder clash than smaller antlers, but a spindly six-point rack will definitely get results.

There's also a good deal of cactus-country romance involved in how to "treat" or "tune" antlers to produce just the right sound. During hunting season, Bill Carter soaks his rattling horns in water every two or three days to produce a "live" ring. Bob Ramsey treats his horns with linseed oil to keep them from becoming chalky.

Most experienced deer rattlers use a grinder to remove the burrs from the antler bases to make them more comfortable to handle. Removing the brow tines lessens the chance that you will accidentally gore yourself when meshing the antlers.

The best way to transport rattling horns is to drill a hole through the base of each antler and connect them with a length of cord 18 inches to two feet long. Drape the cord over your shoulder so that one antler hangs down in front and the other in back. This keeps the antlers from clacking together when you slip into a good spot.

There's another important point about antler rattling and hunter safety. If you plan to rattle in an area where there are other hunters, wear Blaze Orange. As an added protection, spray-paint your rattling horns fluorescent orange. In public areas, it's possible to rattle up other hunters as well.

Ramsey, who once rattled up 38 bucks in a five-hour period, has a few tips.

"The setup is more important than rattling technique," he explains. "If possible, two hunters should participate—one to handle the horns, the other to shoot. As many as 100 times, I've had deer come in so quickly that I didn't have time to put down the horns and pick up the rifle.

"I like to take advantage of cover, at least by sitting next to a tree that will break up my outline and preferably by backing up under some low-hanging limbs to hide me from deer. Climbing a tree makes a lot of sense because the deer aren't apt to see or smell you when you're up off the ground. Hunting from a tree or some other high stand is about the only way a bowhunter is going to do it.

"A mature buck that comes to rattling is almost always going to come from downwind. When you set up, try to make sure there's a clearing downwind of your position. I don't rattle without putting out skunk scent to mask my odor. Otherwise, the deer are going to come in, smell you, and leave. You'll never even know you rattled a buck."

Tink Nathan, who markets sex lures for whitetail hunting, takes this scent business a step farther. He uses a cover scent to mask his own odor and a sex lure made from the urine of a doe in estrus.

"I've discovered that I'm many times more successful at rattling if I use a sex lure," Nathan says. "Bucks fight over does, so it's just natural and reassuring for a buck coming to the horns to smell a doe in heat. Rattling without the use of a sex lure is an incomplete technique."

Back to Ramsey and the mechanics of horn rattling: "If you're right-handed, turn the left antler so that both antlers are like half circles pointing toward the left. You're a lot more likely to hurt yourself if you rattle point to point.

"Wind up and hit the antlers together as hard as you can—really hit them hard. Then fight them; twist them together like two bucks pushing against one another with all their strength. Try to get one wrist to overpower the other. Get a sneer on your face and work up a sweat grinding those antlers together for about 20 seconds. Then really rake the ground hard and thump the antlers on the ground. Reach up and fight a bush. The whole sequence should last about 45 seconds maximum. Now put the horns down, pick up your rifle, and start watching."

Bucks come to the sound of a fight with varying zeal. Some charge in like a bull going after a matador. Others sneak around the scene, trying to get the wind in their favor.

Ramsey waits and watches for five minutes. If he sees nothing, he tries to goad cautious bucks by gently tickling the tips of his rattling horns together.

"You don't want to rattle hard again," he tells other hunters. "The first time you hit the horns together hard, every deer within hearing heard you. By just tickling the horns gently together later, you may prompt action by a buck that's standing close by in the cover.

"I don't generally stay in one spot longer than about 30 minutes before moving on to my next spot. Many times, though, I've stood up after rattling and spooked deer that I didn't see, even though they had come in pretty close."

Ramsey, Carter, Dutch, and any number of other Texans who sing the praises of horn rattling, do their hunting on private property where there are plenty of mature deer and a good buck-to-doe ratio. The typical, American whitetail hunter will be fortunate to rattle in nine bucks in an entire season, much less nine bucks at the same time, as Bob Ramsey has done. Noel Feather's Illinois hunting is more typical in terms of available deer. Feather sometimes hunts four or five days at a time without even seeing a deer, but he's an ardent supporter of the rattling art. After all, he has rattled up and killed three record bucks, and it would be hard to find a Texan who has equalled Feather's feats.

The "secret" of horn rattling, the experts agree, is to rattle in the right place at the right time and to have confidence that the controversial technique will attract deer. But there's another secret to horn rattling: It works very nicely in states other than Texas. Perhaps that's the real secret, and it's one that a few knowledgeable hunters would prefer to keep to themselves.

The Master Of The Bucks

By Larry Mueller

The slow, unmistakable *tick-tick-tick* of a deer walking through downed leaves reached Noel Feather's ears . . . from behind him. The back of his neck tingled. He wanted to jerk his head around to see, but he fought the urge—he had been spotted by a buck once before in this tree stand at the bottom of a swale. A deer leaving the field of standing corn 150 yards up the hill behind him would be at eye level until close to the tree.

It was Thanksgiving morning 1982. Noel had just gone through his three-minute antler rattling sequence for the second time that morning and, as is his practice, he quickly hung the antlers on the stub of a limb and grabbed his bow to get set. Bucks sometimes charge in hellbent for battle. This deer wasn't running, though, and it had come from the wrong direction. Feather had elected to watch two big scrapes and a well-worn trail instead of the cornfield.

Noel waited. He was standing on a wedge, and a nylon rope circled his torso and the fork of the tree he stood in. After the deer walked past, Noel would lean out against the rope. It would allow him to shoot in nearly any direction—if, of course, he wanted the animal. Noel Feather has become extremely selective in the past 10 years.

Gradually, the ticking in the leaves changed direction. Still 25 yards away, and still on high ground, the deer would pass on Noel's left. Noel strained to see the whitetail out of the corner of his eye without turning his head.

The deer's massive right antler was the first part of the animal that he saw, and now there was an urgency: The buck was within 20 yards, would get no closer, and might always be able to see Noel's movements.

Painfully slowly for a man in a hurry, Noel raised his bow and tried to ease it back without seeming to move. But he couldn't get the compound bow to "break over." He was cold and stiff, sure, but . . . and then he remembered. He usually sets his bow at 70 pounds pull for shooting from a tree. But he had just gotten back from an elk hunt and hadn't wound it down from 80.

The buck stopped and stood broadside. There was a four-foot opening to shoot through. But when the buck moved, there would never again be another clear shot. Noel gave the bowstring all the power he had, putting the 20-yard sight pin on the buck's chest in the same quick motion as the arrow came back to full draw.

The animal ran, as deer often do when first hit, but after three big jumps, he just walked off up the hill. Beginning to doubt the accuracy of his quick shot, Noel stood watching the trophy of a lifetime as it was about to vanish into the cornfield. And then the deer collapsed.

Noel Feather stared at the buck from his tree for a full 20 minutes, not daring to believe how big the deer looked—and almost afraid to come down and learn that it wasn't. Finally, he climbed down to see the deer that would score 220⅛ non-typical; the deer that would make him the only recorded hunter to rattle in and take three Boone and Crockett record-class whitetails (two with a bow); the deer that would make him 1982 Hunter of the Year in the Outdoor Adventure Club.

That buck's antlers will be officially scored by the

60

"I've been hooked on calling ever since I was a youngster," he said.

The Grunt

Dougherty had an excellent opportunity to use his grunt call in Alberta this past year while on a bow-hunting trip for one of the province's big whitetails.

"My call makes a guttural sound," he explained. "This cross between a grunt and a growl has been effective for me."

How effective? On one particular hunt, after locating a primary scrape and applying a dose of doe-in-heat scent to his moccasins, Dougherty walked straight into the scrape. He stood smack-dab in the middle of the scrape before walking down the faint trail to a tree he'd scouted earlier for use as a stand. He climbed up and waited. Soon, he saw a good buck running in the distance, but it was on the opposite side of the woods line from the trail and scrape. Dougherty yanked out his 'grunt' call and sounded off a few times.

"That buck stopped so short, it looked like he'd been yanked up tight around the neck with a rope," he told me later. "He started coming right to me when he hit the scent line I'd laid down with my moccasins. He followed the scent to the scrape, then out again, and came right on down the trail. He finally passed right under my tree, presenting a 12-foot shot.

The buck missed the Pope and Young record book by a scant one inch.

Although Jim doesn't use calls every time he goes deer hunting, he likes knowing that he's got something up his sleeve.

"No doubt about it. Calling's a good trick to have," he said. "Using a deer call *in moderation* won't scare deer away and it *can* make a big difference. I especially like to use it when I can see a buck from a distance and it looks like he isn't coming my way anyhow. I feel that, under those circumstances, I have nothing to lose, so I might as well give it a shot. And there's no bigger thrill than calling in an animal that's as wary as a whitetail."

Grunts seem to work during the rut because they signify one of two things: Either two bucks are facing off—getting ready to fight—or a buck will use the grunt, together with pheromonal and visual cues, to get the attention of does in heat. The grunt sound is important enough to buck behavior to warrant some careful consideration by deer hunters everywhere.

Bill Wadsworth, chairman of the board of the National Bowhunter Education Foundation, has bagged 10 deer during the past three years while experimenting with calls. One of his favorites is a variation of the grunt. He calls it "the morning after call" because it sounds like someone losing their breakfast. Bill calls twice, not too loudly, then waits. There might be something to this kind of calling. I tried it once and not a half hour passed before a dandy six-pointer charged down the hill in front of me. It stopped 10 yards away and I collected it easily.

The Aggressive Snort

Deer will snort when frightened, which is called an alert snort. Deer will also snort when they're in a fighting mood, which is known as an aggressive snort. The aggressive snort consists of from two to six snorts made in quick succession. In nature, it occurs during or after a lunge between sparring bucks or while a buck is tearing up the turf when working over small trees. In Dr. Jacobson's study, the researchers were able to provoke noticeably aggressive males into lunging and snorting. Therein lies the

All deer are vocal and, therefore, susceptible to various calling techniques. Factory-made mouth-blown calls can work well.

value of the aggressive snort. It's hard for a red-blooded buck to pass up a challenge. A hunter can play on this to take deer.

Billy Freeman, a factory representative for Lohman Manufacturing in Neosho, Missouri, swears by the snort call. While using it for only the second time, he called in a big-racked, 12-pointer for a fellow he was guiding. The buck came in from 300 yards, as if on a string, and headed straight for the pair. The excitement was too much for the hunter, though, who was gripped with the worst case of buck fever that Freeman has ever seen. He was shaking so badly, Freeman finally took his rifle away.

"I began to believe all the stuff I'd been hearing about the snort call right there and then," Freeman said. "On opening day of rifle season here in Missouri, I gave a few snorts while waiting in my tree stand above a scrape. I was hunting a narrow creek bottom and out came this dandy eight-pointer just like he owned the ground. He was spoiling for a fight, and my deer season was over right then."

Bill Harper, Freeman's employer and the owner of Lohman Manufacturing, developed the snort call eight years ago with Jack Lohman. Harper believes in the snort call, too, and his method for scoring on whitetails incorporates many little tricks that he has learned through the years.

First, he locates an active scrape. He gets to the

scrape early and digs up the earth with his heel. Then, he sprays doe-in-heat scent right on the scrape, and drips it randomly back downwind to his stand. He applies it to bushes and trees, as well. When he reaches his stand, he douses a cotton wad with a few drops of skunk scent, puts it in a baby food jar or empty film cannister, climbs into his stand, and waits for daylight. When it's light enough to see, he snorts four or five times, sometimes rattling antlers a bit, too, and waits.

Last year, this method brought in five does during the first 25 minutes he spent on stand. Then, a small forkhorn wandered by at 8 a.m. and, at 9:30 a.m., a good eight-pointer walked right up to the scrape to nose around.

Harper got his buck, and explained that the secret to calling in deer with the snort call is to "imagine what a rank ol' buck would be doing if he was challenging all comers to a brawl."

Harper doesn't always use antlers along with the snort call, but he thinks that sometimes the two together make powerful medicine—the kind bucks can't ignore.

Earl McNutt from Sterling, Kansas, thinks differently. He likes the snort call. Period. He's been hunting whitetails along the Kansas River flats for the past 15 years—as long as a huntable population has existed. When Jack Lohman and Bill Harper built their first prototype snort call, they sent it to McNutt to field test. McNutt's a self-proclaimed "call nut" who has no doubts that this snort call not only works, but works fantastically well. He's been using the snort call exclusively for the past five years and has bagged bucks with 10 points or more every year. He doesn't quit calling once his buck is in the smokehouse. He keeps right on calling in deer for his own enjoyment, and he's called in 20 to 30 bucks in this manner each season. McNutt hunts the hard way; he doesn't use a stand or scent of any kind. He only hunts after the first good frost when the rut's in full swing.

Kansas River country is wide and flat in areas where the stream winds through lush bottom fields and sand hill plum thickets. McNutt stands on the high ground at the edge of the flood plain, where he can overlook the flats, and observes bucks on their way to feeding and bedding grounds. It has to be fairly still for the sound of the snort to carry effectively but, when conditions are right, McNutt can call a buck in from a half mile away. He likes to watch the buck's reaction; it helps him to decide what to try next.

McNutt terms himself "an active caller" and keeps snorting in one place every 30 seconds for about five minutes. If he doesn't see or hear a buck coming within five more minutes, he gives up and tries somewhere else. If he can get a buck really worked up, it will come in from 300 yards in a couple of minutes.

"If the call's going to work, it's going to work real fast," he said.

McNutt wears camouflage and tries to blend in with his surroundings but, when he riles up the whitetails, they sometimes come busting right on in, throwing caution to the wind. McNutt once had five bucks come charging in at once, see him standing there, and yet be reluctant to leave because they were so fired up. Another time, he got so excited that he missed on all six of his arrow shots at one buck. He then had to wait for the buck to leave so he could retrieve his arrows, and snort the buck back in for another chance.

McNutt feels the good buck-to-doe ratio where he hunts improves his odds of successfully challenging bucks. He tries to hunt open terrain, so he can watch what's going on, and he always calls upwind and keeps his attention focused primarily in that direction. In his experience, he's never had a buck in rut ignore the call.

The success of the call was something I wanted to see, so I asked a neighbor of mine in St. Louis County, Missouri, Jim Holdenried, to demonstrate his technique. Holdenried, a well-known local bowhunter, has called in approximately 100 deer during the past three years. In fact, he called in two bucks to within 20 yards of his tree stand during the opening weeks of Missouri's 1983 bow season. We went to a nearby wildlife area to give it a try.

Although Holdenried usually uses the bleat call while hunting, he was unable to attract any deer the morning we went out. However, when we switched locations and he tried the snort call, our luck changed. Within 30 minutes, a good eight-pointer came creeping in suspiciously and got to within 60 yards of us. We were at a disadvantage because we were both on the ground. When the buck came in, he was looking for the source of the sound and soon discovered us there waiting for him.

Holdenried recommended that two people work as a team when calling deer. One person should call while the other waits 20 to 30 yards upwind. If the deer comes in to the caller's location, the second hunter can intercept it. According to Holdenried, a lone hunter should call from one location and then move to a different spot so that the deer will travel warily to the first site.

Deer calls are manufactured by all the big name call manufacturers, such as Lohman, P.S. Olt, Burnham Brothers, and Western Call and Decoy. Although their products vary somewhat in appearance, all are capable of producing the calls that are appealing to deer. Cassette tapes are also available to aid in mastering the use of these calls. Some hunters have experienced success using makeshift calls such as cellophane bread wrappers, leaves of grass, and the teeth of plastic combs.

Remember, deer calling is no substitute for good workmanship. But, when practiced with good outdoor skills, deer calling could help you be a more successful hunter. Experiment—because this is one area of deer hunting open to all sorts of daring innovations. No matter what call you try—the bleat, the grunt, or the snort—deer calling may be the card that will stack the deck in your favor. 🦌

How To Score In A Crowd

By Bruce Brady

The doe had not yet pushed the panic button, but it was obvious that she did not like the looks of things. She was 40 yards below me and picking her way through a cutover hollow. The area was so dense with underbrush that I could only see her when she moved. A light but steady breeze fanned across my face, so I was certain she hadn't scented me. When she reached a tiny clearing in the brush, she paused for several seconds before trotting across it to vanish into a wall of weeds and briers.

Ten minutes passed as I wondered who could have agitated the doe. Then, the snapping of a twig commanded my attention. I soon made out the form of another deer following the same trail the doe had walked. When it ducked its head under low-hanging vines, I saw a flash of antlers. The buck eased along more cautiously than the doe, and I fought off a compulsion to drive a bullet through the veil of brush that obscured his body. I reminded myself to wait for the buck's pause at the clearing but to be ready in case this didn't happen.

As expected, he stopped, and I put the crosshairs on his exposed shoulder, let out half of the breath I had been holding, then squeezed the trigger. Instinctively, I racked the bolt of my Model 70 Winchester, but a second shot was unnecessary. He was a 3 year old with a nice, eight-point rack.

I leisurely field-dressed the buck, lay my gun at the base of my tree, and then returned to my stand. I had a couple of hours before I was to meet my partner back at the truck. Only one buck a day was permitted, but I figured more deer might travel the hollow and I could gain more information by observing their movements.

It was midmorning and the sun was warm on my shoulders. I could see my dressed buck from where I sat and it was satisfying just to rest there chewing tobacco and feeling all the pressure drift away. My reverie was short-lived, however, for I soon heard the noisy approach of a man pushing his way through the brushy ravine. I kept silent in hopes that he would not discover me or my buck because, even though this was public ground, I didn't want to share this spot with anyone. It was a place I knew I could take other bucks on future hunts.

When I heard him say to himself "Well I'll be darned," I knew that he had seen my deer. I stood up and gave a call. He was a nice enough fellow, but I knew he was inexperienced when he told me that he was tracking this buck and that if I had not "lucked-up," he soon would have killed it. I listened politely to his speculations and didn't bother to tell him that this was the third buck I had "lucked-up" and killed in this same hollow from the same stand.

For many years, much of my hunting for whitetails has been on property open to the public. Public grounds offer good opportunities and, to me, there is something appealing about hunting where anyone can hunt—almost in direct competition. I enjoy a special sense of satisfaction when I get a buck in a public area.

For a long time, hunting pressure was light on

state and national forests, wildlife management areas, and corporate lands open to hunting. It was much like hunting huge tracts of land that were my private domain. Ten years ago, it was possible to hunt from dawn until dark on most public areas and not encounter another hunter. Those days, though, are gone with the wind.

As more land has been posted, more pressure has been transferred to public whitetail coverts. To meet this demand and to better distribute hunters, more access roads are being built, which opens large blocks of once-remote forests. When access roads were few, it was simply a matter of getting off the beaten path in order to find an undisturbed area. Today, hunters must compete for available bucks in almost any area, and competition is keen.

The remarkable whitetail, though, has adapted to increased hunter pressure with ease, and bagging the current edition of a whitetail buck is a thorough test of any hunter's skill. Still, it is possible to be consistently successful where pressure is heavy. Tactics that are productive where deer are undisturbed, however, are seldom effective where hunter traffic is heavy. New strategies must be used if a hunter is to put meat in his freezer. He must learn to use hunter pressure to his advantage.

The eight-pointer I mentioned earlier was bagged as a result of putting another hunter to work on my behalf. The cutover hollow that my stand overlooked headed up more than half a mile away near a bunching ground at the end of a logging road. Bunching grounds are forest clearings where logs are collected for loading on trucks. This particular one was a mile away from the public road and was a popular parking spot for hunters with four-wheel-drive vehicles. The ridges that bordered the hollow were covered with big white oaks and were therefore preferred feeding areas for deer. When easing along these ridges at dawn, I noted that the deer I jumped always broke down into the hollow and ran westward. I scouted in that direction and located a 20-acre strip of dense cutover—the perfect escape cover. By following the escape trail into this cover (often on my hands and knees), I located that tiny clearing. Next, I found a stand on the ridge above that provided an unobstructed shot at any deer that would cross the clearing.

The hunting along that hollow was so inviting that I knew any hunter parking at the bunching ground would not be able to resist moving along the ridges above it. I was confident that any deer jumped by hunters would react the same as the ones that I had jumped, and I intended to be in position when a buck headed for the escape cover I had located.

The first time I sat on that stand was on a Saturday. I arrived 1½ hours before dawn and left my truck well away from the bunching area so as not to discourage another hunter from parking there and hunting down the hollow. I moved into position using a flashlight and waited for sunrise. I dropped a spike an hour after dawn and, although I didn't see another hunter that morning, I knew one had pushed that buck to me. That was three years ago and my strategy has worked every year since. Incidentally, all of these bucks were taken on Saturdays when hunter pressure is greatest. I have spent numerous days on that stand and I have seen far fewer deer on weekdays when the pressure is light.

Knowing the area intimately and being able to anticipate deer movement makes that particular hollow a consistently productive spot. And so it is with other places on public ground where I hunt deer.

The first thing I do on any public area is to locate the most remote spot in the tract. Detailed maps are helpful, but they must be used in conjunction with on-the-ground inspection for which there is no substitute. I walk my area out, searching primarily for escape cover in remote regions. I roam over tracts without access roads, which is just the opposite of what most hunters do. I inspect the largest areas first—with a preference toward wooded blocks with a minimum of two sections about two square miles large. Within this area, I locate all prime escape cover. To find such cover, you must think thick, dark, dirty, and wet. The most common forms of escape cover include cutovers, canebrakes, thickets, weed fields, swamps, and evergreen plantations. I search out escape trails leading into such cover and mark them down on maps that I draw myself.

Escape trails are seldom major trails like those that connect feeding and bedding areas. These trails are smaller and usually traverse hillsides and hollows rather than ridges. In virtually every case, an escape trail will snake through brushy cover and not open woods.

Whitetail bucks prefer to move very cautiously once they are alerted to danger. Even when shot at, a buck will rarely run more than 100 yards or so—that is, if cover is adequate to put him out of sight of the intruder. Once the protective cover of an escape trail is reached, he will stop and check his back-trail for any pursuers. He may break away down-wind, but you can bet a new can of Skoal that he will soon be moving into the wind and along an escape route that will take him into heavy cover. When spooked, a buck does not run in terror without plan or destination. The cover along his escape trail will allow him to move slowly and to stop often. A buck's nose is constantly working but, when he is moving, it is difficult for him to detect movement and to pick up sounds foreign to his environment. Therefore, he makes frequent pauses.

As I go about learning the lay of the land, I pay close attention to the spots where I jump deer and note carefully the direction of their movement. Any prevailing winds are taken into account, as well. I mark each deer's location and its actions on my map.

While scouting for escape trails and cover, I keep my eyes open for tracks, droppings, crossings, and areas with preferred browse. I note carefully all crossings on creeks and other waterways. Deer use them far more predictably than other crossings.

I do most of my roaming around immediately before hunting season opens so that the data I collect will be pertinent come opening day. I seldom find fresh scrapes and rubbing trees this early in the fall, but I look carefully for evidence of last year's activity. Experience has shown me that bucks will return to the same rutting areas year after year. And if the buck that made last year's scrapes was bagged, his area will be up for grabs and another buck will soon claim his territory. Prime rutting grounds seem to have universal appeal from one generation to the next, so I mark every one I find on my maps.

I seldom hunt over scrapes on public ground with the hope of dropping a sex-crazed buck as he makes his rounds. Heavy hunting pressure alters normal behavior patterns and I have come to believe that most rutting activity on public areas occurs at night. Nevertheless, scrapes and rubbing trees tell me that, in all likelihood, I am standing within 400 or 500 yards of a bedded buck. And, too, there's always the chance that, come the rut, I may be in position when a buck's ardor simply overcomes his caution.

The more useful and fresh data I can collect, the more I can turn the odds of seeing a buck in my favor. Biologists tell us that a buck spends 90 percent of his time in only 10 percent of his range.

When I have located a concentration of sign and escape trails leading into dense cover, I pre-select my stands and determine if a tree stand is needed to effectively hunt the area. If so, I note wind direction and select the best tree for my portable climbing stand. Here, let me repeat the importance of remote areas. Prior to deer season, areas with easy access may be loaded with sign but experience has taught me to ignore them. Once 4WD and all-terrain vehicles begin grinding into these spots and the hunting pressure mounts, deer will quit them except during the dark hours.

No matter how remote a spot may appear, you can expect some competition. Sooner or later, hunters will move through. Don't be discouraged because this is movement that you can use to your advantage if you have learned the country and observed the reactions of the animals that you have seen.

I can count on the fingers of one hand the deer hunters I have known who could remain on stand from dawn until dark. Sitting on a stand all day can be uncomfortable and deadly dull if the deer are not moving. If it is very cold, the agony is compounded. The boredom is unmatched by any other outdoor activity save trolling for billfish when the fish won't rise.

Nevertheless, on public areas it pays to stay put. Let the other guy stalk if he must. Rest assured that your fellow hunters are in the process of making drives, building fires, checking with their pals, and just trying to get unlost. All of this activity is working to your advantage as you wait along a hot trail leading to escape cover. Deer will be jumped and moved, particularly from midmorning until midafternoon, and it is during this period that your chances of taking a buck are best.

A couple of years ago, I was sitting atop my tree stand at noon when I heard the voices of two men and some commotion in the distance. Moments later, a four-point buck jogged out of the brush and hit the creek crossing that my stand overlooked. It was an easy shot and I dropped him with one bullet through the ribs. The men came to my shot. I was gutting the buck when they arrived. They were dragging a ladder-type tree stand to a new location and their racket had put the buck in my lap. They remarked on the "luck of some guys," but I just grinned and went about my work.

Hunters will move deer during midday, but there is also a natural movement of deer during this time period. Deer rise from their beds to stretch cold muscles, to relieve themselves, and to feed for a brief period if browse lies in close proximity to the bedding area. Where pressure is intense, this natural feeding period may be greatly abbreviated, but it still occurs. The more remote the area, the more likely it is that the midday feeding period will be extended.

Keep in mind that not all remote areas are large and far removed. A remote area can be defined as any area with good cover and minimal hunting pressure. Bucks, and especially older bucks, seem to have an uncanny ability to differentiate between normal human behavior and hunting behavior. Every fall, scores of huge bucks are killed in unlikely places.

A pal of mine collected a 250-pound, 10-pointer in a tiny covert formed by intersecting gravel roads. That little thicket lies in the midst of huge corporate holdings, but I doubt if another hunter's boots ever made a track there. It was just too small for hunters, but it was just right for a trophy buck to use as a remote area.

Another friend who does not hunt deer told me of a big buck he saw almost every day of the late hunting season as he drove to work. At daylight, this deer would bed in a tiny weed patch in the corner of a pasture within 100 yards of the highway. The weeds were not high enough to hide the buck's rack. Every morning, my pal looked for those antlers and, every morning for more than three weeks, they were there. I scolded my friend for not passing this information along to me while the sason was in progress. He replied that he would have gladly helped me get the deer but that, in fact, I did not cross his mind. By not keeping in touch with someone who lives in the midst of deer country, I had missed some "insider" information.

To me, insider information is data collected from folks who live or work around whitetail coverts. In addition to farmers such as my friend, state and national foresters are good sources of information, as are corporate woodland managers. The directors of wildlife management areas are anxious to put you in areas where your chances to score are good and where their successful management practices will be documented. Don't be bashful about asking for help. Do not expect directions to their pet areas if they are hunters, though.

I always ask these insiders where they have seen a buck recently. Often, I am not only told about a sighting but am given the exact location, as well. Most of these sightings occur at dawn and at dark as bucks cross area roads. I ask the time of day and the direction of movement, too. I know a buck on the move at dawn is likely to be moving toward his bedding area, while a buck moving at dark is probably leaving a bedding area and heading for a feeding area. A running deer usually indicates that the deer was jumped by hunters, and his direction can be indicative of a prime bit of escape cover.

In unfamiliar country, I always ask for directions to remote areas that don't have easy access. I know that bucks, and especially big bucks, will migrate to these areas as hunting pressure continues and the season wears on. Once on the area, I pinpoint escape cover and wait for other hunters to arrive and push deer to me. When locating escape cover, remember to think thick, dark, dirty, and wet.

Hunting on public ground is not without its danger. Invariably, there are numerous hunters without previous experience or competent supervision who will share the area. Regardless of what the regulations require, I always wear ample fluorescent-orange clothing and sit with my back to a suitable tree.

It takes some extra effort and special strategy to take your buck on public ground, but the hunter who succeeds can take pride in the fact that he has scored where the competition is toughest and the deer are as smart as they come.

Deer Hunting Weather Or Not

By John O. Cartier

If you successfully hunt deer on enough occasions from the same spot, you're bound to learn a lot about how they react to weather conditions. Much of this knowledge can be key to putting venison into your freezer. Misunderstanding the principles involved can lead to hours, or even days of wasted hunting effort.

During the past 15 years, for instance, I've shot seven whitetail bucks from the same spot on my property in northwestern Lower Michigan. I just happened to be standing on that knoll when I killed the first of the seven. A couple of years later, I was sitting there with my back to a beech tree when I dropped the second buck.

By then, I realized that the spot was a natural place for a stand. For the next several years, I built temporary blinds there from cedar and oak branches. After I killed two more bucks, I built a permanent blind from weathered boards so I wouldn't have to bother with setting one up each fall. Last year, I got my buck the first morning of our November deer season at the same spot.

I keep notes on weather conditions during all of my outdoor activities. Some years, I was surprised to discover that I'd never seen a deer at the knoll when the wind was from the north, when a very strong wind was blowing from any direction, or when heavy rain or snow was falling. Now I never waste my time hunting there when these conditions exist.

A rainy day is, by all odds, the best time to hunt whitetails. Scent, hearing, and travel are disturbed, giving you the edge.

To help explain my first weather discovery, I'll describe the lay of the land. The knoll is the highest place on a series of east-to-west-running hardwood hills and ravines that slope down to a large inland lake. The lake's shore is 300 yards downhill from my blind. Behind my stand, relatively level woodlands of mixed hardwoods, aspen, and hemlock run south for several hundred yards to typical Michigan farm country. The area's whitetails feed in or near the cropfields and bed in various thick edge covers or in the woodlands near the lake.

Think as a deer would when it was confronted with a north wind blowing across the lake and into the woods surrounding the stand. Of most importance, the animal knows that hunters are almost bound to approach from the south and not from the lake that's to the north of the woods. The north wind robs the deer of its ability to scent danger coming from the south. Deer normally avoid bedding on a slope facing north when there's a wind from the same direction.

An opposite situation applies when a south wind blows. Then the deer want to bed in my woods because they will be downwind from the danger areas and they can bed in comfort.

My notes and my experience from many years of hunting have enabled me to draw many conclusions on how deer react to various weather conditions. Last winter, I categorized my notes and thoughts and came up with weather-related information that I consider important to deer hunters across the nation. Then I cross-checked my thoughts with some of the country's best deer hunters. Following is a boiled-down version of our observations.

Wind Velocity

Bruce Brady, an OUTDOOR LIFE Editor-at-Large, has hunted whitetails in almost every Southern and Southeastern state.

"The worst possible time to hunt deer is when a very strong wind is blowing," Brady said with emphasis. "During such conditions, the animals will lay up and won't move. All deer rely on the senses of sight, sound, and scent to warn them of danger. When a strong wind is blowing, bushes, tree branches, and loose bits of ground cover are moving. Strong winds make noise and produce crosswinds that temporarily blow from various directions. In short, deer won't move in high winds because their three most important senses for survival are at least partially destroyed. Most people hunt when they have the time, but statistics show that they almost never kill deer during strong wind conditions."

Heavy Falling Rain Or Snow

Brady, along with many other experts I talked with, agrees that deer seek shelter whenever precipitation is heavy. The animals much prefer umbrella-type protection such as stands of thick pines. Many biologists feel that deer seek such protection because heavy precipitation limits their ability to hear, see, or smell danger—not because they get chilled. If you hunt when strong winds are mixed with heavy rain or snow, you should hunt in the thickest cover you can find.

Light Rain Or Mist

Many years ago, when a veteran deer hunter told me that a rainy day is, by all odds, the best time to hunt whitetails, I thought he was putting me on. Now I know better. Paul Mickey, one of the best deer hunters I've ever met, is emphatic about how good deer hunting can be when there is a light rain. Mickey has taken more than 12 outstanding trophy whitetails. His best, a non-typical giant scoring 238⅜, is the best non-typical ever taken in Michigan, and it ranks 35th in the listings for North America. Mickey killed that buck on a rainy day in 1976 in Bay County, Michigan. Many of his other big bucks have been taken during rainy or misty weather.

"Most serious deer hunters know that rain dramatically reduces use of the two senses that deer rely on most heavily for safety—hearing and scent—but many of them aren't aware that it also disturbs a whitetail's travel schedule to such a degree that it abandons normal caution," Mickey told me. "When a night is clear, it takes up to an hour for full darkness to turn into dawn. On a rainy night, the period of darkness to dawn is much shorter, sometimes as short as 15 minutes. The sky doesn't gradually lighten. Instead, shooting light seems to come on very rapidly.

"On rainy mornings, deer tend to stay in feeding fields much later than usual," Mickey continued. "Then, when daylight comes on fast, they suddenly realize they have to hurry to reach daytime security cover in bedding areas. This situation makes even the wariest deer much less cautious. A buck that would normally stop every 20 yards or so to test for danger with his eyes, ears, and nose now may travel more than 100 yards between stops.

Mickey also pointed out that, in really nasty weather such as freezing rain or wet snow, bedded deer become very uncomfortable. Therefore, they'll begin moving toward feeding areas much earlier in the afternoon than normal. Nasty weather urges deer to move later in the mornings and earlier in the afternoons. Both situations offer a hunter longer periods of shooting light than on clear days when deer hate to leave security cover until near-darkness prevails.

Light Snow Vs. Snow

Jim Zumbo, a long-time OUTDOOR LIFE Editor-at-Large, lives in Vernal, Utah. His home is relatively close to several other Rocky Mountain states, which enables him to hunt mule deer in as many as five states each fall. Zumbo hails from the East where he put in many years hunting whitetails before he switched to mule deer.

"We seldom get rain in the mountains after October 15, so we're usually dealing with snow during deer seasons," Zumbo told me. "Light snow has about the same affect on mule deer as light rain does on whitetails. The precipitation doesn't repress normal deer activity, but it does make the animals much more vulnerable to knowledgeable hunters. After I first moved to Utah, I heard veteran stillhunters and stalkers say that they always tried to hunt during a light-to-medium snowfall. They claimed that falling snow bothers a deer's ears and interferes with its

Photograph by Fred and Dora Burris

Jim Zumbo claims that light snow makes deer much more vulnerable to knowledgeable hunters. Heavy snow brings even better hunting!

hearing. It also cuts down on its vision and helps to cushion the sounds of a hunter's approach. I also believe that any precipitation tends to drive a human's scent in to the ground.

"I like to stillhunt and stalk along. I guarantee that these methods work best when a light snow is falling. The very best mule deer hunting in the mountains, though, comes after a heavy snowfall that stays. We get early heavy snows that soon melt, but the first one that doesn't melt drives migrating mule deer crazy.

"Some sort of sixth sense tells high-country muleys that heavy snow is extremely dangerous," Zumbo continued. "The deer know they have to get down to lower elevations to survive. When they begin migrating, they don't stop for anything. Any hunter who knows of a mule deer migration route, and who can be there the first day after the first heavy snowfall that stays, will get hunting that can simply be incredible."

Zumbo's statement is easy for me to understand. Some years ago, I hunted out of Collbran, Colorado, with outfitter Ray Lyons. He told me several times while we were riding horses into our hunting area that I should definitely hold out for at least a fine four-pointer.

"There are lots of migrating muleys on the slopes we'll hunt," Lyons said. "You'll see more big bucks in one day than most hunters will see in a lifetime. Wait for a really big one."

I did. I dropped a massive four-pointer in his tracks using a 100-grain slug sent on its way with my Winchester Model 70 .243.

Warm, Calm, And Sunny

Despite what I've written so far, many seasoned deer hunters will claim that they see more deer on nice days than on nasty ones. They're right. Deer are most active on nice, clear days. Some of the most convincing proof of this fact comes from Al Hofacker,

When you know how deer will react to weather, you'll know where they are likely to be and what they will probably be doing.

a record keeper for the Stump Sitters, a nationwide group of deer hunters. The group's data come from the many thousands of hours that its hundreds of members have spent observing deer.

According to Hofacker, hunters saw an average of 41 deer per 100 hours of observation on partly cloudy days, 45 per 100 hours on overcast days, and 59 per 100 hours on clear days.''

''I was surprised at how the figures added up,'' Hofacker said. ''Until I studied our data, I had assumed that deer moved best on cloudy days. Now I know that our members are seeing more deer on clear days.''

A few years ago, the Stump Sitters cooperated with the University of Wisconsin at Stevens Point on a research project involving deer activity with relationship to weather variables. Results showed that, in general, whitetails are fair-weather creatures. Observers saw the most deer during periods of clear skies, light wind, and no rain or snow.

All of this seems logical because, under such weather conditions, deer can take maximum advantage of their superior senses of hearing, sight, and scent to alert them to potential danger. It also follows that, although hunters see more deer in nice weather, they'll be much more successful in bagging them if they hunt when the weather conditions dull the animals' abilities to sense danger. Weather variables can increase your chances, too.

Depth Of Snow

Jim Zumbo said that mule deer in one given area may move completely out of that location as soon as the snow depths exceed one foot, but that deer in another area may not migrate until the snow is 18 to 20 inches deep.

''I have no idea why this is true,'' Zumbo told me, ''but I know it's a fact from my years of observation in many mule deer areas. One of my best hunting areas becomes worthless as soon as the snow gets more than one foot deep. It took me a few years to discover this pattern. The hunter who keeps accurate records of his observations can eliminate hunting in the wrong places.''

In general, deep snow forces deer to change their feeding locations. Stump Sitter data, according to Hofacker, indicate that whitetails will continue feeding on ground foods such as acorns or waste grain in snow that is up to six inches deep. The animals can paw the snow away from such foods without a great deal of trouble. But when the snow becomes considerably deeper, the deer will switch to brush browse. Choice browse may be far away from choice ground food. A harvested cornfield that attracted dozens of deer in November may be deserted in December.

You'll do well to keep in mind that there can be exceptions to any rule. Several years ago, in my area

Photograph by Fred and Dora Burris

of Michigan, we had a very hard freeze before the first snowfall. During the first few days of deer season, I hunted from a stand near a harvested cornfield. I spotted a few deer each day, but not nearly as many as I saw a few days after the first blizzard. The snow was more than one foot deep. Fierce winds produced drifts topping four feet, but the strong winds also blew that frozen field almost bare of snow. The easy-to-reach waste corn drew deer like a magnet.

Clear Vs. Dark Nights

The long-held belief that deer feed heavily on clear—especially moonlit—nights apparently is more myth than fact. Biologists point out that a deer's night vision is so good that the animal can actively feed on the darkest of nights. Deer are likely to feel safer in the open during dark nights. The degree of light intensity at night will probably have little bearing on the success of your hunt the next day.

Storm Fronts

One popular belief that isn't a myth is the theory that deer usually go on feeding binges the day before major fall storms hit. Rapidly falling barometric pressure precedes these storms. Biologists agree that deer activity picks up significantly as the barometer drops. Whitetails, in particular, tend to roam and feed heavily before storms, so this is obviously an excellent time to be on stand near feeding areas.

The best place to be on stand the day a storm hits is near dense cover. As I noted earlier, deer want to move into heavy cover when a bad storm arrives. So, when the storm is close, get on a stand that overlooks a runway or runways that lead to extremely thick cover and wait for deer to move to you.

The harsher the storm, the thicker the cover the deer will seek. Lyle Laurvick, a gunsmith friend of mine who lives in Superior, Wisconsin, hunts with a group that has a very high success rate, especially when they hunt a particular area at a certain time.

"The place is close to the very remote Lake Superior shoreline," Laurvick said. "It's so junglelike thick in there that we cut some trails before each deer season. There are few deer in that big swamp during normal weather conditions, but that changes fast when big storms hit. We hope for a major blizzard before the deer season closes. If we get it, we know we're going to take home a lot of venison."

Laurvick and other veterans are quick to emphasize that there are three phases to hunting storm fronts and storms. During the front, which occurs prior to the storm and is when the barometer first begins to tumble, deer are most interested in feeding heavily and have little concern about cover. Hunting from a stand that's in or near a good feeding area is the way to go. As the front passes and the storm begins, though, take your stand near thick cover. When heavy rain or snow is falling, the animals want to be holed up until the precipitation passes.

There are many bits of knowledge that can help the weather-oriented hunter. Most sportsmen have been indoctrinated to believe that deer always travel upwind so that they can scent danger ahead. The thinking hunter knows that the animals must sometimes travel downwind, and that this usually happens when the best travel route to a preferred feeding area runs downwind from a bedding area.

When whitetails are faced with this situation, they'll almost always follow ridgelines because air currents tend to swirl over uneven land contours. By traveling through such air currents, the animals are offered some security because they can use their noses to scent danger from all directions. The hunter who is aware of this principle hunts along ridgelines whenever the weather dictates that he should.

All deer—being very hardy creatures—don't pay nearly as much attention to temperature changes as do humans, but temperature extremes can help a hunter. Most deer seasons aren't open when it's extremely hot, but many hunters have to cope with extreme cold. From what I've heard from many veteran hunters, and from my own observations during more than 40 years of deer hunting, I don't think deer want to move before full dawn after a very cold night.

A deer can curl up into a very small circle and maintain body heat in the coldest temperatures—if it doesn't move. It follows that a deer won't want to move until full sunlight is shining, and that it will most likely bed in an area where the day's first sunlight will hit. A weather-wise hunter expects deer to bed on ridges or slopes with a southern exposure during cold nights, he expects them to still be feeding during late morning hours, and he expects them to favor sunlit areas that are out of the wind as long as there is an extreme cold snap. He also knows that he should be patient on stand because deer won't move as often or as far as they will on warm days.

This is the type of thinking that takes the success of your hunt out of the "luck" category, because you're depending on knowledge. When you know how deer react to weather, you'll know where they're likely to be and what they're likely to be doing. With that kind of knowledge, you'll know where it's best to hunt and you'll know whether you should take a stand, stillhunt, stalk, or organize a drive.

PART 3

HUNTING MULE DEER AND BLACKTAILS

The One-Year Plan For Muleys

By Ed Park

When Will Henderson told taxidermist Neil Rodgers that he had located a mule deer buck with antlers that would measure 30 to 32 inches and then added, "I'll bring him in when I get him," Rodgers discounted it as the normal preseason enthusiastic exaggeration he hears so often.

Anyone who knows anything at all about trophy mule deer, knows you don't predict taking a buck that size—especially in Oregon, a state not known for trophy mule deer.

For example, the widest typical rack listed in the latest edition of *Records Of North American Big Game,* the Boone and Crockett Club record book, has an inside spread of 32⅞ inches. A quick glance down the listings shows most record-book muleys come from Colorado and other Rocky mountain states. Of the 564 total mule deer listed in the book, only 17 are from Oregon and only one of those—a nontypical buck—has a spread of more than 29 inches.

So you can imagine Neil's amazement when Will Henderson came back a few days later with a mule deer rack measuring 31 inches across. The buck was the one he'd mentioned on his first visit.

It cost me a beer but Neil finally introduced us. Before long I was visiting Will Henderson, examining his photos and antler collection and trying to learn how this man is able to bag tremendous mule deer in a state not known for yielding many.

I first learned that Will hunts in four phases. Phase I involves hunting—not shooting—year-round. Most

Photographs by Ed Park

of Will's spare time is spent looking for oversize deer. He wanders the backroads for tracks and hikes the canyons searching for shed antlers that might indicate the general home range of a whopper buck.

Will also frequents taxidermy shops, sporting-goods stores, feed and seed stores, and other places where hunters, ranchers and farmers might pause to exchange yarns. When a rancher swears he saw a buck the other evening in his alfalfa "that had horns like this," while holding his hands a good four feet apart, Will figures its worth checking out—even after he subtracts about 18 inches for enthusiasm.

That evening and during the next few days, you're apt to find Will hiking through the rough stuff near the rancher's place, looking for deer.

Will is also a firm believer in antler traits being passed on genetically. He can cite several examples of occasions on which he located big deer with unique antler configurations in the same area where he had taken deer with identical antler patterns. The genes are passed along, so Will hunts where he's seen or taken big deer before.

Will Henderson is not a once-a-year weekend hunter—he searches for deer throughout the year. When I jokingly asked him what a hunter should do if he has to work and can't get out a lot, Will seriously replied, "Change jobs."

If you doubt his sincerity, consider that Will has 18 years seniority at the plywood mill where he works and could work any shift he wants. Just so he can have daylight hours off to look for deer, Will has chosen to work the graveyard shift, from 11 p.m. to 7 a.m. If a hunter who works regular hours is serious about his sport, though, Will insists there is plenty of time before and after work or on weekends.

Phase II begins in late summer when antlers are full grown. Based on clues picked up year-round, Will now starts looking for specific tracks.

"I've been fooled a few times by bigfooted does," he says with a laugh, "but most of the time big tracks mean big bucks."

Phase II is where Will's bicycle comes in. He has a low-geared wide-tired 10-speed bike—the low gears are for ease of pedaling uphill, the wide tires are for dirt roads.

Will uses his bicycle for several reasons. It's quiet. He can cover a lot of country easily. It helps condition him for later rough hunting. And he can see more tracks from a bicycle than from a pickup.

Once he locates tracks, Will follows them until he gets a good look at the deer. The idea is to see if the buck measures up to Will's personal standards.

Once he actually spots the buck and makes his personal judgment, Will backs off and goes looking for another big buck.

"When I first started this hunting method years ago, I made the mistake of locating just one big buck," he told me. "I was on his track opening morning and he trotted across the blacktop where some guy driving by shot him. Now I always try to locate at least three or four.

"The most important part," Will emphasized, "is

that by locating these bucks ahead of the season, I *know* there's a good buck in a particular area. I could tell other hunters about the buck but they don't know for certain that he's there, so they are not as likely to see him during the season. Because I *know* he's there, I'm much more apt to see him."

Phase III begins about two weeks before the season opens, which in Oregon is the Saturday nearest October 1.

With the arrival of this phase, the hunting becomes intense. Will changes from ordinary clothing and lightweight boots to camouflage clothing and heavy boots. The camo clothing is partly to keep others from seeing what he is doing and the heavy boots help to slow him down. He also applies a cover scent at this time. These modifications are mostly part of Will's technique for psyching himself up for the approaching hunting season. Will knows that the switch of clothing means an increase in hunting intensity.

He then begins doing everything he'll be doing during the hunting season—with the exception of pulling the trigger. All this effort helps Will learn in detail the nature of each buck and how it will react to his approach.

For example, Will feels that most of these older and smarter bucks tend to bed twice. They'll leave the fields or other feeding areas well before dawn and move back only a short distance—maybe just a couple hundred yards. They'll lie there until after dawn, then get up again and move maybe a couple of miles to their day-long bedding area.

He feels that individual deer habitually bed in certain types of habitat. Some prefer high open sage, others bed alongside fallen dead trees, and still others in pockets of brush. By learning the characteristics of each of his bucks, he'll be better prepared when the season opens and will be more apt to outguess just where that specific deer will be.

When jumped, individual deer also tend to follow specific patterns. One will jump, then run across, down and up a slope. Another will head right uphill. A third might run only 20 yards then stop behind some brush. Knowing how your buck will probably react moves the advantage to your side.

Phase IV, of course, is the actual hunt. Will puts on his heavy boots, his scent and switches to red clothing for safety.

He laughs when he admits to few successes on opening weekend.

"The influx of hunters keeps the deer all stirred up and changes all my carefully studied patterns. I try but don't succeed too often. I find my type of one-on-one hunting really doesn't work well until about the fourth day of the season, when most hunters have gone home and the woods return to normal."

But even though he rarely takes his buck the first couple of days, he uses this time to study their tracks and discover what they did and where they moved under heavy hunting pressure. Each evening he also makes a few phone calls to sporting-goods stores and

Will Henderson believes camouflage is essential, even when scouting. His clothing and gear all meet his requirement.

taxidermists, to see if anyone has reported taking a big buck that matches the description and general locations of those he had spotted. Usually nobody has.

When I asked him what he thinks of the generally held opinion that opening-day pressure tends to push the smart bucks clear out of the area, Will replied with a grin, "I love that! All that opinion does is lessen hunting pressure. Sure, those bucks may leave for a while, but they don't go far and they come right back. I've taken many of my best bucks on Wednesday or Thursday—in areas that had been hunted to death opening weekend—right where those deer had been the week before the season."

Will's actual hunting involves locating tracks early in the morning, then dogging them. He moves along pretty fast until the tracks indicate the buck is thinking of bedding. Here again his pre-season hunting has told him the particular buck's habits.

"For example," he explains, "when approaching a draw, one old buck would either go right on across, or loop back and follow it along the edge. If he went right on across, I knew he hadn't picked the draw. But once he started that looping business, I knew he'd chosen that particular draw to bed in and he'd be near the head of it."

Once the tracks change to indicate that the buck is bedding, Will shifts into extremely slow gear, for he knows he's within a quarter mile of his trophy. Hunting now demands absolute silence and complete attention to the wind and every object within sight.

"It doesn't matter how long it takes," Will says. "You have all day. You've been studying that deer for weeks, so another couple of hours won't matter."

The intensity of Will's hunting can be measured by noting how slowly he hunts at this point. That last quarter of a mile stalk might last four hours. He'll take one or two steps then search the area for a long

time. He uses binoculars continually and spends a lot of time crouching or on his hands and knees, looking under low-hanging limbs. He's looking for sign of bedded deer—an antler tine, an ear, a white rump, a gray side or one shiny eye. He usually spots them in their beds but most of the time the deer spot Will first. The big bucks are rarely completely fooled.

If eye contact is made at close range, the buck knows instantly he's been spotted and will be up and gone in one motion. The shooting can be tricky, especially if the timber is rather thick, but Will is also skilled at snap shooting.

If Will's not in a good position to shoot when the buck is first spotted, he often backs off and pretends to be doing something non-threatening.

"When I know one jump will bring that buck to safety, I pretend I'm wandering around looking for arrowheads. It doesn't fool a smart buck often but I try."

If Will spots any lesser bucks bedded, he stalks them, too, because the odds are good that the big one will also be bedded nearby. He's been surprised more than once to stalk and jump a forkhorn and, in the process, jump a half-dozen other deer—including the big one he had been hunting.

Will's equipment is basic. He hunts with a .270 Parker-Hale or a .257 Roberts sporterized Mauser. In the .270 he shoots handloads with 130-grain Nosler solid-base bullets and, in the .257, he uses 100-grain Nosler solid-bases. Each rifle is topped with identical Weaver 4X scopes.

Will carries his binoculars and a rifle year-round. Doing so gives him greater familiarity with the weight and feel of his equipment so they are not strangers.

Central Oregon may not harbor many bragging-size bucks, but any that do exist there won't be living a life of secrecy once Will Henderson finds out about them and gets on them, one on one.

Big Bucks I've Hunted

By Walter L. Prothero

The big muley buck had simply vanished. Earlier, watching from a canyon to the east, I had seen the buck come off a high ridge and into the wide, bare, rolling draw where the only cover was sagebrush. Now, on the lip of the draw, I scanned slowly with binoculars.

The sun had set some time ago and frost was settling on the tawny grasses and blue-gray sagebrush. The light was fading fast. I shrugged and walked back up the ridge toward the truck. On the ridge, I scanned the draw one more time. The buck was in the bottom. He was stretching like a big dog, rump in the air and forefeet extended in front. I was too far away for a shot and, by the time I worked close enough, it would be dark. The big buck had been there all the time, lying in the short, 20-inch sagebrush, watching me. Looking at him through the binoculars, I could have sworn he was grinning.

That was only one of several hundred encounters I have had with big muley bucks. He was one of the many that got away. I have hunted deer for 20-odd years in five Western states. I've bagged more than 40 good bucks. In these hunts, I've run across some pretty unusual bucks—smart, equipped with incredible patience and steady nerves and, above all, unpredictable.

Perhaps the smartest buck I have ever hunted was the one I named the "Sheepherd Buck." He lived in the canyons draining into Sheepherd Canyon in northeastern Utah. I hunted this buck for four consecutive seasons. Each year, I saw the buck at least once and usually twice. Each time, I got a chance and, each time—except the last time—I was outsmarted.

One time, early in the deer season, I came upon the buck in a thick growth of maples. I could see him sneaking away. I ran to the opposite slope of the small draw and watched. Nothing happened. After a-while, I walked back to the maples and picked up the buck's tracks.

He had crossed the ridge beneath two big spruce trees, the only place he could have gotten out of the draw without my seeing him. I followed the tracks. In the next canyon, he had joined up with five other bucks. As I crossed the ridge, I saw the bucks silhouetted against the snow in thick maples on the opposite slope.

Five bucks were browsing unaware. The sixth deer, the Sheepherd Buck, was watching me. I moved down the slope toward the bucks, using the scrub oak for cover, but I didn't fool the big one. He continued staring. One by one, the other bucks picked me out. They were within rifle range but in thick brush. The big buck had gotten behind the other deer. Then they ran, slowly at first, then more quickly as they became panicked. The Sheepherd Buck kept the other deer between himself and me.

Just before the fleeing bucks were about to cross an opening, the Sheepherd Buck took off at a right angle and ran up through the thickest brush on the hillside, zigzagging from one stand to the next. The last I saw of him that year, he was crossing the ridgeline 600 yards away.

Another time, while watching some horseback hunters who were "brushing" the opposite slope of a canyon more than 500 yards away, I again saw the buck perform some incredible feats of patience and intelligence. He lay in a tangle of maple and willow

Photograph by Mike Francis

while three horseback hunters passed within 10 yards. After they passed, he stood up and slowly and deliberately walked up the slope. He laid down in a clump of willow. A few hundred yards below, more hunters were riding up the canyon. They rode right through the place where the old buck had been bedded earlier. After they had passed, the buck stood up and casually walked down to his first resting place.

On opening day of the following deer season, I got into the buck's favorite draw across from his favorite stand of maples long before daylight. I sat on the opposite slope. As the light began to come I saw a buck disappearing into the brush. Was he the Sheepherd Buck? I waited. Big, heavy clouds raced by from the northwest. Finally, I moved down into the draw and circled around the growth of trees. For some reason, just before moving down into the maples I looked back across the draw to the place where I had been. A few feet from where I had been sitting, the Sheepherd Buck stood. He twitched his tail and walked over the ridge. I guess he figured the safest place to be was the one I had just come from.

There were other adventures with the Sheepherd Buck, and most of them made me the dunce of the encounter, but the big buck finally made a mistake. He was getting old, I knew, and his antlers were a little smaller than they had been the year before. I saw the buck standing in a small clump of brush on the opposite slope. He was staring down toward the lower end of the canyon. Hunters were coming up the bottom a thousand yards away from him. The Sheepherd Buck stared in the direction of the noises and perhaps his preoccupation with the advancing hunters was the reason why he did not detect me. I was a long rifle shot away, but I didn't want to shoot into the brush. Then the buck stepped into an opening, perhaps trying to better sense the oncoming danger below. I settled the crosshairs of the .270 at the top of his shoulder and squeezed. The buck leaped at the shot and came down a few yards lower on the slope. He didn't seem to be hit, and he had located me. I raised the crosshairs to a few inches above the top of the buck's shoulder and squeezed again. This time the buck jumped into the air and came down running. I was sure I heard the bullet strike flesh. He ran into some brush and then tried to make it over the ridge. He died trying. The 130-grain bullet had taken him through the heart. The buck had a 33-inch spread and very high-reaching antlers.

A buck I once killed in Nevada's Ruby Range perhaps best illustrates a muley buck's steely nerves. I camped in my pickup beside a small stream at the base of a long, bare slope that led to a ridge. The ridge, in turn, led to some steep canyons and jagged peaks to the south. A little farther than midway up the slope, in a slight depression, was a small, thick tangle of willows and aspens that was perhaps 15 yards across and maybe 20 long. Surrounding the tangle was open slope, grass, and wind-stunted sagebrush—nothing over 10 inches in height.

I had been hunting for more than a week and had seen only does and small bucks. Each morning, I walked by the patch of brush on the hillside on my way to the ridgetop and the canyons to the south. I often walked next to the brush and I always passed within 10 or 15 yards of it.

One afternoon, on my way back to camp, I stopped a few yards from the patch of brush to enjoy the panorama of the valley below. The aspen and cottonwood leaves were like phosphorescent gold in the afternoon sun. Sitting slightly above the patch of brush, I idly tossed rocks into the aspens and willows. I had tossed a half-dozen stones when an incredible commotion broke out. The tops of several 20-foot saplings swayed violently, brush popped, and then an immense buck broke out of the other side of the growth. I was so startled, I fired the first shot in the air. He headed across the slope with all the speed he could muster. A bullet caught him in the back of the neck as he was disappearing over the curve of the slope.

Later, I checked the tangle of brush in detail. The buck had been staying in the patch. The whole interior was trampled with big deer tracks. Willows had been heavily barked by antler polishing. There was a small water seep near the center of the tangle. Several of the rocks I had tossed were lying on the main bed. Perhaps I had hit the buck with one of them. From all of the sign in the patch of brush, it seemed the buck had been there all the time. I had passed within a few yards of him every day.

One summer, not too long ago, I was able to find time to fish the upper reaches of Causey Reservoir in northern Utah nearly every evening. I would paddle my canoe the four or five miles to the back of the rugged, steep-sided reservoir and fish until dark. A big buck lived in a small draw high up a steep, brush slope broken by gray, limestone cliffs. I saw him browsing on cliff rose and mountain mahogany nearly every evening. He was there through August, September, and early October. (The Utah deer season opens in the last half of October.) I figured I had a sure thing. I even made wagers on it, but I lost. The buck had somehow sensed the advent of deer season, perhaps because of the appearance of hunters and the sounds they made, perhaps simply because of the time of year. The buck disappeared several days before the season opened. I hunted hard but I didn't see him.

In early November, a week or so after the deer season had closed, I paddled the canoe up the reservoir to have a last try at the browns that were still spawning in the feeder creeks. Looking up the slope toward the big buck's haunt, more out of habit than anything else, I was pleased to see the old deer. He was feeding on the slope just as he had during the summer and early autumn. I have had similar experiences with other muley bucks. Maybe they become nocturnal in their movements or maybe they move to rugged or inaccessible areas come hunting season.

One summer, I made several backpacking trips onto Buffalo Plateau in southern Montana's Absaroka Mountains to scout for elk. During that time, I found a monster buck that hung out in the rocky ridges at the end of Elk Creek Basin. I was sure the buck would make the record book. I saw him a number of times that summer, always within one-quarter mile of the ridgetop. I packed in two weeks before the opening of elk and deer season to scout and enjoy the Indian summer weather. The buck was still there, and there were several bull elk in a basin to the south. Things looked good.

As opening day approached, outfitters began moving hunters into and through the country. The buck just disappeared. I shot a nice bull elk, packed him out to the truck and horse trailer 20 miles to the north, and headed home to Utah.

I drove home through the northern part of Yellowstone National Park, actually only seven or eight miles from where I had been hunting though more than 100 miles by road. In Yellowstone, next to the highway near Tower Junction, I saw the buck. He was being photographed by several tourists as he browsed. He had not gotten big by being a dummy. There was no mistaking the buck. He had five long, heavy points on each side and his antlers were perfectly matched. He was the largest buck I had ever seen, and I'm sure he would make the top 10 in the record book.

One deer season about 12 years ago, I came across a buck with very unusual habits. During the summer, I had heard about a big buck that hung out with a herd of sheep. I didn't put much stock in the story, though.

That deer season was hot and dry. I hunted hard but hadn't seen one decent buck and only a few small ones. Each evening, I hunted a small draw in the head of Utah's Magpie Canyon. Over the years, the place had consistently yielded good bucks, and I'd always seen deer there. One evening, I reached the ridgetop and peered over. The draw was full of noisy, smelly sheep. The herders were moving their flocks out of the mountains for the winter. I stood up and cussed, pondering my next move. Then I saw a tawny flash in the brush below and, a moment later, a great buck bounded up the opposite slope. I dropped to a sitting position and fired at the buck. The first shot grazed his neck; the second entered between the shoulder blades and exited through the brisket. The buck fell three feet from several sheep. He had jumped up within less than 10 feet of several others. Later, I talked with the herders.

"Sure," one said in heavy Basque accent, "he been with the sheep all summer."

I had never believed any selfrespecting buck would even be in the same canyon with sheep, let alone travel with them. And because many hunters don't believe it either, that's probably the reason he survived so long.

Even more unusual was the buck I hunted during the 1981 season. I had set up camp on a ridge over-

looking the North Fork of the Narrows of the Ogden River in northern Utah. The country is rugged—steep canyons feed into the headwaters of the Ogden River, which flows in a steep, limestone gorge 1,000 feet below. Because of its ruggedness, the place gets little hunting pressure.

I scouted the country several days before the opener. The weather had been perfect—mild days and cold, crisp nights. I had seen a number of deer from camp through the spotting scope. One was a good buck. I saw him near a peculiar, orange, sandstone cliff. At the base of the cliff grew a huge, old Douglas fir. Surrounding it was a thick growth of scrub oak.

Opening mornings found me across the draw from the orange cliff. I was within easy rifle range of the place where I had seen the buck. After watching for a while to no avail, I crossed the draw and checked out the rock. There were large, fresh deer tracks. I felt sure they had been made that morning—probably before light—but there was no sign of a deer bed. A ledge crossed the face of the cliff 20 feet up. I moved out of the brush and back across the draw. The big Douglas fir covered much of the face of the cliff but, from what I could see, it looked as if the ledge crossed from one side to the other. I hunted back toward camp and had lunch.

I watched the ridges and canyons from camp with the spotting scope that evening. Just before dark, the big buck was again feeding at the base of the orange cliff. One moment, there was nothing; the next, as if by magic, there was the big buck. It was as if he could appear and disappear at will. I hunted back to the orange cliff in the morning. Still no buck. I couldn't figure it out.

I clawed through thick oak brush to the ledge. There were big tracks on the ledge. I eased along the ledge and sat down next to a large, cavelike hollow. There was a sudden, loud, shrill, whistling snort and a flash of gray rocketed past me and over the ledge. The buck landed in the scrub oak 20 feet below and crashed down the draw. I was so startled, I nearly fell off the cliff. I never did get a shot at the buck. From across the draw or from camp with the spotting scope, I couldn't see the hollow because it was hidden behind the fir.

On the last day of deer season, I again approached the cliff. I was on top of it and began dropping stones onto the ledge below, hoping to spook the buck out. I dropped several stones before I heard a movement in the brush above and behind me. I turned just in time to see the buck disappearing over the ridge. For all I know, that buck still roams the rugged canyons above the Narrows of the Ogden River.

The intelligence of big whitetail bucks is legendary. But the whitetail is more predictable; the muley buck is apt to do anything. Where the whitetail is highstrung and spooky, a big muley has nerves of steel and seldom panics. The only rule that works in hunting big mule deer bucks is to be ready for anything.

Migration Muleys

By Jim Zumbo

Snow pelted down furiously as I trudged along the ridgetop. The clouds looked like they meant business. Three other snowstorms dropped snow, but they were only temporary efforts. This blizzard had the makings of winter in all its glory.

It was early November, and I was hoping to bushwhack a muley high in the Colorado Rockies. I'd hunted the area before, but never during a hard snowstorm. I was delighted with the snow, though, because I'd be able to read deer sign easily. I'd also be able to spot deer more easily against the white background.

I approached a place that is choked with quaking aspen and that I know always holds deer. Moving carefully, I expected to see deer scattered about as they spooked. Twice, I'd jumped good bucks from this spot and I'd taken them both.

This time, however, I drew a blank. Although snow was falling heavily, there were no tracks in the stand of trees. It appeared that the area had been vacated by deer well before the storm, or at least in the midst of it.

The same was true as I pushed along the ridge, visiting places that had always supported deer. Nothing.

I left the ridge and headed for a wide valley. I thought that perhaps the deer were along the sidehills feeding on mountain mahogany and oak brush. Snow piled deeper as I walked. It was rough going.

I stopped abruptly when I crossed the valley bottoms. A fresh trail in the snow indicated plenty of deer in the area, and they were just minutes in front of me. I hurried along the trail, marvelling at the number of deer that had to be using it. One of those animals might be the kind of buck I was looking for.

I left the trail and climbed a sidehill to look over the ridge, hoping to see deer in front of me. As I topped out, I looked into the face of the storm. Snowflakes reduced visibility to just a few dozen yards. I couldn't see a thing.

Night was coming on, so I decided to watch the trail in the event more deer would be heading down. It was a fruitless effort. Nothing showed.

The next morning, I visited the valley-bottom trail again, but it hadn't been used. The snow had quit, and blue skies were promising a bright day. I backtracked up the trail and realized that it was apparently used as a migration path by mule deer herds leaving the higher country. Smaller trails funneled into it from several ridges.

It didn't take me long to figure out that I'd just missed a full-fledged migration. If I'd been five minutes earlier, I might have ambushed a buck the day before. I'd heard of migrations before, but had never seen one while I had a tag in my pocket.

Muleys move to the low country when winter comes. If the hunting season is late enough, this fact will help you score.

Photograph by Mike Francis

86

I hunted the rest of the day in vain, wallowing through knee-high snow. I kept hoping I'd blunder into a tardy buck that hadn't left the high country, but all I saw was a skinny coyote.

The next day, I hunted lower. I had an idea where the deer were going, and I planned on spending two days in the area. It was winter range where deer spent the cold months after snow covered their feed in the higher elevations.

My strategy worked. As soon as I arrived in the lower elevation, I spotted fresh deer sign. After an hour of sneaking through cedars and pinyon pines, I jumped a herd of deer that included a smallish three-point buck. I let him go, confident that more deer would be showing up. Later that afternoon, I tied my tag to the antlers of a fine four-point buck that I surprised in the cedars. He was bedded with a half dozen does and fawns.

In much of mule deer country, migration is an annual event. Once high elevations are converted from grassy glades to inhospitable spots covered by several feet of snow, deer must move lower to where feed is substantial.

Muleys instinctively migrate when winter approaches and they don't necessarily require a deep snow to force them out. The area they live in often determines the timing of their migration. For example, I know places where muleys are on the move after a few light snowshowers. In other areas, a heavy snow gets them traveling.

Summer range in most Western states is much more abundant than winter range. Therefore, deer must funnel into the winter ranges from miles around, and they usually travel the same routes each year. By nature, winter ranges must be places where deer can feed from about November to March or April. The area must have comparatively light snowfall with adequate browse. Sagebrush is often the predominant food plant eaten by muleys.

Wise hunters can take advantage of this annual migration and the muleys' need for browse to waylay a buck that's headed for the lowlands. Hunters must have two elements in their favor, however. First, state regulations must allow hunting late enough in the fall to coincide with the migrations and, second, deer must be forced out of the high country by winter conditions.

What triggers this move to the low country? Probably the same instinct that gathers waterfowl and other creatures together for a mass departure from a given area. A heavy snowstorm is usually enough to start the movement, but biologists have also studied herds that begin heading down before a storm. Most of these herds live in very high elevations of 11,000 to 12,000 feet.

There are several ways to hunt migrating deer. The most exciting is to ambush a buck as he's trailing out of his summer quarters. Timing, of course, is essential. You must be located precisely along the route when deer are moving by. The incident that I mentioned at the outset of this article makes me sit up in bed every now and then and daydream about the size of the bucks that wandered down the trail. Some of the tracks were enormous, and it's amazing to consider that an entire population of muleys moved over one path in the snow during the course of a few hours.

Several years ago, a large party of hunters accidentally stumbled into just such a massive deer migration in northern Utah. As they told the story, a herd of about 60 deer swarmed over a saddle along a ridge during a driving snowstorm. The hunters were about to call it quits when the deer appeared. After the action was over, each of a dozen hunters had killed a nice buck. They loaded the dressed bucks in two pickups and created quite a stir along Vernal's Main Street. This was in the mid-70s when muleys were tough to find. During that period, a westwide decline in mule deer was responsible for low harvests.

Another technique to hunt migrating mule deer is to intercept them as they fan out between summer and winter areas. Although they'll normally trail out of the high country and move along rapidly, they begin to dally and nibble here and there as they escape the deep snow. It might take weeks for them to actually make the journey to the wintering spot.

River valleys, sagebrush flats, thick stands of low-elevation oak brush, and cedar forests are traditional winter areas. It's possible to hunt deer on the winter range itself, but the season often ends before the deer are down. In states where seasons end early, however, a heavy storm often puts deer in places where they normally aren't. I've seen deer show up overnight after an unseasonably heavy storm up in the high country.

Once, I was hunting cottontails in early November along a brushy desert wash. I was well acquainted with the area and never saw a deer track. Two days after a blizzard in the upper elevations, I saw seven big bucks trailing through the greasewood. They were moving directly toward a traditional wintering area five miles away. I lamented the fact that I was carrying a scope-sighted .22 rather than my .30/06. Deer season was still on, and I hadn't filled my tag yet. I hurried home, grabbed my deer rifle, and killed a modest three-point buck in the same area.

Deer migrations are the source of much study among biologists. Interesting facts are turned up as scientists probe this annual mule deer behavior pattern. Studies show, for example, that migrating deer often follow routes so precisely that they swim the same rivers at the same spot each year. Before 90-mile long Flaming Gorge Reservoir was impounded on the Utah/Wyoming border, deer swam the river to cross the Uinta Mountains into the Green River bottoms where they wintered. After the lake filled, deer continued to cross by swimming the reservoir exactly where they waded before the dam was built. The reservoir was constructed in the early '60s. Now, 20 years later, deer still swim it at the same spot.

Deer migrations often coincide with the breeding season, giving hunters yet another advantage. Mule deer normally begin thinking about reproductive duties around mid-November, with the peak of the rut occurring around Thanksgiving. The rut period varies with elevation, climate, and other factors, though the last week in November and the first week in December will cover it in much of the West.

Big bucks turn their interest to does during this time, and they make mistakes that they normally wouldn't. They readily show themselves in the open and often show little fear of humans.

A few years ago, I was hunting elk and deer with outfitter Keith Rush in Montana's Centennial Mountains. Though I was hoping for a good bull elk, I didn't intend to ignore a nice buck if I had the opportunity.

While hunting early one morning with Kevin Rush, Keith's son, I spotted a herd of deer in a sagebrush pocket. A close look revealed a fat five-point buck cavorting with a half dozen does and fawns. I made a 20-minute stalk and peeked over a knoll where the buck had disappeared. He was so interested in a doe, he never knew what hit him when I squeezed the trigger.

I was able to capitalize on the rut because Montana's general deer season normally extends into late November. Had the hunt been a week earlier, that buck might have been slinking around the timber on the ridgetops.

Mule deer behavior being what it is, does and fawns often inhabit lower elevations during the autumn, while warier bucks are high. If snow doesn't kick bucks out of their lofty domains, the rut often starts them on an early migration. They'll head to the does instinctively.

In some states, special late hunts are held in November. In Utah, for example, a muzzleloading season traditionally begins in November after the general rifle season closes. It's amazing to suddenly see big bucks showing up in the same spots that were heavily combed by hunters just a couple of weeks previous. The big deer seem to come out of the woodwork.

Those bucks are merely following nature's call. If deep snows fall during their quest for does in heat, so much the better. They'll be out of the inaccessible back country quicker.

Figuring where deer migrate need not be a mystery. There are ways to find out. One of the simplest and most ignored is a sign that is placed along a highway by the transportation department to warn motorists that deer migrate across that particular stretch of road. I'm not going to suggest that you plunk yourself against the signpost and wait, but I'd recommend that you investigate the general area if you're serious about waylaying a buck when he's fleeing the high country. Local inquiry about migration times will often produce enough information to plan a strategy. Ranchers, farmers, and game wardens are good sources.

Determining winter range areas is often easy because wildlife agencies usually have them well lo-cated. Wintering regions are critical to mule deer herds, and biologists keep close tabs on their conditions. In fact, state wildlife agencies try to buy up winter areas to protect them from urban sprawl. Countless deer herds have declined or disappeared altogether because winter ranges were bulldozed or turned into cabin sites or shopping centers. You can often request to see maps showing winter ranges in wildlife offices. Federal agencies, especially the Bureau of Land Management and the U.S. Forest Service, make attempts to preserve winter areas, as well. Wildlife personnel within those agencies can be helpful in pinpointing migration routes and wintering grounds.

If you're hunting and run across unusually large numbers of cast-off antlers, you're in the midst of an important winter area. File this information mentally, and make a point to look into the area during a late hunt. Try to figure a logical migration route that mule deer will use; then concentrate your efforts between the winter area and the high country when heavy snowstorms are blanketing the upper elevations.

When bucks begin their migration, they often travel for days through timbered forests. If you can find a fresh track left by a big buck, you might be able to stay with him long enough to make him yours. If he's lined out straight and heading in one particular direction instead of feeding and wandering about, chances are good that you're following a buck moving down to low country. If the deer seems to be staying the same distance ahead of you, you're not moving fast enough to gain on him. If you know the area, try to circle ahead and cut him off, especially if he's on a ridgetop and following a trail.

Don't take foolish chances when hunting in the winter. If possible, hunt with a companion but, if you go alone, tell someone where you're hunting and what time you'll be home. Take along a daypack with survival gear as well as plenty of clothing. Plan your hunting strategy so that you'll be out of the woods in good time.

Hunting migrating deer involves a different type of pursuit as compared with general-season hunting. The most obvious difference is the fact that you're after *moving* deer that are intent on a particular goal. You won't be doing any deer driving but will be glassing and searching for signs of traveling herds or single animals. It's a quiet hunt, one that involves a lot of theorizing, second-guessing, and plenty of hoping. But it's a hunt that offers a special challenge in outwitting a buck and ambushing him after he's been safe in his high-country hideout. He can't cope with the deep snows of the long Western winters, and he must leave his summer domain or die of starvation. He makes himself vulnerable as he heads for winter territory. You can capitalize on that vulnerability by being at the right place at the right time. And if you do so, you might draw up face to face with the biggest buck of your life.

A Hunter Is Born

By Brian Kahn

Even a quarter-mile distant, the buck looked huge. His long body stood out black against golden aspens and, when he raised his head, the massive antlers glowed in the first sun of morning.

"Just look at him!" Don whispered, breaking the stillness.

I realized that I'd been holding my breath.

"That's about as big as they come," I said softly, as much to myself as to my friend.

It was the first morning of our Nevada bowhunt, and we watched the big buck through different eyes. For Don, this was only his second deer hunt, and his first bowhunt. He'd hunted once before with me and had taken an exceptional buck with a rifle. But the hunt had been easy—perhaps too easy—and I wasn't certain whether Don was really committed to the sport. I'd been hunting bucks for more than 25 years and, though Don and I were best friends since our high schools days—and were partners in our upland and waterfowl hunting—he'd resisted my efforts to get him to hunt deer for years.

On that first trip, we had seen few deer and he'd killed the first buck that he had ever glassed. The hunt seemed over before it had really begun and, while during the off-season Don agreed to go again and waxed eloquent over the venison that he'd provided for his family, I didn't sense the enthusiasm that he usually brought to his hunting.

I gave a great deal of thought to that next hunt— there was a lot riding on it. Good hunting partners are hard to find, and I felt that, unless Don got the full flavor of deer hunting, he might not pursue it any further.

Instead of inviting him on another rifle hunt, I chose the bow. In my two bow seasons, I'd seen many more bucks than during rifle hunts. And on each hunt, I had made stalks—taking hours to move in close. The experience of being close to deer, of watching them at length in an undisturbed state, had impressed me, a jaded deer hunter. It had heightened my respect for the animal that I pursued and had made me more intensely aware of the age-old interaction between predator and prey.

On a bowhunt, I felt confident that Don would see and stalk game, and I hoped that the experience would win him over to the sport. But bowhunting

Blacktails also provide hunters with excellent opportunities to make record books because minimum record-book qualifying scores for these deer are relatively low. The minimum for the Pope and Young Club bowhunting record book is only 90 points, and an average three-point (Western count) buck will score that well. The minimum score for the Boone and Crockett record book is 130. That's a fine buck, but deer of that status aren't really rare. Over the past few years, I've seen hundreds, maybe thousands of mule deer, yet I've never seen any that would make Boone and Crockett. I've seen far fewer blacktails, yet I've seen close to half a dozen that would make the record book. I think that's because competition for blacktails hasn't been as high, so the minimum score has remained relatively low.

If you're after a record-book buck, you must know how to judge the quality of a deer's rack. Blacktail antlers are measured like mule deer antlers, but the dimensions are smaller. With a mature blacktail, the tip-to-tip ear spread measures about 17 inches. To score 130, a buck just about has to have a 16-inch inside spread. Many listed in Boone and Crockett were wider than 20 inches. As a rule of thumb, the main beams (between the front points) must, therefore, be at least as wide as the horizontal spread ears. The buck must also have four even tines, plus eye guards (five points total) on each side. The tines should be seven to eight inches long, and the eye guards two to three inches. A blacktail's ears measure 6½ to seven inches long, so you can use them as a ruler to gauge the length of points.

At one time, Jackson County in southern Oregon ranked as the premier region for trophy blacktails, but record-keeping organizations have changed the boundary lines, and now most of the best blacktails from Jackson County must be scored as mule deer. I think the best places for trophy blacktails now are among the foothills along the east side of Oregon's Willamette Valley, south of Portland. That country hasn't produced the most Boone and Crockett entries, but it definitely has some of the biggest blacktails. Five of the top 10 bucks listed in the Eighth Edition of *Records Of North American Big Game* came from this general vicinity.

My second choice would be the wilderness country west of Redding in California's Coast Range. The highest number of record-book bucks has come from this region, primarily from Mendocino, Trinity, and Siskiyou counties.

The current world-record blacktail buck, which scored 182⅜ points, was killed in Lewis County, Washington, in 1953. Washington has produced other large bucks but, overall, its trophy buck production can't compare with that of California and Oregon.

Blacktails offer a hunting challenge matched by few other deer, and the hunter who can take big

In the Coast Range of California from Los Angeles northward past San Francisco, the country is covered with dense, dry chapparal.

blacktails regularly has a lot of hunting savvy. I've had some experience with whitetails, often touted as America's smartest deer, and I'd bet on the average blacktail's craftiness in a contest with the average whitetail. I think they're spookier and are less likely than whitetails to linger to find out what made a suspicious noise or a vague movement.

Blacktails are often said to live in brush—a statement that is not completely true, as we'll see later. In their typical brush-country haunts, special hiding tactics are required. From Southern California north to the San Francisco Bay area and farther, the brush comes in the form of crackling dry chaparral that bristles over the convoluted terrain.

In the Coast Range jungles of Oregon and Washington, the brush is equally thick, but there it's wet. Giant ferns, moss-bearded Douglas firs, salal bushes, and evergreen huckleberry growth are so thick that they make the chaparral country of Southern California look bald. These zero-visibility confines call for special techniques, too.

Probably the most underrated method is to take a stand—more specifically, a tree stand. Any Eastern whitetail hunter will think this odd because whitetails and tree stands go together so well. Western hunters, though, still think a tree stand is something to hold up a Christmas tree; few seriously employ tree stands, and that's a mistake.

If there's any "secret" to killing a trophy blacktail, I would say it's hunting from a stand. At least that's true in thick country where, nine out of 10 times, the deer see a hunter on foot before he sees them. In that situation, the tree-stand hunter is like a great blue heron waiting to spear a frog. Even the oldest, wariest bucks fail to see the quiet hunter above them.

George Shurtleff, a retired security guard hunting with a bow and arrow during general seasons in competition with rifle hunters, killed two of the largest blacktails ever taken. One scored 172⅔, which makes it the second-largest blacktail ever recorded and the all-time record for bow and arrow. That buck was also listed as No. 1 in the Eighth Edition of Boone and Crockett's *Records Of North American Big Game*, although it has since been replaced by a buck from Washington. Shurtleff's other buck ranks second in the Pope and Young record book and would place in the top 10 of Boone and Crockett. It scored 163⅞. Shurtleff has taken other huge blacktails. No other hunter, rifle or bow, can claim that kind of record. Shurtleff has taken all his trophies while on stand, either tree stands or ground blinds.

Boyd Iverson, an Oregon rifle hunter, set out with the express purpose of killing a Boone and Crockett blacktail. For many years, he hunted on foot, but he finally decided that that method was futile. Even though he used a rifle and scarcely needed the close-range shots made possible by taking a stand, he de-

The open oak foothills of Northern California and Oregon provide plenty of room for open-country techniques.

The tree stand may well be the "secret" to trophy blacktail hunting. A safety belt prevents serious injury.

All blacktail hunting does not take place in tangled cover. In many places, particularly in central California and the valleys of southern Oregon, blacktails are quite visible because they live in open oak forests and grasslands. They live in even more open country in the Coast Range of northern California, roughly from Clear Lake north almost to the Oregon border. Three Wilderness Areas—Yolla Bolly, Trinity, and Marble Mountain—lie along the backbone of this range in true alpine settings, and plenty of similar high country borders these designated wilderness areas. These blacktails are mountain deer, pure and simple, and they can be hunted just like mountain mule deer.

I've hunted that alpine country with rifle and bow, and the same method has worked beautifully during both seasons. I perch on one side of a steep canyon and use binoculars to watch the far side for movement. By far the best time is from daylight until 8 a.m. or 9 a.m. The blacktails are feeding and are quite "seeable." However, on heavily overcast days, you'll often be able to spot blacktails feeding near the edge of cover all day long, and they emerge to feed following a heavy rain.

At first, the country may seem lifeless but, if you study it, you see a black-topped tail flicking in a sparse clump of firs. Then you notice a flicking ear. Next, you spot a gray body. Soon, you pick out deer all over the hillside. I've spotted as many as two dozen bucks and innumerable does in one morning

I caught this four-point blacktail during Northern California's general rifle season in October.

cided that he should hunt from stands if he was ever to see the really big bucks. He took to the trees. Right from the start, he saw and passed up many blacktail bucks that would give most hunters the shakes. Only a few years later, he killed a buck that scored 145⅛, well above the Boone and Crockett minimum.

Of course, Iverson did more than take a stand in a tree. He studied maps to find isolated locations that might harbor old bucks. He then scouted promising areas to study sign. He finally settled on one location that showed abundant tracks—and some big tracks.

Then he combed that one area to learn the locations of feeding sites, bedding cover and, most importantly, the trails that led from one to another. He also studied prevailing wind currents. After he fully understood the area, he placed a stand in a tree on the downwind side of a prime trail intersection.

After the season opened, he hunted mostly in the evening when the deer emerged from their thick bedding cover to feed. He wore camouflage and blackened his face with camo paint, even though he hunted with a rifle. Oregon law does not require hunters to wear Blaze Orange. Any time the wind was wrong, he stayed away from the area. He left nothing to chance. It paid off.

of glassing. Those are pretty good numbers of deer that supposedly live only in places where visibility is 10 feet or less.

Once you've spotted a buck you want, it's a matter of studying the country to plan a stalk. Always look for other deer. In open country, blacktails seem to cluster together in big, loose-knit bunches, and unseen does have given me real headaches in trying to stalk big bucks. Blacktails have an aggravating lack of curiosity. In brush country, blacktails try to sneak away undetected but, in open territory, when one spooks, every deer on the hillside takes off without looking back. More than once I've watched a veritable stampede as more and more deer popped out. Look carefully to locate hidden deer that might spoil your stalk at the crucial moment.

Even in typical dense forest country, you can employ open-country methods. Like other deer, blacktails like edges and flock to openings that break up the brush or timber. Near Stoneyford, California, government agencies have teamed up to control-burn the bristling chamise chaparral hillsides. Burns are made in small irregular patches and blacktails feed heavily on new growth in these burns. From a well-chosen vantage point on one side of a canyon, you can easily spot deer in these burns and then plan a stalk.

The same thing is true of logging clear-cuts in Oregon and Washington. Clear-cuts 2 to 8 years old serve the same function for low-country blacktail hunters as do natural alpine openings in the high country. They provide a clear view where you can spot deer. You can set up a spotting scope or use binoculars to pick out deer feeding on opposite hillsides. If you're alone, you can plan a stalk; with other hunters, you can plan a drive. Whatever approach you take, spotting the animal before you make a move puts you in the driver's seat.

Calling also works well. During early seasons, some hunters call blacktails by bleating or screaming with a predator call. Why deer sometimes come to a predator call is a mystery, but they do so often enough to make it worth a try.

Antler rattling is a proven method. Although blacktails apparently don't systematically make scrape lines like whitetails, they do make scrapes. I've talked to several hunters who have found blacktail scrapes and, by rattling near them, have pulled in blacktail bucks quite often. Place a tree stand near a fresh scrape and rattle two antlers together to simulate the sound of two battling bucks. But some hunters don't bother with scrapes. They move through likely areas and take ground stands. Then they rattle and paw and stomp the ground so that they sound like two bucks in combat. Several companies now market instructional tapes on antler rattling for whitetails, and the techniques described work with blacktails, too. Many of these tapes also reproduce the grunting sounds made by whitetails, and these odd noises also can be used in blacktail hunting. Jesse Stalcup, an Oregon bowhunter, told me that he and several friends have grunted up

In the oak-shaded grasslands, where I'm hunting here, you can spot deer with binoculars and stalk them on foot.

bucks during the rut without rattling at all. The Oregon rifle season takes place in the early rut, and the bow and muzzleloader seasons in Oregon and Washington are also open during the rut.

Virtually any rifle suitable for other deer will do the job on blacktails. Terrain and vegetation are the major factors in selecting a firearm. For brushy country, a low-velocity rifle equipped with open sights or a low-power scope is more than adequate but, in more open alpine or clear-cut areas where you might shoot across a canyon, a good mule deer rifle such as a .270 or .30/06 with a 4X or a variable scope sighted in for 200 yards is best.

Heavy bullets aren't necessary because blacktails are smaller than mule deer or whitetails. However, I think that many writers make more of their small size than is warranted. The average field-dressed weight of blacktail bucks is probably 100 or 120 pounds, but lots of big mountain bucks field-dress at 150 pounds or heavier. Average weight depends largely on the kind of food available, just as it does with other deer species.

I can't make you respect the blacktail deer just by talking about him. You have to meet him for yourself. Whether you find him in the popcorn chaparral of Southern California, northern California's alpine wilderness, or the rain forests of Oregon and Washington, rest assured that Mr. Blacktail will teach you to have respect.

PART 4

FIREARMS AND BOWS

The Man Behind The Gun

By Jack O'Connor

Last spring a pal of mine was toiling through the Indian jungles behind his gentleman shikari (guide, to you) when suddenly he heard a rather strange noise. He turned toward it and what did he behold but a large and indignant-looking tiger barreling right at him, flat out.

Now this pal of mine is a good shot and a pretty cool citizen as cool citizens go. With one motion he unslung and mounted his .458 and let the tiger have one. The shot turned the tiger and it headed to the left. My amigo manipulated the bolt of his rifle, held for a juicy shoulder shot at about 35 yards, pulled the trigger.

Not a thing happened. For a moment my pal was stunned. Then he became conscious that the hinged floorplate of his rifle was hanging open and the nice shiny .458 cartridges that had been in the magazine were on the ground. The recoil of the first shot had kicked the magazine open. The cartridges had dropped out and he had operated the bolt on thin air when he thought he was feeding in a second cartridge.

Now this friend of mine is of Irish descent—or at least he has an Irish name. For more than 1,000 years the Irish have been renowned and eloquent cursers and, by inheritance, temperament and practice, my friend was pretty good at invective. He cut loose with a string of oaths that blew out bicycle tires in Jabalpur, a town about 85 miles away. Several monkeys fell out of nearby trees stone dead and all over the

100

Illustration by Leon Parson

The better the serious hunter knows his rifle and his ammunition, and the more realistically he can appraise his own skill, the better off he is and the less apt he is to come a cropper in the field.

I can remember some pretty sad occasions when insufficient care in checking has caused grief. Once in Arizona a friend and I went antelope hunting. At the first glimmer of dawn on the first day of the season we drove out into the middle of the antelope country, parked our car and left in different directions. We agreed to meet at the car after we had got our bucks. It was high country with grass and scattered junipers almost a mile and a half above sea level. In due time, I managed to keep a juniper between me and a buck until I was within fairly decent range.

When I lugged my antelope back to the car my companion was waiting for me and wearing a very long face. He had no antelope. Just before we left Tucson he had loaded up some ammunition. He had used a bullet seater set for one make of bullet, but he loaded another make of bullet of the same weight but with a different ogive. He had not run any of his newly loaded cartridges through his magazine and chamber—something which every handloader should do as a matter of routine. When we had left the car that morning, he had fed a cartridge into the chamber and had put the safety on. Later he had decided to remove the cartridge from the chamber. The case came out without the bullet and scattered grains of powder through the magazine. The bullet was stuck in the lands at the lede.

He could have worked a bullet in another cartridge loose, pulled it and inserted the case with powder into the chamber behind the bullet. Then he could have shot the bullet out. But he didn't think of that. He decided to whittle himself a cleaning rod and poke the bullet out from the muzzle end. He got his homemade rod stuck in the barrel and gave up. He said that on the way back to the car he saw a dozen bucks with big black horns. At camp we tried to poke the piece of branch out with a cleaning rod but it was really stuck and we couldn't move it. My friend killed a buck antelope that afternoon with my rifle. Later, a gunsmith got that whittled rod out of the bore with some sort of a gadget he made especially for the job.

Something I always do when I am planning to take handloaded ammunition on a hunting trip is to run every cartridge through magazine and chamber. Cartridges that chamber a little hard should be set aside and used for practice. The rifleman should make certain the bullets are seated deep enough in the case so that there is no chance of the cartridges hanging up in the magazine—something that happens if they are a hair too long. Cartridges used in hunting should seat in the chamber and extract easily.

The man who knows his rifle thoroughly knows how it performs with bullets of different weights. Some rifles will shoot bullets of all practical hunting weights more or less to the same point of impact—

central-Indian highlands sacred cows gave premature birth to young.

I wish this story had a happy ending but it does not. The tiger was never seen again and my friend, alas, departed from India without a tiger.

My tiger-hunting friend had carefully sighted his rifle in but he had done so by feeding the cartridges into the chamber one at a time. It had never occurred to him that, with the magazine full, the hinged floorplate might unlatch. Yet that is not an uncommon ailment, particularly with rifles of heavy recoil. A latch that will keep the floorplate closed when the magazine is empty may fail when it is full. My friend found he could have one cartridge in his magazine and the floorplate would stay put when he fired a shot, but if he had more than one cartridge in it the recoil would open it every time. Not long ago I got back a pre-1964 Model 70 in .338 Winchester Magnum that had been restocked and altered by putting the release button for the floorplate in the trigger guard. The first time I fired the rifle the floorplate flew open. I am glad I wasn't shooting at a grizzly when that happened.

so close, in fact, it is feasible to interchange bullet weights with confidence. Some, alas, will not.

Two somewhat innocent young men of my acquaintance were on an elk hunt when one of them spied an enormous black bear about 250 yards away across a canyon. The bear was rooting around unsuspectingly and the lad who had first seen him was about to level down on him when his companion handed him a cartridge loaded with 220-grain bullets.

"Heck," he said, "you can't kill a big ol' bear like that with a little ol' 180-grain bullet!" So the other lad slipped the cartridge loaded with the 220-grain bullet into the chamber, took a rest over a log and squeezed one off. An exceedingly astonished bear took off untouched. Later the lad who had missed discovered that, at 250 yards, the 220-grain bullet in his .30/06 struck almost two feet lower than did the 180-grain.

I am continually astonished at the great number of people who go off on long and expensive hunting trips, not only without knowing their rifles, but just about without having been introduced to them. Many have not fired a box of cartridges through their rifles and some have not fired them at all. It is common for hunters to ask gunsmiths and sporting goods dealers to sight their rifles in for them. Ralph Young, the famous brown bear guide and outfitter who operates out of Petersburg, Alaska, tells me that fully half of his clients who have come after the big bears with some powerful rifle like the .338 or the .375 have never fired a shot through them. "Oh, hell," they say. "The gunsmith has it sighted in. I don't want to get kicked around by that cannon any more than I have to."

It is getting more and more difficult these days to do much rifle shooting, particularly at ranges of more than 200 yards. Sometimes sporting goods dealers or gunsmiths have access to 100-yard indoor ranges for sighting in but generally they do not. They "sight in" by lining up bore and scope with an optical collimator or by bore sighting. They make sure that the line of bore is pointing a little higher than the line of scope sight—to allow for bullet drop—and let it go at that. Or at least some of them do. Often such sighting puts the bullet close enough to where the scope or the iron sights look so that game can be killed if it isn't too far away, but even the best bore sighting cannot take into account barrel vibration. The most a careful and conscientious bore sighter can guarantee is that, after he has lined up bore and sights, the bullets should strike somewhere within six or eight inches at about 100 yards. Often the shots will be closer than that but you cannot depend on it. Sometimes the bore-sighted rifle is right on the money but generally it needs correction.

Here is a story that wrung my heart a generation ago. A high-powered executive, the president of a big and well-known corporation, decided he must get himself a desert ram. He wrote me, asked me to recommend an outfitter, and also asked me what I would suggest in the way of a first-class rifle for desert sheep. I wrote that if I had my druthers I would select a 7 × 57 or a .270 with a 2½ or 4X scope, a 22-inch barrel and a sling. The rig would weigh from 7½ to eight pounds. My busy correspondent had the rifle built by a famous gunsmithing firm in the East and left them instructions to sight it in. When he picked the rifle up he was assured that it had been sighted in to put the 130-grain .270 bullet three inches high at 100 yards.

So the high-powered executive landed in the desert with his beautiful and expensive rifle. He had booked a 21-day hunt. For 19 days he and his guide climbed around through the rocks and thorns of some of the most beautiful and difficult sheep mountains in North America. Then they saw THE ram—a gaunt old fellow that looked all horns. The points of his massive horns came up over the bridge of his nose and were broken and rubbed wide and blunt at the ends. The guide whispered that they'd go close to 40 inches around the curl. They made a long stalk and finally peeked over a ridge not more than 100 yards from the ram. The hunter pushed his new rifle out in front of him, held carefully about one-third of the thickness of the ram's body up from the bottom of the chest and right behind the foreleg, and squeezed the trigger. The ram stood there for a few seconds in shocked surprise and the hunter got off another shot. Another miss! Then the ram was over the ridge and gone. They never saw it again.

Gloomily the hunter and the guide came down off the mountain and headed across the desert to their camp. Then the guide had an idea. He suggested that the hunter sit down, squeeze a careful shot off at a hole in the trunk of a giant cactus about 100 yards away. He did—and the shot was 18 inches high. He was, of course, ready to shoot the man who was supposed to have sighted his rifle in for him but he should have targeted the rifle to assure himself it was right before he left the East. He should also have shot it as soon as he got to his desert camp. His guide should also have insisted that he shoot it. If there is anything that brings an honest hardworking guide down with chills and fever it is to work a dude up to a spot where he can get a good shot at a trophy and then to have him muff it.

On a long hunting trip a rifle should be checked now and then. Jiggling around on a saddle horse or in an automobile, being bumped, or getting dropped can cause a rifle to change point of impact enough to miss even a large animal at no very great range. The hunter should always take along screwdrivers with blades so ground and of proper width to fit the guard screws and the screws in the scope mount. Every few days he should go over his rifle to see if the screws are drawn up tight. A test that is simple and easy and that should not be neglected is to see if there is any play in the scope. On my first trip to Africa I missed a good trophy simply because I had neglected to check the screws in the scope mount I was using. It had 13 screws in it and every one of them was loose.

I had another very sad mishap in Africa in 1959. Made spooky by the unfortunate experience on my

first safari, I checked the scope and guard screws every day while I was trying to shoot a suitable leopard in northern Tanzania. To be doubly sure I wouldn't make a miscue, every day I had a gun bearer make a blaze on a tree with a panga 50 yards from the hunting car. Then I fired one careful shot across the hood of the hunting car with my .30/06 rested on a seat cushion. The bullet landed just where it was supposed to every time—one inch above point of aim.

We had several leopard baits out. There were a good many leopards in the area and I could afford to be choosy. We turned down a couple of females, one young male. One morning we found that a leopard was feeding on another bait. His tracks showed he was a big male. Along late in the afternoon Syd Downey, my white hunter, and I would hide behind a big rock and, when the leopard came for his dinner, I'd bushwhack him. Possibly it was because my .30/06 had shot so dependably day after day or maybe I was excited over the prospect of getting a crack at a leopard, but that day I didn't fire my one shot at a mark on a tree.

Along about 5 p.m. the leopard appeared. Before eating he decided to lie on top of a termite hill, enjoy the late-afternoon breeze and think pleasant thoughts. He appeared to be a little over 50 yards from our rock. (It afterwards turned out to be 62 paces.) I put the crosswires behind his foreleg and about one-third of the way up from the bottom of his chest and squeezed the trigger. The leopard let out a coughing grunt, shot at least six feet in the air and took off. It turned out that I had barely burned him along the bottom of the chest as we found a few hairs but no blood.

So then, too late, I fired my daily shot. The bullet struck five or six inches low at 50 yards. Examination showed a bright mark on the eyepiece of the scope. Apparently a gun bearer, when cleaning the rifle, had dropped it the night before—and had dropped it hard enough to bend the aluminum arm of the scope mount. On this occasion luck was with me. The next morning, yet another big male leopard found the bait, and, when along about sundown he came back for a snack, I nailed him.

When certain types of safeties are improperly installed on rifles with Mauser actions and the trigger is pulled when they are on safe, they will fire when the safety is taken off. This is a bad and dangerous situation, and anyone with such a rifle should find out about it and have the fault corrected. My wife and I were once hunting bears on the coast of British Columbia with a friend who had not done much hunting and who was of a nervous disposition. When he saw a nice plump glossy black bear chomping grass on a hillside, we suggested that our friend and the guide complete the stalk and shoot the bear while we watched. We sat down to see the fun. Our friend got down on one knee, trained his rifle on the bruin and then gave a tremendous flinch. The rifle was on safe. Realizing what had happened, he pushed the safety lever down with his thumb. The rifle went off and both he and the bear almost jumped out of their pants. The bear tarried not on his going and, although our friend plowed up considerable hillside with .30/06 bullets, he didn't cut a hair.

Tom Burgess, the Spokane, Washington, gunsmith, tells me that this condition can occur with two types of safeties made for the Mauser action,

and that the cause is careless installation and failure to check. He also tells me that the instructions that come with one make of safety specifically warn against this and tell how the condition is to be avoided. In case anyone has a safety that lifts up under the scope tube on a Mauser action, it might not be a bad idea to check it. Cock the rifle, put the safety on, pull the trigger. Then take the safety off. If the firing pin is going to fall under those conditions, it is well to find it out.

We all know that the line of sight is always higher than the line of a rifle bore. In the case of scope sights it is considerably higher—from 1½ inches to three inches or a bit more in the case of high-mounted scopes or scopes with large objectives. On a big-game rifle a high line of scope sight is of no particular moment and generally its only apparent effect is to flatten the trajectory a bit. However, a high line of sight complicates the problem of shooting the heads off game-birds, such as grouse, for the pot. This is a stunt that is not difficult if a rifleman knows exactly at what point the path of the bullet crosses his line of scope sight. Using a .30/06 with a scope mounted so that the line of sight is 1½ inches above the bore and sighted in with the 180-grain bullet to strike the point of aim at 225 yards, the bullet first crosses the line of sight at 25 yards. But suppose you have a scope mounted so the line of sight is three inches above the bore and you sight in to put the 180-grain bullet

at 2,700 fps on the point of aim at 225 yards. Then your bullet will first cross the line of sight at 50 yards. With the higher line of sight the trajectory is apparently "flatter." With the high sight line, the bullet rises only 2½ inches above the line of bore, whereas with the lower line of sight, it rises about 3¼ inches.

An amigo of mine had not given much thought to the fact that he was using a rifle with a scope mounted fairly high. He stalked a bunch of unsuspecting rams, got into a good steady prone position so he would have the ram with the best horns dead to rights. As he lined up on the ram through the scope, making certain that the intersection of the crosswires was right on the ram's ribs, he didn't pay attention to much else. Alas, about 10 feet in front of the muzzle was a jagged stone. It was out of focus in his scope and he could see the ram sharp and clear above it. My pal, excited as he was, did not realize that although that chunk of rock was not in the line of sight, it was in the line of bore. Because of the way his scope was mounted, the path of the bullet did not cross the line of sight until it had traveled 50 yards. Anyway, my sheep hunter squeezed the trigger. The high-velocity bullet struck the stone right in front of him. There was a tremendous crash, a great white puff of powdered stone and he was showered with rock fragments. The rams took off and my friend was so unhinged by the mishap that he didn't recover in time to get off another shot.

I am often struck by the fact that many hunters really don't know their rifles and prefer to shoot them as little as possible. Many a hunter has no notion of how accurate his rifle is, what its trajectory is, how much the bullet drops at the longer ranges. Likewise, he doesn't know his own capabilities.

If the rifleman has access to a range where he can shoot at 300, 400, and even 500 yards, he should shoot at those ranges—not only to discover how much the bullets drop below the line of sight at those distances but also to see how well he himself can shoot. It is just as important for a man to know himself as it is for him to know his rifle.

I am a great believer in the lessons that holes in paper targets teach. The man who pops away at a stump of undetermined size at an unknown distance doesn't learn much, either about his rifle or about his own skill. An old hunting pal of mine once told me how he'd seen a mutual acquaintance bang away at a stump. He fired three times and, from the flying fragments, apparently hit each time. Onlookers regarded his incredible feat with awe and wonder. Now this pal of mine is a cynical fellow as well as a skilled and knowledgeable rifleman. Just for the hell of it he went over and took a look at the stump. It was five feet tall. The rifleman had hit it once near the top, once near the bottom. One shot had missed it entirely and had hit another stump nearby. At that distance and with that skill, the rifleman whom all had thought was a ring-tailed wonder could easily have missed a moose entirely. But he would have hit an elephant somewhere—if it had been a large elephant! 🦌

Are You Overgunned?

By Rich LaRocco

A couple of summers ago, I was discussing with one of my closest friends a particularly serious problem he was trying to solve. He wasn't concerned about an impending bankruptcy, and his wife wasn't cheating on him. His house had not been destroyed by fire, and he wasn't about to lose his job. No, he perceived his problem to be far more serious than that. You see, he'd been hunting deer for almost 10 years but he still hadn't managed to bring home any venison. It was getting to the point that hunting acquaintances would snicker whenever they saw poor old Charlie.

"You seem to fill your tags pretty regularly," Charlie said. "What do you figure I'm doing wrong?"

I thought for a moment. I'd gone hunting with Charlie several times, and he seemed to be a fair hunter. He lacked patience, but he was a quiet still-hunter and knew how to use a pair of binoculars. He didn't have much difficulty getting within rifle range of a buck. But that's when Charlie's troubles always began. To put it plainly, he was a rotten shot.

Take, for instance, the time I led him on a hike into my favorite canyon in central Utah. A particular ridge there is covered with mountain mahogany and juniper trees that attract muleys the way blood draws sharks. I positioned Charlie on a high point overlooking the intersection of several deer trails and told him to rest there because we'd be packing out his first deer that afternoon. Then I wandered farther down the ridge in search of a monstrous buck I'd seen there during the summer bow season. Not 10 minutes had gone by when I heard Charlie's .30/06 roar. I grinned with satisfaction and turned to hike back to see Charlie's buck. But then another shot rang out. And another. And another. And still another. It sounded like a sniper in Beirut. Was Charlie letting another deer get away?

As it turned out, the answer was yes, for when I got to my pal, he was shivering in the warm October sun as though it was January, and he looked more sheepish than a merino.

"I missed him," my forlorn friend muttered. "And he was only 70 yards away. I can't believe it. I missed again."

"And again and again and again," I said, but Charlie looked so sad that I quickly retracted that. "Just kiddin'. You probably got him. Let's check for blood."

We investigated the area, and that's when we found out that Charlie hadn't missed at 70 yards. He'd missed at half that range—*seven times.*

I was pondering that sad day when Charlie snapped me back to reality. "What do you think," he repeated. "What am I doing wrong?"

"I think it's your shooting," I replied. "Come on, grab your rifle and let's go to the range. I'll give you some tips."

Charlie grimaced as if I'd smacked his funny bone with the flat end of a hatchet.

"Practice shooting with my '06?" he asked. "I can't stand shooting that thing. It kicks like a mule. I'll grab my .22 instead."

So that was Charlie's problem: He was simply overgunned. When we arrived at the range in the foothills above town, I stapled a target to a cardboard box and watched Charlie pump seven or eight .22 bullets into the black at 20 yards. Then I picked up his sporterized .30/06 Springfield and pretended to load the chamber.

"Watch it," I said as I handed him the rifle. "She's loaded. Now let's see how well you can shoot."

Charlie screwed up his face the way I do when changing diapers. Then he took the gun, aimed it at the target, flipped off the safety, and took in air as

though he expected it to be his last breath. When he yanked the trigger, his eyes were closed, and every muscle in his body was tense. The barrel jerked several feet off to his right.

"You son of a gun!" he said.

Eventually, I got Charlie to shoot my .243 Winchester, which is much more pleasant to shoot than a .30/06. And, before the hour was out, he was keeping all his shots inside a four-inch circle at 100 yards. When I saw that his confidence was growing, I offered to lend him the rifle for the deer season, which was only a few weeks away. I did so on one condition: that he invite me over for a fresh deer steak in November. Charlie kept that promise. My invitation came early—the day after deer season began. When I arrived at Charlie's house, he told me how he'd killed his buck with a shot through the chest. Then he showed me the tiny antlers, grinning as though admiring the world-record mule deer rack. After a delicious venison dinner, he posed the question: "How about selling me that .243?"

The above story is true, but the name has been changed to protect the guilty. Sadly, this isn't an isolated case. If what many gunsmiths, game wardens, and outfitters have told me is any indication, I'd dare say that at least one-third of the 11 or 12 million deer hunters in America are overgunned. That is, they're afraid of their rifles because the guns kick too hard and bang too loudly for enjoyable shooting. Consequently, they seldom practice with their big-game guns and haven't learned to deal with their heavy recoil and deafening noise. There's a very good chance that you're one of these hunters. And, if you hunt bigger game than deer—such as elk or black bear—the odds are even better that your gun is simply too powerful for you. Waterfowl hunters, too, tend to think that bigger is better.

Many sportsmen are introduced to high-powered centerfire rifles in the wrong way. In my case, for instance, I was about 12 years old when I decided to try my dad's old .30/06. I propped the heavy, uncut military piece on my knees, chambered a round, and pressed the trigger. The recoil threw me onto my back. When I was 16 and old enough to hunt deer in my state, I tried some target shooting with a friend's .270. The bruises that quickly appeared on my right shoulder were not quickly forgotten. In short, I developed a phobia of high-powered rifles early.

When I was growing up it seemed that almost every deer hunter in my neighborhood had a .30/06, partly because hundreds of military rifles in that caliber were available for $40 and $50. I wanted a .30/06, too, but when I had a chance to buy a .243 Winchester at a good price, I spent my money on that, instead. I'm grateful I did. Because of the .243's light recoil, it didn't take me long to overcome my fear of centerfire deer rifles, and soon I was even using the gun for varmint hunting. At first, I partly believed rumors that a .243 was too low powered for deer but, after I'd shot a few muleys with it, my doubts vanished. The 100-grain factory loads were

especially deadly at close range. I clearly remember the two deer I shot that were facing me at a distance of about 70 yards. Both reared up and crumpled without taking a single step. The rifle was also very flat shooting. I usually sighted it in to hit zero at 300 yards. That meant I aimed for the heart from point-blank range to about 250 yards. From that distance to 350 yards, I held for the center of the chest cavity. At 400 yards, I aimed at the back line. That way, even if I overestimated the range by 100 yards, I'd still hit the deer in the vitals. It wasn't until I began hunting elk and black bear that I decided to get a heavier gun.

Too many sportsmen think a 10-gauge shotgun or a large-caliber rifle is the mark of a real man. Real men might not eat quiche, but neither do they mash their shooting shoulder into pulp.

While hunting whitetails in New York, I met many hunters carrying rifles such as the 7mm Remington Magnum, the .270 Weatherby Magnum, and even the .300 Winchester Magnum. A few fellows used such traditional brush guns as the Savage Model 99 in .300 Savage or the Winchester Model 94 in .30/30, but most chose rifles in .30/06 or .270. This was in the Catskill Mountains, where most shooting is done at ranges under 100 yards and where shots of more than 200 yards are rare. What seemed especially odd to me was that many of the .30/06s and .270s were unscoped. The flatter trajectory of these cartridges—as opposed to the .30/30 or the .300 Savage—did those shooters very little good because it is extremely difficult for a typical rifleman to shoot deer at more than 200 yards with iron sights. Now I'm not saying that the .30/06 or the .270 is a poor choice for whitetail hunting. However, my experience has been that most shooters cannot deal with the recoil of these rifles and would be far better off with something they could shoot more accurately. A whitetail deer simply isn't difficult to kill—neither is a mule deer or a blacktail, for that matter.

Bigger is not necessarily better, and that's true even if your quarry is a large beast or bird. Some Canadian and Alaskan grizzly and moose hunting guides grimace when they see a client arrive in camp with a spanking-new .375 H&H Magnum or .300 Weatherby. Here's how one Alaskan guide was quoted in a recent article in *American Hunter*:

"Some guys will come up here with a bad case of flinchitis and, when they line up the crosshairs on a game animal, they'll jerk the trigger and pull the shot. Often, that means a wounded grizzly. If a hunter is used to a magnum rifle and can shoot it accurately, he's one step ahead of the game. But if he's flinching badly, he'd be better off shooting 220-grain bullets in a .30/06."

If you suspect that you're recoil shy, try this trick sometime. Load a dummy cartridge using good components, except for the expended primer. Then toss the shell in with your live ammunition next time you sight in your rifle or shoot claybirds. Believe me, when the firing pin falls on that dummy cartridge, you'll know whether you have a flinching problem.

Photograph by Tom Brakefield

(Don't forget to keep track of that dummy load. You wouldn't want a misfire when the whitetail buck of a lifetime is in your sights.)

Let's suppose you do flinch badly. What can you do about it? Well, you have three choices: Switch to a more shootable gun or load, alter your gun so that it has less recoil, or learn to overcome the problem. Even if you switch to a lighter-kicking and quieter

gun, you might have to practice many hours to overcome your tendency to flinch.

There is a widespread notion that the bigger the hole in the end of the barrel, the better the killing power of the gun. Other sportsmen subscribe to the theory that speed is all important. These ideas are akin to trends in passenger cars in the '60s and early '70s. I never could understand what good it would

CALCULATING KICK

For the mathematically minded, here's how to calculate your gun's recoil.

1. Measure the powder charge in grains Avoirdupois and divide by 7,000.

2. Multiply the result of Step 1 by 1.75 if the bullet velocity at the muzzle is equal to or greater than 2,500 fps. If the muzzle velocity is less than 2,500 fps, multiply by 1.5. Don't round out any of these figures.

3. Now weigh the bullet or the shot charge plus

the wad in grains. Divide the bullet weight by 7,000.

4. Add the result of Step 3 to the result of Step 2.

5. Multiply the result of Step 4 by the bullet velocity at the muzzle in feet per second.

6. Multiply the result of Step 5 by itself.

7. Weigh your gun in pounds. Multiply the weight by 64.348.

8. Take the result of Step 6 and divide it by the result of Step 7. Sound simple? I didn't think so.

Cartridge	Bullet Weight (grains)	Free Recoil (ft.-lbs.)	Recommended Uses*
.250/300 Savage	100	8.7	a,b
.30/30	170	9.4	a
.257 Roberts	117	9.7	a,b
.32 Winchester	170	10.1	a
.243 Winchester	100	10.4	a,b
.35 Remington	200	10.9	a
8mm Mauser	170	12.7	a
.300 Savage	180	12.7	a
6mm Remington	100	13.2	a,b
.30/40 Krag	180	13.7	a,c
.303 British	180	13.8	a,c
.45/70 Government	405	14.2	a
7 × 57	150	15.3	a,c
.25/06 Remington	120	15.7	a,b,c
.308 Winchester	150	17.1	a,b,c
.240 Weatherby Magnum	100	17.6	a,b,c
.308 Winchester	200	18.0	b,c
.358 Winchester	200	18.0	b,c
.30/06	150	19.8	a,b,c,d
.358 Winchester	250	20.5	c
.270 Winchester	130	20.9	a,b,c,d
.30/06	220	22.5	c,d,e
.257 Weatherby Magnum	117	23.0	b,c
7mm Remington Magnum	175	25.5	b,c,d,e
.300 H&H Magnum	150	25.6	b,c,d
7mm Remington Magnum	150	26.7	b,c,d
7mm Weatherby Magnum	154	29.5	b,c,d
.300 H&H Magnum	220	30.6	c,d,e
.300 Winchester Magnum	220	33.1	c,d,e
.300 Winchester Magnum	150	34.8	b,c,d,e
.338 Winchester Magnum	250	39.0	c,d,e,f
.300 Weatherby Magnum	220	41.3	d,e
.375 H&H	300	47.6	d,e,f
.300 Weatherby Magnum	150	47.7	d
.458 Winchester Magnum	510	63.3	e,f
.378 Weatherby Magnum	300	78.0	e,f
.460 Weatherby Magnum	500	147.9	e,f

* Note: a = deer within 200 yards; b = deer at long range; c = elk, black bear, moose within 200 yards; d = elk, black bear, mountain goat at long range; e = grizzly bear; f = dangerous African game.

do my Mustang to have a 400-hp engine that could make the car stand on its hind wheels and rocket down the highway at 140 mph. So it is with a gun that generates more bullet speed and power than is necessary for the purpose at hand. Jack O'Connor, the late Shooting Editor of OUTDOOR LIFE, said it best when he wrote, "I am often asked which is a better killer, a .270, a .30/06, a .264, or a 7mm Magnum. The answer is that any of them is adequate with well placed shots and inadequate with poorly placed shots."

So the first step is to select a cartridge that can perform the job you want done without producing excess recoil and noise in the process. Using a computer, a standard formula to calculate recoil, and ballistics tables provided by ammo manufacturers, I have compiled the following list. It shows some popular rifle cartridges suitable for big-game hunting, along with the foot-pounds of free recoil. Data is based on the use of a rifle that weighs eight pounds, including the scope.

Besides changing cartridges, there are other ways to reduce recoil and muzzle blast. When I decided to start shooting a 7mm Remington Magnum, I did several things to prevent myself from becoming recoil-shy. The first step was selecting a fairly heavy rifle with a straight, classic-style stock. Some rifles with high cheekpieces kick upward as well as backward, giving the shooter a sore cheekbone. It's much better to direct all the recoil directly to the shock-absorbing shoulder. And I made sure the stock fit me. Often, it's a poorly fitting stock that creates flinching problems. I learned this the hard way when I bought a short-stocked pump shotgun while still in college. I'd been a fair wing shot until acquiring the gun, but because the comb whacked me in the face every time I shot at a duck, I soon began missing more ducks than I hit.

Recoil drops proportionately as you increase the mass of the gun. That's one reason some shooters install metal cylinders or tiny flasks of mercury inside their stocks. I didn't want to do that to my new 7mm, so I did the next best thing: I mounted a heavy variable scope. I also made sure my rifle had a good rubber recoil pad. Then I selected a light bullet for deer and elk hunting—a 145-grain soft-point boat-tail—and my first loads for it were light.

Whenever sighting in the rifle, I did so in heavy hunting clothes with extra padding, such as a towel, over my shooting shoulder. Some shooters use commercially available recoil-absorption pads for this purpose, and I've been told that bags of lead bird shot work well, too. I avoided shooting in the prone position. I never shot targets without wearing good ear protection, either. Many shooters are not so recoil-conscious as they are muzzle blast-conscious. The roar of a high-powered rifle forces many sportsmen into bad shooting habits.

Whenever possible, I shot the rifle at varmints and small rocks in the mountains near my home. This not only helped me to gain confidence with the rifle and to lose my fear over its recoil and report, but it also allowed me to learn the bullet's trajectory over various ranges. Much of this shooting was done off-hand, which is a good position for absorbing recoil. The result of all this is that I enjoy shooting my magnum. Of course, I didn't select one of the really hard-kicking magnums, either. In fact, the load I settled on doesn't kick much harder than a .30/06.

Some handloaders try to get the maximum velocity from their rifles but, if they realized what that does to recoil, they might think better of it. Let's take a look at my 145-grain 7mm bullet. With a light load that moves out at about 2,600 fps, recoil is about 14.3 foot-pounds. With a 300-yard zero, the slug strikes about 14 inches low at 400 yards. A hot load that pushes my bullet to 3,200 fps flattens the trajectory very little but *more than doubles* the recoil. With the same zero, the bullet hits about nine inches low at 400 yards. Would you rather aim five inches higher or put up with twice the Boom Boom Mancini sock in the arm? Remember, hot loads often are not as inherently accurate as moderate loads, and it's also rare to find a rifleman who can make a heavy-recoiling gun perform to its capability.

Shotgunners, too, should be careful about which loads they select. A table in Edward Matunas' book, *American Ammunition and Ballistics*, compares recoil of some common 12-gauge loads. A 1⅛-ounce shot charge ahead of a 2¾-dram equivalent charge generates about 17.4 foot-pounds of free recoil energy when a 7½-pound gun is used. Even with an eight-pound gun, a three-inch magnum load of 1⅞ ounces of shot blasts the gunner with 47.7 foot-pounds of terror!

The moral of the story? Don't use maximum loads unless you really have to. I myself won't have to be told twice. I well remember my first duck hunt. My boyhood friend Kevin Dawson and I had decided to splurge and buy 1⅞-ounce three-inch magnum shells. I fired the first shell while walking in a shallow pond. The recoil threw me off balance and I had to sink to my knees to keep from toppling over backwards. Then Kevin and I ventured into a large lake in our fiberglass canoe. Each time one of us shot, we were in danger of swamping.

Switching to a smaller shotgun gauge does not always solve the recoil problem. A heavy 20-gauge charge shot from a featherweight gun actually generates more recoil than a light 12-gauge charge shot in a standard gun.

If you're a beginning shooter, try to avoid firing a gun with more than 12 foot-pounds of recoil energy. Even most experienced shooters should avoid firearms that generate more than 18 foot-pounds of recoil. If you must use a magnum cartridge, shoot moderate loads and stay away from light-weight rifles. If it suits your needs, get an autoloader, which spreads recoil out over more milliseconds, giving the impression of much less recoil. And practice, practice, practice. If you won't do that, maybe you don't really need a magnum. Get something you enjoy shooting, and you'll be a much better marksman and hunter for it.

The Grand Ballistic Illusion

By Jim Carmichel

It looks like we made something of a mistake. When I say "we" I don't mean only OUTDOOR LIFE but just about every outdoor magazine and shooting journal and all the firearms books and catalogs that have been published over the past 100 years or so.

Actually, the mistake wasn't really an error of fact. It was a failure to fully explain what we were talking about. It caused many, if not most readers to have a faulty understanding of a bullet's flight. The printed word—or picture—seldom fails more miserably.

The error crashed down on me again a while back when I was drying my boots over a tent stove somewhere along the Turnagain River in northern British Columbia. One of my fellow hunters was a pleasant fellow from Germany who, like most of his tribe, loves guns and will tell hunting yarns until the last drop of schnapps is wrung from the bottle. He was well versed on rifles, ammunition, and related equipment, and quoted from memory the velocities and energy figures of a wide range of cartridges. That's why I was surprised when he insisted that when a bullet exits the muzzle of a rifle, it climbs above the bore line. According to his understanding of a bullet's flight, it is as though a bullet had wings and could rise upward during the first part of its flight.

When I explained that this is impossible, he grinned in triumph.

"Ah, Mr. Carmichel, I will now show you where you are mistaken," he told me.

After digging through his expensive leather duffle, he came up with a German shooting catalog and eagerly flipped the pages to a section on ballistics and presented me with the irrefutable evidence.

"And now what do you say?" he asked.

And there it was—as plain as bear signs on flat rock. It wasn't proof of his argument; rather, that diagram, and others like it, cause the endless calls and letters I receive that usually begin: "My hunting pal and me have a bet we want you to settle. He says a bullet climbs when it leaves the barrel. I say it goes flat . . ."

The drawing in the German catalog seemed clear at first sight and was almost identical to hundreds of other such illustrations that we've all seen in hundreds of shooting publications. The drawing showed a hunter aiming his rifle at a moose that was said to be 300 meters distant. Two dotted lines issued from the rifle. One, identified as the line of sight (sometimes the line of bore was used), went straight to the animal's shoulder. The other, identified as the bullet's path, angled upward from a level rifle bore and then curved downward so that it intersected the line of sight at point of impact on the moose's shoulder.

Obviously, anyone who takes this diagram, and those like it, at face value—without reading the fine print—immediately concludes that a bullet begins climbing as soon as it spins out of a rifle or handgun barrel. No wonder my companion and thousands upon thousands of other shooters are willing to bet the farm that bullets rise like skyrockets. As I said, the blame rests with guys like me and with ballistic

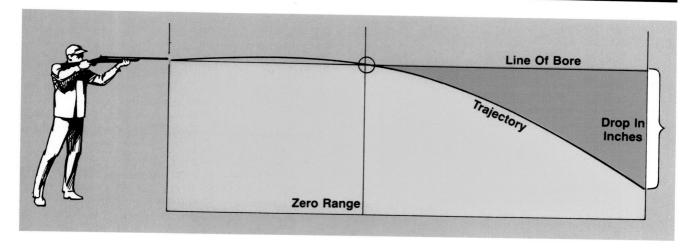

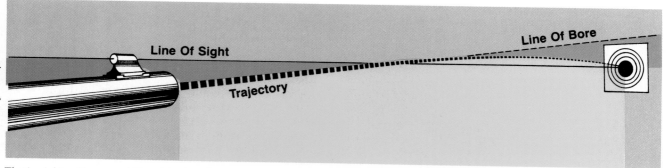

Illustration by Adolph Brotman

That's right—it's wrong! Top drawing shows one form of erroneous trajectory drawing that often appears in shooting publications. Rifle's bore is horizontal, and yet the bullet's flight rises above line of bore before curving back down to hit target. This is impossible because gravity affects bullet on exit from muzzle. Bottom drawing shows reality. If rifle is zeroed to hit at a given range, bore is angled slightly upward so that bullet crosses line of sight at about 25 yards and then comes back down to hit target. Note that bullet does not rise above line of bore.

diagrams that don't tell the whole story. We apologize.

Now let's set things right. We'll start with the classic example of a rifle that is held so that the bore is perfectly level and horizontal to the earth's surface when the bullet exits the muzzle. What happens? Old Man Gravity takes charge and immediately begins pulling the bullet downward. This is caused by one of the earth's favorite, and oldest, laws, and there's no way we can avoid gravity, except by cheating.

If you're interested in *seeing* how fast gravity makes a bullet fall, just hold one in your hand and drop it. The same gravity that makes a bullet fall immediately when dropped from your hand makes a high-speed bullet come to earth. The classic demonstration is a level rifle held at a given height above level ground and a bullet held in your hand at the same height. If you drop your bullet at the same instant that an identical bullet leaves the muzzle of the rifle, they will hit the ground at *almost* the same instant, even though the bullet from the rifle will also have traveled several hundred yards. (The reason I say *almost* at the same instant is that some funny things happen to a speeding bullet but, for all practical purposes, they hit at the same time.)

Why do all those pictures make it look like a rifle bullet angles upward? The reason is that we try to cheat gravity by tilting the rifle's bore slightly so that it is inclined upward by a fraction of a degree in respect to the line of sight. In other words, we actually launch the bullet at a slight, upward angle. It doesn't rise by itself. That's the part that isn't made clear in most trajectory diagrams.

The reason we launch the bullet at a slightly upward angle is to increase the range at which we can hit a target. Remember back when you played Little League center field and tried to pick off runners at home plate? You didn't throw the ball in a level straight line because, if you had, it would have fallen far short of the target. To increase your range, you threw the ball at an upward angle and it came back down to reach the catcher at the right height. It's the same with rifles. In fact, a bullet fired on the level falls surprisingly fast. For example, a streamlined 180-grain bullet fired from a .30/06 drops about 2½ inches below the bore line by the time it goes 100 yards. At 200 yards, the bullet has fallen nearly a foot and, at 300 yards, it has dropped more than two feet. Obviously, this would make it pretty hard to hit a deer at long range. Therefore, we cheat gravity just a little bit.

Cheating Gravity

We do this by inclining the bore in relation to line of sight so that the bullet hits, say, two inches above where we aim at 100 yards. We don't really cheat gravity this way. Actually, we get it to cooperate with our ploy. Gravity takes hold of our bullet and pulls it back earthward in a beautifully curved line called a trajectory. Thus, by angling the .30/06 barrel upward so that the bullet is two inches above point of aim at 100 yards, we can count on Old Man Gravity to bend the trajectory downward so that the bullet hits right where we aim at 200 yards and is less than a foot below where we aim at 300 yards. This gives us a much better chance of hitting a distant target. This is what those confusing trajectory diagrams were trying to make clear.

This hunter will bring home his buck if he has learned the truth about a bullet's trajectory.

Photograph by Richard P. Smith

Do you know that a bullet's trajectory doesn't always follow a curved path? The curvature is most pronounced when we hold the rifle level—meaning parallel with the ground. As we elevate or lower the muzzle from the horizontal, the curve straightens out gradually. If we shot straight up or straight down, the bullet's path would be perfectly straight. This is why we tend to overshoot our target when shooting uphill or downhill. The trajectory simply doesn't have as much downward curve as it does when we shoot over level ground.

If you were to aim your rifle straight up with the bore perpendicular to level ground, the bullet would travel upward in a straight line, come to a stop, and then fall straight back down along its original path. It's unsafe to try this yourself, but rest assured that the bullet would seldom fall back into the gun barrel. First of all, it's almost impossible to aim a rifle perfectly straight up and, even if you could, some atmospheric turbulence would almost always blow it off course.

Other Puzzles

And that brings up another topic of campfire debate. If you fire a bullet straight up, will it fall with the same speed and energy with which it went up? The answer is both yes and no. If you tried this trick in a vacuum, the falling bullet would indeed be traveling at the same speed with which it went up. For example, if the bullet was launched at 2,000 fps, it would be traveling at that speed when it came to earth. But, when we try the trick in our normal atmosphere, the bullet doesn't come down nearly as fast as it went up. This is because of air resistance. The falling bullet reaches a terminal velocity that is a "sort-of" balance between the pull of gravity and atmospheric drag. Anyone who has been hit on the head by falling shotgun pellets in a dove field or duck blind knows that this is a mighty good thing because the shot merely tickles. The shot would hit at muzzle velocity if it had been fired straight up in a vacuum.

The question that begs to be answered when a rifle bullet is fired straight up is: Will it still be spinning when it falls to earth and, if so, will it fall point first or base first?

As it so happens, a bullet retains its rotational speed more efficiently than its velocity. When the bullet reaches the apex of its straight upward climb, it is still spinning rapidly and retains much of its gyroscopic stability. Thus, it falls base first. But, if the bullet isn't fired straight up—say, for instance, that it's fired at about 85° angle or less—it performs a gyroscopic progression that causes it to have a point-forward attitude throughout its flight.

Gravity does some ugly things. It makes it harder for us to hit a distant target. It causes our wrinkles to sag and our bellies to hang over our belts. I even understand that some women become acutely annoyed by gravity when it causes some of their prize parts to migrate from place to place. But look at the bright side. If it weren't for gravity, we'd fall off this beautiful earth.

Iron Sights Are Here To Stay

By Jim Carmichel

If this column were being written in the late '40s rather than the mid '80s, it would be about coming to terms with an oddity called the telescopic sight. Gun writers of that happy time busied themselves by trying to convince their readers that scopes might be more than just a passing fad, and makers of the newfangled gadgets spent their days trying to lick the myriad problems of fogging, insecure mounting, and indifference on the part of rifle manufacturers.

What has happened during the intervening decades has made history. Scopes are so much a fact of the shooting and hunting scene that it's hard, if not impossible, to imagine life without them. There's a whole generation of baby-boom shooters, now trudging toward middle age, that never hunted without a scope and can't even remember those virile days when scopes held more water than a canteen and were inclined to fall off a rifle just when you were supposed to be aiming at a bull elk. Nowadays, a good scope can lie at the bottom of a river for a year and still get your shot on target, and mounting systems are as tough as a white-oak floor. Even so, there are times when some other way of aiming a rifle might work as well as a scope—or even better. What are these options, how well do they work, and who can use them?

The ever-smoldering question of alternatives to scopes is: What kinds of iron non-magnifying sights can be used on rifles that also have scopes attached?

In the good old days, even the makers of scopes conceded that their products might fail, so the market offered all sorts of "quick detachable" mounting systems. If a scope fogged or went haywire just as the hunter was eyeball to eyeball with a grizzly, the scope could be snatched off or flipped out of the way so that iron sights would save the day.

As scopes have become increasingly rugged, the quick-detachable concept has given way to sturdier scope-mounting systems. However, the suspicion that something *might* go wrong with a scope still lurks among us and has spawned a system of "tunneled" mounts that hike the scope above the rifle so that the open sights are visible beneath it. I'm no fan of this sort of mount and I'm sure that, by pointing out the system's failings, I've made no friends with the good people who make these mounts. The logic, however, is overwhelming. If a rifle is scope equipped, the scope is the primary aiming device and the iron sights are only accessories that might be used for one shot out of 50. By using tunnel-type mounts, which by their very nature have to elevate the scope higher than wanted, the scope is placed so high above your normal eye level that its use becomes awkward and unnatural, thereby reducing speed and effectiveness. Why reduce the effectiveness of the primary aiming device in order to cater to open sights that will be used seldom if at all? How can we have back-up iron sights without diminishing our performance with the scope?

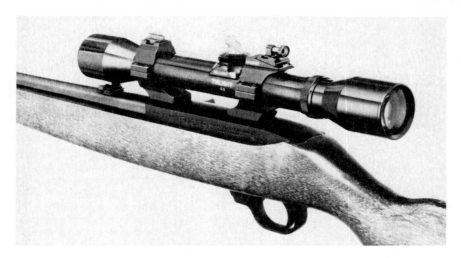

Williams S-O-S (Sight-Over-Scope) puts peep sights on front and rear scope rings. This keeps scope low over the bore where it belongs.

The problem has been solved, to some degree, by the Williams Gun Sight Company (7389 Lapeer Rd., Box 329, Davison, MI 48423). The Williams S-O-S (Sight-Over-Scope) system simply mounts an ordinary bead front sight on top of the front ring of the scope and an adjustable aperture sight on the rear ring. They are used in the same way that you aim any aperture or "peep" sight. Since the sight radius is rather short, you cannot aim as precisely with the S-O-S as you can with aperture sights on a rifle's barrel, but accuracy is plenty good for almost any hunting—especially at close ranges where the target may be out of focus through the scope. Of course, the Williams S-O-S aperture sights are quite high, meaning that they will be a bit awkward to use, but this is a much better choice than having the scope too high. The Williams brothers offer their S-O-S mounts for most of today's rifles and also offer a conversion kit for hunters who are already using Williams rings.

Despite the widespread use of telescopic sights, most of today's rifles come furnished with some sort of old-fashioned iron sights. But iron sights a generation ago were securely dovetailed into the barrel. Many of today's standard-equipment iron sights are held in place with a couple of screws. This is done out of consideration for scope users who often want to remove the iron open sights so the barrel will have a smooth, clean contour. This same sort of thinking on the part of some gun makers has also led to a "they're not going to use 'em anyway" approach to the design and manufacture of open sights. Conversely, there's also a trend among some manufacturers to be a little too cute with their iron sights, as if they are only bizarre forms of decoration rather than working necessities. A while back, for instance, I spent a half-hour trying to decide how to aim with a peculiar type of open sight, and then another hour trying to figure out how the adjustments worked.

Probably the most useless sight combination for a hunting rifle is a square-topped front post with a square-notch rear. This is a great combination for target shooting with a handgun because it presents a well-defined sight picture and allows precise alignment correction. But for rifles, it's next to worthless because the sights have to be held *under* the target. Otherwise, they block too much of it. Bullet placement is difficult if the target is moving or of irregular shape. All in all, the old-fashioned open sights with a bead front and a V or U-shaped rear notch are hard to beat.

Back when I could afford such extravagances, some sharpshooting pals and I would bet a dime a shot on a game we called "tack driving." The object was to drive in a nail with .22 Rimfire bullets from a distance of 50 feet. According to our rules, no scopes or peep sights were allowed, so we filed our front sights to needle sharpness and made rear sights to match. These superfine sights were great for tack driving but when I took my rifle squirrel hunting one misty morning, I couldn't see the sights.

That experience points up the centuries-old problem faced by open-sight users. With a small front bead and corresponding rear notch, we can more precisely determine where our bullet will hit, especially at longer ranges. But the difficulty with small or "fine" sights, as the local Tennessee mountain folk call them, is that they are hard to see, particularly as we get older and our eyes lose their ability to rapidly shift focus from sight to sight to target and back again.

Express Sights

Here of late, I've come to the conclusion that a hunter who wants to use open sights on his big-game rifle will be better off if he uses an oversize (one-eighth-inch to 3/16-inch) gold or ivory front bead with a wide V-notch rear. Although a front bead that large covers much of the target and makes precise bullet placement difficult at longer ranges, there really isn't a problem. Hunters who anticipate shots at game beyond, say, 150 yards generally use a scope anyway. So what we're talking about is open sights at closer ranges. After all, most shots at timber-dwelling big game are fired at 75 yards or less. Big-game hunters in Africa thought the problem out generations ago and came up with the so-called ''express'' sights for fast shooting at dangerous game at close ranges. The oversize, easy-to-see front bead, coupled with a wide, shallow V rear that obscures little of the target, is the fastest, surest combination for affairs with charging lions and is also wonderful for whitetails in brush, especially for us guys who can't see like we used to. Aligning the big bead in the shallow rear sight is fast and more accurate than you might suppose. I've seen two-inch groups fired at 100 yards using these express sights.

Sadly, a good, low-cost express-type combination is not offered by any of the domestic sight makers or, at least, any that I know of. Williams offers an express rear sight of sorts that is called the B type, but what we really need is a copy of a good British sight.

An express sight, by the way, is not, as some people believe, a set of folding leaf rear sights that flip up according to the target's distance. These folding leaf sights were useful for long shots at game back before good scopes were available. Naturally, in order for such sights to be practical, they have to be mounted on a rifle of light to medium caliber that is capable of long-range hits. Folding leaf sights on a dangerous-game rifle that will always be used inside 100 yards are nothing but window dressing. Though a series of folding sights may be combined with an express sight, an honest-to-goodness ''working hunter's'' express sight is a single, rock-solid rear blade that has been dovetailed, pinned, and soldered in place so nothing can knock it loose. Professional African hunters who face dangerous game regularly steer clear of sights with moving parts. They figure that, if it moves, it can go wrong, and if it can go wrong, it will do so at the worst possible moment. The one allowable exception is an extra-large, flip-up front sight, usually faced with ivory, for shooting in poor light.

A few years ago, when I had a dream rifle made up by the David Miller Company of Tucson, Arizona, I specified a plain, rigidly mounted, express-type rear with a large-diameter gold bead at the front end. They made something even better. The simple, wide, V-notch rear sight was machined from solid steel and then dovetailed into a quarter rib that is *integral* with the barrel. It's a very fancy piece of gunsmithing, seeing as how quarter ribs are usually attached to the barrel. The front sight ramp, or foresight, as the English say, is attached by soldering *and* by a band that encircles the barrel, a double fail-safe precaution. The foresight blades are dovetailed into the ramp and held in place by a spring catch, making it easy to change from daytime to nighttime beads in a second or two. Both front and rear are so solid that they couldn't be pried loose with a tire tool, and an oversize hood further protects the front sight. It's better to have a front hood that's too big than one that's too small. Those dinky little hoods that come on some of today's rifles only crowd the sight and block out the target. You're better off without them.

The Folding Tang Sight

A very classy, accurate, and easy-to-use sight that we could make good use of these days is the old-fashioned folding tang sight. These were once made in the United States by Lyman, King, and Marble sight companies and several custom shops, but they have almost faded from the scene except for hand-made models and a 19th Century blackpowder type by Thompson/Center. The best tang sights were simple peeps on adjustable pedestals mounted on the tangs of pump, autoloading, single-shot, and some lever-action rifles. The beauty of a tang sight is that it is mounted close to the eye for speed and convenience, has the accuracy of peep sights, and folds down out of the way for carrying or storage. Wellmade .22 Rimfire lever rifles such as the Browning BL-22, Marlin's Model 39, and Winchester's

Peep sights are little used nowadays, which is a pity. This is the Williams FP-GR-TK mounted on a Winchester Model 9422 lever-action rifle.

Tascorama sight projects a glowing aiming dot on the target. It is especially useful for shooting in very dim light.

Model 9422 would benefit both in appearance and shooting if fitted with a nicely finished tang sight.

Mounting these sights is a simple matter of drilling and tapping a couple of holes in the tang. Once attached, the rear sight is mighty secure. Considering today's trend toward classic rifles and quality accessories, a well-made tang sight such as the old Lyman No. 1A might be a hot-selling item.

Aperture Sights

An interesting type of rear sight that enjoyed a brief moment in the sun was the so-called cocking-piece sight. It was a miniature, adjustable peep mechanism mounted on the cocking piece, or striker, of Mausers, '03 Springfields, Krags, and a few other bolt-action rifles. This was a neat arrangement because the sight was small and out of the way while, at the same time, it offered peep-sight accuracy. It also put the peep aperture close to the eye for fast sighting, and the shooter didn't have to worry about getting poked in the eye because the sight jumped forward with the striker when he pulled the trigger. The additional weight on the striker was a drawback, however, because it slowed down lock time and, eventually, these interesting and well-made sights passed from the scene.

What with all the flap about ultra-lightweight rifles these days, I wouldn't be surprised if we see a trend toward aperture-type receiver sights. Commonly known as peep sights and weighing only one or two ounces, they offer excellent accuracy. Compared to scopes, they are inexpensive. If someone wants to break the five-pound weight barrier with a rifle that puts a bullet on target out to 300 yards, a bolt-action, fiberglass-stocked, *peep-sighted* rifle would be the way to go.

Quite a few shooters say they don't care for peep (aperture) sights, but most problems stem from an improper approach to their use. A hunter who has been shooting with open sights will usually try to aim peeps the same way. He shifts his eye's focus from sight to target and back again. But focusing on a peep sight tends to block out the target and that's where first-time users go wrong. The trick is to simply look *through* the peep, not at it. As long as you are looking through the aperture, you're automatically aligning the sights, so all you need to do is put the front bead on the target and the sight picture is complete. Shooters with eyes that no longer focus clearly on open sights will find they can aim more easily, faster, and more accurately with peep sights. It is important that the peep be positioned close to the eye for speed and convenience.

Interesting alternatives to both scopes and iron sights are the non-magnifying optical sights, which are aimed by means of a battery-powered sighting dot. Since these sights have no magnification, the field of view and eye relief are virtually unrestricted, making them ideal for shots at running game. They can even be mounted on shotguns for use with flying targets. When the unit is switched on, a glowing dot of light appears in the field of view, indicating where the bullet will hit. This simple arrangement makes aiming extremely fast and convenient. These units are also small and light in weight and don't interfere much with the portability of a rifle. Probably best known is the Swedish-made Aimpoint (Aimpoint USA, 203 Elden St., Suite 302, Herndon, VA 22070). This sight has also made quite a hit in handgun-shooting circles. Tasco (7600 N.W. 26th St., Miami, FL 33122) offers four different models of their Tascorama battery-dot scope for different types of shooting. Mounting and sighting in these space-age rifle sights is almost identical to sighting in ordinary telescopic sights. Both the Aimpoint and Tascorama sights feature a rheostat switch so you can adjust the brightness of the aiming dot.

Scopes are a simple fact of shooting life. But it's also a certainty that iron sights will be around as long as rifles are made. They're a lot more than cheap substitutes for a scope. Be it trick shooting or hunting deer in thick brush, nothing does the close-range job better than a good set of old-fashioned iron sights.

Hunter's Guide To Scopes And Mounts

By Bob Bell

One Wyoming sagebrush usually looks pretty much like another, especially from 300 yards. This particular one held my attention because it had antlers growing out of it. I lowered my binoculars and eased the 7mm Magnum into position, the back of my hand resting against an old broken-off fence post. With the Redfield scope at 6X, I could see the wide-spreading antlers, the ears, and the top of the muley's head. When I twisted the ring to 9X, I could make out the black nose right in the middle

of it all. One strand of rusty wire gave the fence post tenuous support but couldn't keep it from swaying. Nevertheless, I managed to settle things down long enough to squeeze off a shot when the crosswires rested smack on that black nose.

A few minutes later, I was examining one very dead mule deer. My handloaded 160-grain Sierra spitzer had centered the throat, just under the chin, for an instant kill.

Actually, it wasn't a difficult shot with the equip-

Photograph by Bob Bell

Author takes aim through a Leupold 6½X-to-20X variable mounted on a Remington 7000 in .22/250 caliber.

Bushnell's 3X-to-9X Banner Wide Angle Riflescope, also available in 4X-to-12X (above), is equipped with Bullet Drop Compensator and Prismatic Rangefinder. Game-spooking glare is minimized on Leupold scopes with Matte finish (left).

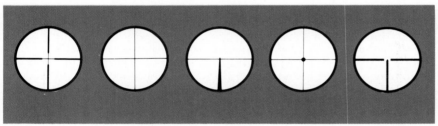

Reticles come in a wide variety of styles, but hunters most often choose the type at the far left.

ment I had. But even with the best iron sights, it would have been impossible. I just couldn't have seen the deer through them. That's why practically every rifle sports a scope nowadays.

Open iron sights completely conceal everything beneath the top of the rear sight, and the front sight covers a lot of the animal—all of it on an end view at long range. It also seems to shift sideways, depending on which direction light falls on it. Furthermore, such sights require the shooter's eye to rapidly and repeatedly shift focus from the rear sight to the front sight to the game in order to keep things aligned. Youngsters can adjust, but older hunters, whose eyes have lost their powers of accommodation, have trouble. Most open sights are also difficult to sight in very accurately. Aperture (peep) sights eliminate some of these problems but still do not supply a bright image under gloomy conditions. Only a good scope does that.

The primary advantage of a scope is that it presents a sharp, enlarged view of the target and its surroundings, even under poor light conditions, with an aiming point seemingly pasted right onto the target. And it will do all these things at any range at which today's high-velocity cartridges are effective. But without a scope, we might just as well use a .30/40 as a .300 Weatherby Magnum. The old Krag load will dispatch most anything we want to shoot at iron-

sight ranges, but a scope makes the magnums effective several times as far. With a scope, the hunter can see better, and thus aim better and hit better.

So . . . what is a scope? Viewed simply, it is a metal tube containing a series of lenses that create a magnified image, plus an aiming point called a reticle and a means of adjustment so that the reticle's position can be aligned with the arc of the bullet's flight.

A scope must have a large-enough field of view (that portion of the environment seen when looking through it) so that the target is easily found. It must transmit enough light to be usable even in gloomy woods late on a winter day. And it must have enough eye relief (the distance between the rear end of the scope and the eye) so that recoil will not drive the tube against the eyebrow when the gun is fired. Furthermore, the scope's dimensions and weight must be reasonable, as the hunter has to carry it, along with the gun it's mounted on. It must also be completely unaffected by the tremendous recoil shock transmitted each time the gun is fired.

It's not easy to obtain all these qualities. Durability requires weight, which is a problem both in terms of toting the scope with you and in the way it affects the balance of the firearm. For instance, good illumination requires large lenses, yet these add bulk and cost. Boosting power reduces field of view and affects eye relief. Never, in scope design, do we get something for nothing. Therefore, any scope is ultimately a compromise, the end result of the designer's trade-offs.

Fortunately, the nature of things makes scope use practical. Low-power scopes automatically have large fields and long eye relief; high-power models have small fields and shorter, more critical eye relief. However, where quick aim at disappearing targets is necessary—on whitetails, elk, or bear in thick cover, for example—high power isn't needed because the animals are large. Conversely, small targets that require high magnification, such as woodchucks, crows, and prairie dogs, are normally shot while motionless, so the small fields of such scopes are no problem. For situations falling between these extremes, such as typical shots at pronghorns, open-country mule deer, and sheep, medium-power scopes fill the bill because they are compromises in magnification and field.

As a result, scope designers long ago came up with a complete range of magnifications. Those of 2½X, 3X, and 4X are considered conventional big-game models. The 6X is a reasonable choice for big game at long range, though a few experts might go to 8X because their familiarity with such equipment allows them to overcome the limitations of the smaller field and to take advantage of the extra power. Scopes in the 10X-to-20X bracket are normally used for sit-still varmints and competitive target shooting, while the 24X-to-36X models are favored by benchrest shooters.

Even within these basic groupings, it makes sense to match magnification to rifle caliber and type. U.S. Repeating Arms' new M94AE carbine in .356 Winchester caliber, for instance, is an excellent woods outfit but it's not intended for long shots. A small 2½X, such as the Leupold Compact, is a perfect choice for this rifle, whereas for the Model 700 Remington 7mm Magnum, which can handle most big game at most any range, a 4X is probably the best compromise.

Likewise in the varmint realm: There's no need to go higher than a 10X on a .222 or .223 because the magnification will give precision aiming at any distance where these loads are effective. But the .22/250 can benefit from a 16X when working at the ultimate ranges where its higher velocity is useful.

The rifleman's primary goal, of course, is to match his equipment to his normal shooting needs. Yet there are always occasions when he wishes he had a different magnification. That's why variable-power scopes were created. They date back to early in this century in European models, but did not become readily available here until the mid-50s, when Bausch & Lomb's 2½X-to-8X BALvar caught everyone's imagination. Now, practically every line includes several switch-powers.

Early variables had the reticle in the focal plane of the objective (front) lens. Since power change is effected by altering the position and spacing of the erector lenses, which are behind that first focal plane, apparent reticle size varied directly with the magnification. In other words, the reticle got bigger as

the power was boosted. It didn't actually subtend any more of the target, but it was more conspicuous. This characteristic bothered American shooters, who complained so much that the manufacturers, led by Redfield and Weaver, moved the reticle into the second focal plane behind the erectors. Then, when power was increased, the image grew but the reticle wasn't magnified along with it, so it subtended less of the target. This alteration gave the effect that shooters wanted and made variables popular choices for loads such as the .243, which could handle deer in the fall and varmints the rest of the year.

However, under this system, a power change can slightly displace the target image while the reticle stands still. This is due to the mechanical clearance necessary for moving the erector system. As a result, there can be a change in the bullet's point of impact. In the better makes, tolerances are now held so close that this problem has been largely eliminated. But such quality pushes prices up, so anyone considering a variable should be willing to pay a reasonable price for a good one.

Variables also are harder to seal against moisture than straight powers because there has to be an opening in the tube so that a connection can be made between the power-selector ring and the erector lens tube. Again, the better models are pretty dependable, but you have to pay for such quality.

Variables are readily available in four power combinations: 1½X-to-4½X, 2X-to-7X, 3X-to-9X, and 4X-to-12X. There are minor variations of these from some makers, and a few offer higher options—6X-to-18X from Redfield, Burris, and Tasco, and 6½X-

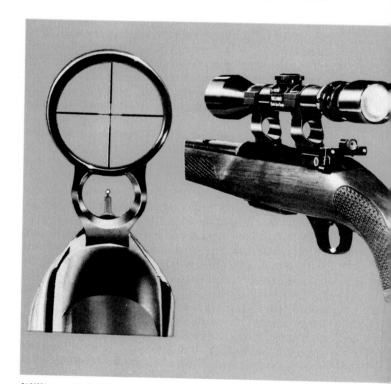

Williams Sight-Thru Mount gives shooters choice of aiming through scope or iron sights.

to-20X from Leupold. All of these have an actual power spread of 1-to-3. A few makers supply variables with a 1-to-4 ratio, notably the new Bausch & Lomb 6X-to-24X and the Kahles 3X-to-12X. This spread requires an unusual optical design.

From all indications, the 3X-to-9X is the most popular, although it shouldn't be, except for outfits to be used on both big game and varmints. To get enough light transmission at 9X requires such large objective lenses that bulk, weight, and cost go up significantly, yet this power is almost never needed for big game. The 2X-to-7X will handle any big-game situation and is the best choice for an all-around big-game gun. For the black-timber specialists who occasionally might get a shot in an alpine meadow or Eastern powerline right-of-way, the 1½X-to-4½X is unbeatable. It's physically small (no enlarged objective), lightweight, and has a tremendous field at bottom power. For years, I have been using this size variable by Leupold, Weaver, Kahles, and Redfield. I recently mounted Weatherby's new Supreme 1.7X-to-5X on a 7mm/08 and it performed perfectly. The small variable has become my favorite type of scope for big-game hunting.

The 4X-to-12X is best used on an open-country deer/pronghorn outfit that will double on varmints, while the larger variables are really varmint rigs with power spreads that adapt immediately to mirage.

No matter which scope is chosen, the proper reticle makes it more efficient. Many designs are available, but the simplest is usually the best.

Crosshairs, which are actually wires, are simple, precise, and generally efficient, particularly on small targets. They can be difficult to see in dark woods. For generations, the post was recommended for big-game hunting, usually with a horizontal wire to reduce canting. It is conspicuous under any light conditions, but can cover too much of the animal at long range. The best shape is a tapered, flat-top design. It gives a constant aiming point, whereas the tip of a pointed post tends to get lost when a fast shot is taken.

To gain the qualities of both crosshairs and post and to eliminate the deficiencies of each, the Middle Europeans long ago came up with a reticle featuring crosshairs at the center and posts at the outer ends. About a quarter-century ago, Leupold refined this design into their Duplex reticle, and now all scope-makers offer it, usually under other names. The posts make quick aim possible, no matter what the ambient light, while the fine crosshair intersection permits precise aim on even small targets. Furthermore, the space between opposing posts, or the crosshairs intersection and one post, can be used to estimate range. These separations are listed in the company's literature or can be determined by comparing with a target of known size at a measured range. If a separation is six inches at 100 yards, it will be 30 inches at 500 yards. And, if an elk's body depth just fills this space, the range is about 500 yards, for 30 inches is about the withers-to-brisket measurement of a big bull. Other possibilities are obvious.

The Duplex reticle also provides two immediately available aiming points—the crosshairs and the top of the bottom post. When zeroed +3 inches at 100 yards, as is common with high-velocity loads, the crosshair zero will be at 250 to 300 yards, depending upon the exact load used. From then on, the bullet will be arcing downward from the line of sight. At some range, it will obviously coincide with the top of the six o'clock post. With most of today's magnums, this point will be reached between 400 and 500 yards. The precise distance can be determined by experimental shooting on the range, or it can be calculated closely from ballistics tables. Once this is learned, the hunter knows that, anywhere from the muzzle to that way-out distance, his bullet is striking somewhere along the wire from the crosshairs intersection to the post, so he has an excellent idea of where to hold.

Many so-called range-finding reticles are available, and they work as well as can be expected. But most require turning the power-selector ring to get a reading and, at such times, a third hand would be helpful. They might be superior at extreme ranges, and I can see their value in some military situations but, for hunting use, I prefer the simplicity of the Duplex system. All in all, the Duplex has more advantages and fewer drawbacks than any other reticle I'm familiar with.

There are others, of course. The Lee Dot is extremely fast and easy to use, and can serve for range estimating when both its angle of subtension and the approximate size of the game are known. For easy visibility on big game, it's important to get a fairly large dot. In a 4X scope, it should be at least three minutes of angle (about three inches at 100 yards). Four minutes is better for woods use. As power goes up, dot size can go down, and vice versa.

Recently, Bushnell reintroduced their Lite-Site reticle in several scopes. This is a center dot of light created by tiny batteries and projected onto the crosshairs intersection. Obviously, it is visible under the

Holden Ironsighter scope mounts can be fitted on rifles or on slug-shooting shotguns.

Side mounts by Griffen & Howe are made for top ejection (near right) or standard models (far right).

darkest conditions so accurate aim can be taken on any animal that can be seen in the first place.

Dan Shepherd's sophisticated 3X-to-9X scope takes a different approach to long-range shooting. Its reticle is a series of circles that are photo-etched along a vertical line, each circle enclosing 18 inches at 100-yard intervals. The circles are spaced to accommodate for bullet drop after zeroing in at 100 yards, so the shooter just selects the one that encloses an 18-inch area of his game (long assumed to be the body size of a deer), and squeezes off a shot.

Once a scope has been selected, it has to be attached to the rifle by means of a mount. During the past three-quarters of a century, countless designs have appeared. Early on, when shooters who didn't fully trust scopes put them on military Mauser and Springfield bolt rifles, high or offset mounts permitted the use of backup iron sights. Gradually, the situation changed and, when underslung bolt handles became common, mounts became lower and iron sights tended to disappear from scoped rifles.

Dozens of mount designs are still available, but the vast majority of riflemen use one of two types: the Weaver and the Redfield. The Weaver utilizes easily detachable rings and a pair of modified dovetail blocks that are screwed to the receiver bridge and ring. The Redfield uses a stiff metal base that bridges the magazine opening of a bolt action. This bridge has an opening on top of the front end that accepts a male dovetail integral with the front scope ring. At the rear, opposing screws make it easy to swing the tube in a short arc. This permits zeroing for windage with the mount, which is a good idea even in this day of constantly centered reticles because it brings incoming light rays through the optical center of the lenses, where they are least affected by aberrations.

Mounts of the Weaver and Redfield types are made by numerous other companies, most of them so close dimensionally that the various parts inter-

change. Different but similar bridge designs are available from Buehler, Conetrol, EAW, Williams, and others.

A few years before his death, stockmaker Len Brownell designed an excellent, quick-detachable top mount. It features lever-locking rings that attach to a pair of action-mounted dovetails. Precise replacement and extra security are provided by teeth on the inner face of the ring sections that engage serrations along the edges of the dovetails. This mount is now available from Kimber of Oregon.

Side mounts, which have a base permanently attached to the side of the action, are offered by Griffin & Howe, Jaeger, and a few others. Two rings situate the scope in normal position but allow it to be quickly removed by means of finger-operated levers, thus clearing the way for iron-sight use. For even quicker access to the irons, Pachmayr long ago designed the Lo-swing Scope Mount, which lets the scope rotate to the side in seconds.

A different approach—or rather a revised old one—came on the market some years back when Jerry Holden's Ironsighter mount appeared. Essentially a pair of metal figure eights, the top circles clamp the scope tube while the bottom circles form a tunnel that permits use of the metallic sights. Clear View, Kwik-Site, and other makers now offer similar designs, and there's no doubt that they can be useful when hunting in bad weather.

There are other systems for attaching a scope to a gun, including the Sako and Ruger dovetails that are integral with the receivers. These are in one way the best of all, for they eliminate the tiny 6/48 screws normally used for attaching the bases.

But all the designs that have survived on the market give satisfactory to excellent results so, as with scopes, it's mostly a matter of finding one that suits your personal requirements and then going with it. Most of the time, the sighting equipment is more efficient and dependable than we shooters are.

Getting Started In Handgun Hunting

By Hal Swigget

If for some reason that I hope never comes up, I should have to limit all my hunting to a single type of firearm, my immediate choice would be a handgun. And I'd never look back.

A bold statement, you say. Possibly. But one day, without realizing what had happened, I discovered that every time I went hunting for myself—just for fun—with no gun to test or ammunition to write about, it was with a handgun.

There is a tendency to think of hunting with handguns as a stunt. Some even make light of the subject. But I guarantee that it isn't that way at all. If anything, it is precisely the opposite. Handgun hunters have to be *better* hunters than those shooting long guns. They have to be far more disciplined because they must be in complete control of themselves at all times.

As a case in point, let's say that you know you can hit a one-quart oil can nine times out of 10 at 45 yards from any shooting position, in any light, and while short of breath from a climb or stalk. Such proficiency would make a shot at a deer 45 yards away a legitimate target for your handgun. A shot at 60 yards *is not* legitimate unless you can do the same thing at 60 yards. That's where discipline comes in. That's also why handgunners have to be better hunters than those shooting long guns.

First-time handgun hunters should start with a .22 Rimfire, autoloader, revolver, or even a single-shot.

My suggestion would be to make that first .22 a revolver or single-shot.

Purchase the best rimfire handgun you can afford. You won't regret extending yourself a bit because any quality handgun will last all your life if you take care of it, and you will discover in later years that a .22 will end up getting a lot of use long after you've graduated to much heavier calibers. Good sights are a must. No one can hit anything without good sights that are adjustable to each individual's grasp and eyesight. No two people hold a handgun alike, nor do we see sights the same way, which makes adjustable sights mandatory on any handgun that's going to be used seriously.

The longer the barrel, the greater the distance between sights. This, in turn, allows for more accurate sighting—within reason of course. I consider four inches the shortest practical length and 7½ inches the maximum. If you feel the need to add an inch, I think you will find it unwieldy. Six-inch barrels are mighty hard to beat for all-around use.

When you've settled on your .22 Rimfire handgun, buy a carton (10 boxes) of standard-velocity Long Rifle ammunition. That's 500 rounds, which may not be enough to make you a good shot but is at least enough to get you started. You will not need high-velocity ammo. This faster ammunition usually isn't quite as accurate, so stick to standard velocity until you have a reason to change.

Try to find a range where you can shoot at no more than 10 yards. Most are set up for a minimum of 25 yards, but this is beyond a beginner's ability, in my opinion, because it soon ceases to be fun if you don't hit the target. Having access to a farm or ranch is an ideal way to start. A few beverage cans tossed against a creek bank or any dirt backstop (always be sure of where your bullets are going) five or six steps away is perfect. *Do not* shoot at bottles. Broken glass left anywhere is dangerous.

Carefully study the instructions that come with your gun before loading. Remember to always point the gun in a safe direction.

Line the sights up, keeping the front sight even with the top of the rear sight and with an equal amount of daylight on each side. Squeeze the trigger, adding pressure when the sights are aligned perfectly and remember to hold that pressure steady when they wander off. Don't be surprised when you hit that can on the first shot. As you gain confidence, increase the distance. That's all there is to becoming a good handgun shot.

As soon as you can hit the can regularly at 20 or 25 yards, you are ready to tackle cottontails and squirrels. Always try for head shots when small-game hunting. This gives you the entire animal to eat—no bloodshot meat—and there's seldom a crippled animal to trail.

Once you've become an accomplished small-game hunter, it's time to move up. If you live where there are coyotes, foxes, javelinas, woodchucks, or prairie dogs, jump in and get your feet wet. But you need more gun.

It's time to look for a .357 Magnum. It will probably be a revolver or single-shot because there are few .357 Magnum semi-automatic pistols. Colt, Dan Wesson, Ruger, and Smith & Wesson are the big names, and you won't go wrong with any of their revolvers. Thompson/Center Contender single-shot pistols are renowned hunting handguns, and the advantage here is interchangeable barrels of some 17 or 18 calibers. You can use one frame and many different-caliber barrels. These pistols are available in .22 Rimfire, I might add, then on up to .44 Magnum and rifle calibers such as .223 Remington, .30/30 Winchester, and .35 Remington.

Everything said about starting with your .22 applies here except that you shouldn't have to start at less than 25 yards. Do start, however, with .38 Special ammunition in your .357 Magnum. Although they sound different, bullet diameter is identical so the lesser round can be safely shot in the magnum. Case length in the .38 Special is shorter—not the other way around. Even if they could be chambered, .357 Magnum ammunition is much more powerful than .38 Special guns can handle and you could easily get hurt.

Recoil and noise will be a factor as you move up to the .357 Magnum, so always wear good ear protection. When shooting on a range in an enclosed area, I always use ear plugs (those with a valve) and then put earmuffs over them. When I'm not in an

Cylinders for both .22 Long Rifle and .22 Magnum are furnished with the single-action version of Ruger's New Model Single-Six Convertible.

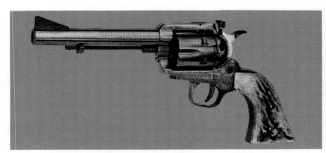

Mossberg's .45 Colt Abilene sixgun is one of the author's favorite handguns.

The Smith & Wesson model 25 .45 Colt double action is fine for medium game.

The Colt Python .357 Magnum is the top of Colt's line of hunting handguns.

Ruger's Super Blackhawk .44 Magnum is one of the most popular hunting handguns.

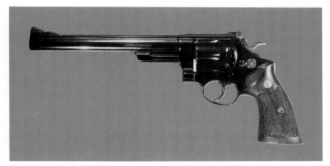

If long-range shooting is your goal, try the Smith & Wesson Model 29 .44 Magnum.

The Colt Diamondback is a great small-game revolver in either the .22 or the .38 Special.

Thompson/Center's Contender, pictured here in .30/30, is a specialized hunter's handgun.

enclosed area, I only use valved ear plugs. It pays off, too. I've been shooting 58 years and can still hear a watch tick, a soft conversation, and have no problem tuning my trumpet for playing in church. Good ear protection will also make you a better shot because most flinching is caused by noise rather than by recoil—though shooters think it's the other way around.

My reason for recommending the .357 Magnum as the next step up is because those soft-recoiling, not-very-noisy, .38 Special loads will help you get used to the heavier gun. And you can always use them for small-game hunting, plinking, and plain fun shooting when more powerful ammunition isn't needed. If a .38 Special revolver is purchased, you may prefer to buy a .357 Magnum later anyway. It's best not to undertake .44 Magnums directly from .22s or .38s but, for serious handgun hunting, .44s are your goal.

Good sights are a must. Some of us like colored inserts in the front sight. Red became standard for the industry a few years back, but most shooters have found black to be just as suitable. I happen to be very fond of yellow and find it does well for me under most light conditions. Green and orange work mighty well, too.

Some of us like white outlined rear sights. For me they are easier to see. Little things like this are individual preferences and can be added only after you have learned to shoot your gun with what you have on it. Change for the sake of change is never worthwhile.

One thing that is a worthy investment, for sure, is a change of grips. Custom grips made for your hand are a bit expensive, but are ultimately worth their cost for the serious shooter. Do not, even on a .357 Magnum, accept grips with sharp checkering. Hot hunting loads will tear up your hands. Many handgunners purchase a Pachmayr neoprene grip. Later, you may want to try custom-fit wooden stocks.

I'm not all that excited about hollow-point loads. There isn't enough velocity to make them expand in a .22, and I prefer not to use them in magnum handguns, either. I am definitely concerned with bullet weight for magnums. I do not believe in light bullets—not for game, at least not for medium or big game. Varmints can be taken easily with 125-grain hollow points in .357 Magnums, but never use that weight bullet on game weighing more than 50 pounds. Nothing less than 158 grains in .357 Magnum should be fired at an animal weighing 100 to 150 pounds—and 180 grains is better. I do not consider the .357 Magnum adequate for heavier game, and under no circumstances is it sufficient for firing on a target that is beyond 60 yards—except, perhaps, for the practiced handgunner who is positively sure of himself when it comes to estimating range and placing bullets.

Scopes can definitely help improve accuracy. However, handgun scopes need not be as powerful as rifle scopes because shooting ranges aren't normally as great. I like 1.5X or 2X for almost all big-

The Ruger MK II .22 Long Rifle semi-automatic gets the nod for small game and plinking.

game hunting. In fact, I'd go so far as to say that nothing more powerful is ever needed with traditional handgun calibers.

Sight in your .357 Magnum to hit point-of-aim at 60 yards. That's where you'll get the most out of it as a big-game hunting handgun. Longer shots at coyotes or woodchucks will require only a little higher hold, yet midrange shots are just as easy with a slightly low hold.

Eventually, you will graduate to the .44 Magnum. There is a .41 Magnum in between, but there is little need to consider it unless recoil is a problem. If so, do consider moving on up to the .41 Magnum rather than staying with the barely adequate .357.

Barrel length is again to be considered. It's best to stick close to middle ground until you become an accomplished handgunner. I still like barrels six inches in length with 7½ inches as the top for revolvers. Single-shots can go to 10 inches and still be shorter than a 7½-inch revolver. My all-time preference in .44 Magnum is a much-worked-over Ruger Super Blackhawk with a 4⅝-inch barrel. It has killed game from cottontails to American bison and has been doing so for a long time.

I have recently had another .44 Magnum worked over. It is a Ruger Redhawk that has been highly tuned and that now wears a 5½-inch barrel. Both Rugers were modified with Mag-na-port vents. The Mag-Na-Port process consists of cutting a pair of slots through the barrel alongside the front sight. The slots reduce recoil somewhat, but their primary purpose is to reduce muzzle jump. They are very effective.

As with the .357 Magnum, I believe in only heavy bullets in .44 Magnum. Factory-loaded cartridges are available starting with 180 grain, but 240-grain loads are better—for big-game hunting, at least. Many of us shooting .44s are now using hard-cast 320-grain

bullets and are moving them out as fast, even a bit faster, than factory 240 grains. This is not really for beginning .44 Magnum shooters, however.

Sight your .44 Magnum in to hit point-of-aim at 75 yards, to get the most practical use of it. This is with a scope or open sights. Though most of us should not shoot that far, .44 Magnum 240-grain factory loads will drop a whitetail or mule deer at 150 yards with ease. My confidence wanes at 100 yards and I'd feel better if yours did, too.

When you get that .44 Magnum, make sure you install a good grip. Checkering here can be painful just as on the .357. Smooth wood or Pachmayr will protect your hand.

Even if you have been shooting full-power .357 Magnum ammunition, it's best to start off with .44 Special ammunition or, at most, with Remington's medium-velocity 240-grain load. It produces a bullet velocity of 1,000 fps out of a 7½-inch barrel. It's a good load, and is capable of handling most .44 Magnum chores with little fuss for the shooter and little wear on the gun.

Big-game hunting with these heavier handguns can be a problem, however. Shoulder holsters are a convenient addition in most cases. It is possible to put a sling on longer-barreled revolvers, particularly single shots. It is a practical method of carrying to be sure.

Since we are talking about hunting with a handgun, let's look at some specialized uses, such as long-range woodchuck or prairie dog shooting. Single-shots come to the front here. I have consistently knocked over prairie dogs at 250 yards with both a Thompson/Center Contender .223 Remington pistol wearing a 6X Burris scope and an M.O.A. Maximum .223 Remington pistol topped with a 4X Weaver scope. Many of these custom-built single-shot barrels will outshoot rifles of the same caliber.

There are some mighty big ones, too. Four of my favorites are .30/30 Winchester, .35 Remington, .300 Savage, and .45/70—all on Thompson/Center Contender single-shot pistols. They're not for the casual shooter but are a definite possibility for the experienced gunner.

One other point is worth mentioning. When I was 6 years old, my grandfather started me shooting. The first gun I fired was a Colt single-action .44/40. I had it firmly gripped in both hands and, with my grandfather's arms around my shoulders and his big hands around mine, he told me, "God gave you two hands, so always use them both when shooting a handgun." That undoubtedly was the best advice ever given a handgunner. I've lived by that credo—two-handed handgun shooting—for the past 58 years and it's been good to me. I encourage all handgunners, and particularly hunting handgunners, to use both hands and, wherever possible, a rest.

Rarely are shots made without the help of a rest, whether it be a tree, stump, fence post, rock, or something else that is close at hand. If these are not available, sit down and shoot with your arms supported across your knees.

Slug A Buck

By Bob Bell

I t looked as though circumstances would force me to leave my 7mm rifle in the rack and hunt deer with a smoothbore and rifled slugs one fall, and I reluctantly decided to find out about shotgun slugs by testing them. The results were better than I had expected, and they may be useful to other hunters.

The one-ounce 12-gauge rifled slug's advertised velocity of 1,560 fps isn't impressive nowadays. Various new .22 rimfire cartridges equal that, but these .22s weigh only 33 grains or so. In standard loadings, a 12-gauge slug weighs close to an ounce (437.5 grains) and, when propelled at 1,560 fps, it generates kinetic energy of almost 2,364 foot-pounds at the muzzle. In addition, the 12-gauge slug has a diameter of approximately $7/10$ of an inch and, therefore, starts out with a greater cross-sectional area than most expanding rifle bullets attain after they hit game. All this indicates that, at short woods ranges, such a projectile should be deadly on thin-skinned big game. Its low velocity can't provide the flat trajectory needed for consistent hits over long unknown ranges, and the deep hollow base of American-type slugs isn't ideal for penetration on heavily-muscled game. But these characteristics are unimportant to most hunters. In their dictionary, "big game" means deer, and there's no doubt a 12-gauge slug will do the job on whitetails or mule deer if properly placed.

The important thing for the hunter who wants to use slugs or who is legally required to do so is accuracy. Will his shotgun produce acceptable groups at normal ranges? Will these groups be located near his point-of-aim if he uses the typical shotgun sight

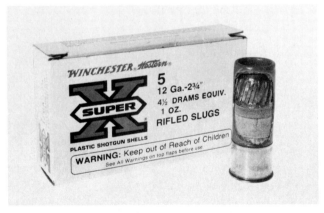

Photographs by Bob Bell

Typical American rifled-slug load (top) has wads that fall away a short distance from the muzzle. Slugs shown are all 12-gauge (from left): Remington one ounce, Federal one ounce, Brenneke (German) one ounce with attached wad, Federal 1¼ ounce.

127

or sights? If he uses a double-barreled gun, will both barrels have a common point of impact? Do barrels of different chokes produce different results?

I doubt that these questions will ever be answered definitively because there's so much individuality among smoothbores. Actual bore diameters and their relationships to slug diameters vary; with doubles, barrels are fitted together differently and influence each other; the way barrels of repeaters fit into receivers also differs. All this means that test results with one gun are probably not completely transferable to another. But if a hunter does some testing with his gun and assorted loads before going into the deer woods, he will surely have a better chance of bringing home some venison. I decided to find out what I could expect from my smoothbores.

I've always preferred 16-gauge and 20-gauge guns for upland hunting, but the 12 has the obvious advantage of heavier slug weight. I have only three 12s: a Model 870 Remington with a 28-inch Modified

barrel and two SKB over/unders—a 26-inch hunting gun bored Improved Cylinder and Modified, and a 32-inch trap gun with Improved Modified and Full chokes. To get some idea of the performance of smoothbore barrels designed especially for use with slugs, I got one of Remington's 20-inch IC slug barrels for the 870. It comes with adjustable open sights, but I wanted to try a scope also, so I ordered a scope mount from B-Square. This mount is installed in minutes by tapping out two pins that hold the trigger group and substituting longer threaded ones that secure a mounting plate. Though a scope may not be necessary at the ranges at which slugs are effective, using a low-powered scope has obvious advantages when aiming at indistinct targets in dark woods. I had a 3X Lyman All-American that was easily mounted for some of the shooting done with the special slug barrel.

All this provided six barrels to work with, and their chokes ranged from very open to very tight. As a

As shown on opposite page, all groups were fired from benchrest. At right are four sample three-shot groups, two groups on each sheet, fired at 50 yards. Group size measured center-to-center of the widest shots was: near right top, 2¼ inches; near right bottom, 4⅝ inches; far right top, 3¾ inches; far right bottom, 6⅛ inches. For details and size of other groups, see text and statistical table.

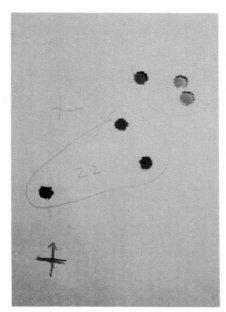
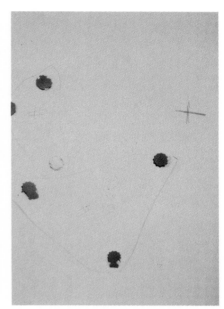

matter of interest, I measured their diameters at the muzzle and the results were as follows: Model 870 special slug barrel—.712; 870 Modified—.703; SKBIC—.721; SKB Modified—.704; SKB Improved Modified—.698; and SKB Full—.689. These measurements aren't necessarily the minimums in these chokes, but they do give some basis for comparison.

Slug designs vary considerably, and perhaps the greatest variety is available in Europe and the United States. The German Brenneke slug was probably the first rifled slug, and dates from just before the turn of the century. It is essentially a square-ended lead cylinder with a small rounded bump centered in the closed front end, angled ribs around the perimeter, and a thick wad attached to the base by a centered screw. This slug gives the impression of solidity. Its normal weight, with wad, is one ounce. One sample obtained by cutting up a shell weighed 469 grains, and its diameter was about .730. Minor variations, mostly in weight, are made in Austria, Belgium, and Spain.

American slug loads came on the market in the mid-1930s. They are normally available from Remington, Winchester, and Federal. Though differing in detail, they are essentially short lead cylinders with closed rounded noses and deep hollow bases. The parallel sides are ribbed like the Brenneke. Some claim these angled ribs induce rotation when the slug passes through the air, which should aid accuracy just as a bullet's accuracy is aided by rifling in the bore. Others feel that whatever accuracy exists is due to the fact that the front end of the slug is heavier than the hollow rear, which keeps it flying point forward.

Prior to World War II, smoothbore loads utilizing solid lead spheres, or "punkin balls," were readily available here and abroad. These rarely gave any semblance of accuracy. Because they were for all practical purposes incompressible, the balls had to be small enough to go through the tightest choke without damaging it, so undersize balls were deliberately loaded. They slid and rattled through the bore, and sometimes hit a deer at 25 yards or so. The hollow base of current American slugs allows them to compress when passing through a tight choke if they are a bit larger than the choke when loaded. The outside diameter of the skirt of the one-ounce Remington was about .690, the one-ounce Federal measured .734, and the 1¼ ounce Federal was .691. I say "about" because measurements taken at the rear end were not always the same when taken at different points around the perimeters. The Brenneke went .730.

The American rifled slugs we examined did not seem to be made with a great deal of care. Bases were not square with the longitudinal axis. The slugs had a noticeable slant when placed based down on a flat surface, and that could not aid accuracy. Chances are the makers assume that a slug's low velocity means it is a short-range projectile at best. As long as it will group within the vital area of a deer, say 10 inches at 50 or 60 yards, there's no point in being concerned.

Nowadays, slugs come in packs of five and they are expensive—70¢ to 80¢ each for American loads, more for Brennekes. This discourages extensive test firing and practice shooting.

Recalling a few previous experiences with slugs, I wasn't sure I wanted to shoot many of them off the bench, so I finagled hunting buddy Bob Wise into helping. Bob is a longtime competitive rifleman. Like most of my friends, he finds it impossible to pass up the chance to shoot someone else's ammo, but this is one project I think he'd just as soon have missed. The 870 was no problem, but the way the SKB bird and trap guns are stocked, each shot from

SHOTGUN SLUG PERFORMANCE

Twelve-gauge slugs were fired from benchrest from shotguns with varying degrees of choke. Unless otherwise noted, each line in the table represents one three-shot group that was measured center-to-center between the two widest shots in the group. Except for the last unit in the table, all shooting was done at 50 yards. The "C-C" column indicates group size. The "V" column indicates vertical displacement of the group center from point-of-aim. The "H" column indicates horizontal displacement of the group center, right or left, from point-of-aim. All on-target measurements are in inches.

M870 Remmington, 20-Inch Special Slug Barrel With Rifle Sights*

	C-C
Remington (1 oz.)	4.4
	3.7
	2.2
Federal (1 oz.)	4.5
	1.7
	4.4
Federal (1¼ oz.)	14.4
	7.5
	8.6
Brenneke	4.1
	5.6
Winchester (1 oz.)	1.6
	3.1

M870 Remington, 28-Inch Modified Barrel

	C-C	V	H
Remington (1 oz.)	5.2	−2	0
Federal (1 oz.)	7.2	−2	R1.5
Federal (1¼ oz.)	13.1	−3	R2
Brenneke	6.5	0	R4.7

SKB 26-Inch Improved Cylinder Barrel

	C-C	V	H
Remington (1 oz.)	5.0	−6	L5.0
Federal (1 oz.)	3.7	0	L6.0
Federal (1 ¼ oz.)	10.8	−3.5	R3.5

SKB 26-Inch Modified Barrel

	C-C	V	H
Remington (1 oz.)	7.4	+4	L3.0
	9.1	+4	L1.0
	3.7	−4.5	L4.0
Federal (1 oz.)	6.2	+6	L4.5
	7.4	−1.5	L6.0
	4.3	+2.5	L1.0
Federal (1¼ oz.)	13.0	+8	0
	11.0	−4	L9.0
Two shots off paper			
	8.7	+8.0	0
Brenneke	6.1	−5.5	L4.0
	4.5	+0.8	L0.5

SKB 32-Inch Improved Modified Barrel

	C-C	V	H
Remington (1 oz.)	5.8	+11	L1
	4.7	+5	R1.2

(SKB 32-Inch Improved Modified Barrel, continued)

	C-C	V	H
Federal (1 oz.)	2.2	+9	R1
	4.5	+6.5	0
Federal (1¼ oz.)	7.5	+5.5	L5.5
Only one shot on paper			
Brenneke	3.2	+9	0

SKB 32-Inch Full Choke Barrel

	C-C	V	H
Remington (1 oz.)	4.8	+8	L1
	5.0	+3	0
Federal (1 oz.)	4.8	+5	R2
	4.0	+6	0
Federal (1¼ oz.)	17.0	0	L6
Only one shot on paper			
Brenneke	3.7	+4	0

M870 Remington, 20-Inch Slug Barrel**

	C-C
Remington (1 oz.)	8.3
Federal (1 oz.)	7.0
	9.1
	8.7
Brenneke	16.2
	8.7
Winchester (1 oz.)	6.5

* Since this barrel is equipped with adjustable sights and could therefore be zeroed in, vertical and horizontal displacement are unimportant and are not listed.

** All slugs were shot at 100 yards, from benchrest, with 3X Lyman AA scope. Since this barrel was equipped with scope, it could be zeroed in and displacement was therefore unimportant and omitted.

the bench banged the comb into the cheekbone, so it took concentration to sit there and squeeze them off, but we spread the shooting over three Saturday afternoons to ease the strain.

On the assumption that slugs will be used mainly for brush and woods hunting, we decided to fire three-shot groups and do most of the shooting at 50 yards. We fired some at 100 yards, though, to cover the odd chance of a long shot. Figuring we might as well get all the information possible, we set up my Oehler chronograph, intending to check the velocity of each round fired.

Bob started with the iron-sighted Model 870 IC slug barrel and Remington one-ounce loads. His first three shots went into 4⅜ inches (center to center) and clocked 1,503, 1,473, and 1,478 fps 7½ feet from

the muzzle. That was a bit slower than you might expect, but the barrel's short length—20 inches—doubtless had some effect on velocity. The group wouldn't have excited a varmint hunter, but three of those big holes in a palm-size cluster didn't look bad for close-range shots at deer. The next shot turned up 1,492 fps, but I got no readings on the following two. The three-shot group was even nicer, 3¾ inches, and I began to think that there might be a place for slugs in my hunting. But I wondered why we had no chronograph readings on the last two shots and began to check the wire connections. When I got to the forward Skyscreen, the answer was all too obvious. There was a one-inch hole in the face of the box. It wasn't caused by a slug—that would have exploded everything. One of the wads had angled off course to do the dirty work. An Oehler repairman later found it inside the box among the scrambled wiring. I've no idea how many rifle and handgun rounds we had chronographed with those screens without incident, but the fifth slug fired put an end to the velocity portion of this report. At least the first four had been close to expectations . . . and Oehler says the screen can be fixed.

We went on with the shooting. Because it was impossible to actually zero in both barrels of the over/unders, our only recourse was to use a target that was large enough to catch all the slugs at 50 yards. For each group, we stapled an aiming point—a four-inch bull's-eye with a two-inch white center—in the middle of a 16 × 20-inch sheet of heavy drawing paper. As it turned out, the 16 × 20 sheet was not big enough to catch every shot fired with the over/unders but, in many cases, it was possible to shoot two groups on a given sheet by marking the holes after firing the first three shots from the first barrel tested. The results of each group—53 were fired—are shown in the table.

Average sizes of all groups fired at 50 yards with the one-ounce loads were as follows: Remington (12 groups), 5.1 inches; Federal (12 groups), 4.6 inches; Brenneke (seven groups), 4.8 inches; Winchester (two groups), 3.2 inches.

Obviously, there is no significant difference among the first three, and it seems likely that the Winchester average would have been similar if more groups had been fired.

The Federal 1¼-ounce load did not shoot as well in my barrels as the conventional one-ounce slug. Individual groups measuring more than 12 inches at 50 yards were common, and several three-shot "groups" had only one shot out of three on the 16 × 20 paper. Admittedly, the results cannot be considered conclusive because of the small number of shots fired, but the results indicate the importance of actually testing different loads in a given barrel.

The averages above were for all chokes. Normally, open chokes are recommended for slug shooting but, in these tests, they did not perform much better than the tighter bores. The small groups of the 870's slug barrel can probably be attributed more to its rifle sights than its IC bore.

The 50-yard groups with the one-ounce loads were not bad, I felt—a man's hand would easily cover the overall average group at that distance—and they would certainly do the job on any deer, assuming that the group was centered close to the point-of-aim. But that, as Hamlet might have said, is the rub. As the vertical and horizontal displacements in the table indicate, group centers in many cases were six to 11 inches away from the point-of-aim, and individual shots in these groups were several inches farther away. This means that, even with a perfect hold and a small-group potential, a clean miss on a deer would not be unusual. Further complications arise when you realize that one barrel of a double can throw a nice group high, while the second barrel may put its equally nice group low.

Some of the best groups fired came from a pump gun with 3X scope in a B-Square mount.

A single-barrel outfit seems less cantankerous than a double. There's nothing new about such a conclusion, but it was interesting and reassuring to see that the 28-inch Modified 870 barrel grouped almost on point-of-aim at 50 yards, and averaged six inches in group size with American one-ouncers. And this was done with only the conventional shotgun front bead. A hunter could do well with that rig.

Of course, a lot of shots at deer are in the 50-to-100 yard bracket in wooded areas, so we did some shooting at 100. The 870 slug barrel with 3X Lyman scope was used for all of these shots. With this sight, it was easy to hold well within the two-inch white center of the bull's-eye. The results, again, are listed in the table. It's interesting to note that, with the exception of one group with the Brennekes, the largest group was 9.1 inches, the smallest 6.5, and the average of six groups was eight inches. That's better than most hunters can hold when shooting offhand. In fact, it's possible to find rifles that won't do better.

I don't know what caused the 16-inch Brenneke group listed in the table. This was a four-shot group that was fired to finish up the available slugs. Two shots were only 1½ inches apart, the other two were six-inches apart, but the two pairs were 16 inches apart vertically. This is the kind of thing that can show up in an individual group and then perhaps not occur again for a long time. But that's what we got, so that's what is listed.

If any conclusions can be drawn from 160 or so shots, it's that factory-loaded rifled slugs are accurate enough for deer to at least 100 yards but that, to make them effective, the shooter must have some way to zero in his smoothbore so he can put his shots where he wants them. He might get lucky with a repeater and have it shoot where he's looking, but life will be a lot simpler with adjustable sights or a scope. With a double that shoots to two different points of impact—who knows.

In the end, the only way that results with a given gun can be determined is through plenty of test shooting. It's better to do it before the season than during it.

Muzzleloaders For Big Game

By Rick Hacker

Each autumn, history repeats itself in the United States. Literally hundreds of thousands of big-game hunters take to forest and field armed with muzzleloading rifles. This "new breed" of hunters comes from all walks of life and encompasses everyone from doctors and carpenters to bankers and truck drivers, for the lure of the front-loader can affect anyone. Moreover, the reason these hunters have decided to lay down their scoped bolt actions for a more primitive weapon are as varied as the individuals themselves: the opportunity to get in on a second deer season, the quest for a greater hunting challenge through the use of open sights and stalking, and the nostalgic feel of history that hunting with a muzzleloader provides.

Many first-time muzzleloading hunters look forward to the big-game season throughout the year and spend much of the preceeding months gathering equipment and reading articles about their intended quarry. Unfortunately, the final choice of what type of blackpowder rifle to take is often left to the last minute, or else the decision is based simply upon what rifle costs the least or is the most readily available at the local sporting-goods store. Ironically, it is that very rifle that can determine the outcome of your hunting adventure. Whether you are merely waiting for an apple-eating buck just a few miles from your home or you are spending hundreds of hours and thousands of dollars in pursuit of elk, bears, or sheep in the wilderness many states away,

it stands to reason that the muzzleloading big-game hunter should give some serious thought to what type of frontloader he will use. This is no easy task, as there are currently more than 50 different styles of blackpowder rifles on the market, representing a far greater selection than our forefathers ever had. However, there are certain characteristics in a rifle that every blackpowder hunter should look for and, by sorting these out, the choice boils down to less than a dozen smokepoles suitable for big game.

Virtually all modern blackpowder guns sold in this country are made in either the United States, Italy, Spain, or Japan. All have been proofed in their country of origin for either blackpowder or Pyrodex RS, the *only* propellants that can safely be used with muzzleloaders. The rifles' design and metallurgy, plus portions of your own anatomy, will not stand up to anything else.

The first concern in choosing a big-game muzzleloader is caliber. Basically, nothing less than .50 caliber should be considered for deer and larger animals. A .54-caliber is my choice for elk, moose, and bear. The next most popular caliber is the .58, which is not as accurate as the .50s and .54s but packs a greater wallop.

Of course, the effectiveness of the caliber is only as great as the powder charge you put behind it. I use 3F blackpowder for my .50-caliber hunting rifles and switch to the coarser-grained 2F blackpowder for .54s and .58s. Each blackpowder rifle is a law

Photograph by Rick Hacker

The author dropped this bull elk in Wyoming with one shot from his .54-caliber Sharps.

unto itself and will develop its own preference for an optimum hunting load. This requires that you spend some time at the shooting range getting your rifle, sights, and loads settled in for the hunt. The goal is to reach a compromise between accuracy and bullet energy. Lighter loads will usually shoot tighter groups but may lack the power to drive your bullet deep into an animal's organs or to shatter bone. Too much powder may blow part of your load out of the muzzle before it burns. It also has a tendency to scatter bullets beyond the limits of hunting accuracy.

Depending on the bullet size I am using, I strive to work up hunting loads that will give me a striking energy that's somewhere around 500 foot-pounds with a round ball and more than 1,000 foot-pounds with a conical at 100 yards. Round balls tend to have a higher muzzle velocity and, in certain guns, can

be more accurate than conicals. But conicals hit with a great deal more energy and are my first choice for large or dangerous game. If round balls are used for big game, you *must* use a large caliber because the bigger the ball, the greater your killing power. This factor is not as critical with deer as it is with thick-skinned animals such as elk or when you're hunting dangerous game such as bear. In these cases, the shot must break bone and anchor the animal in order to assure a quick kill. When using round balls in my .50 and .54-caliber rifles, my hunting charges will usually be 100 to 120 grains of blackpowder; when switching to the heavier-weighted conicals, less powder is needed and these charges usually average 85 grains of blackpowder. (For a step-by-step guide on loading blackpowder rifles see "How To Load Your Muzzleloader" on page 138.)

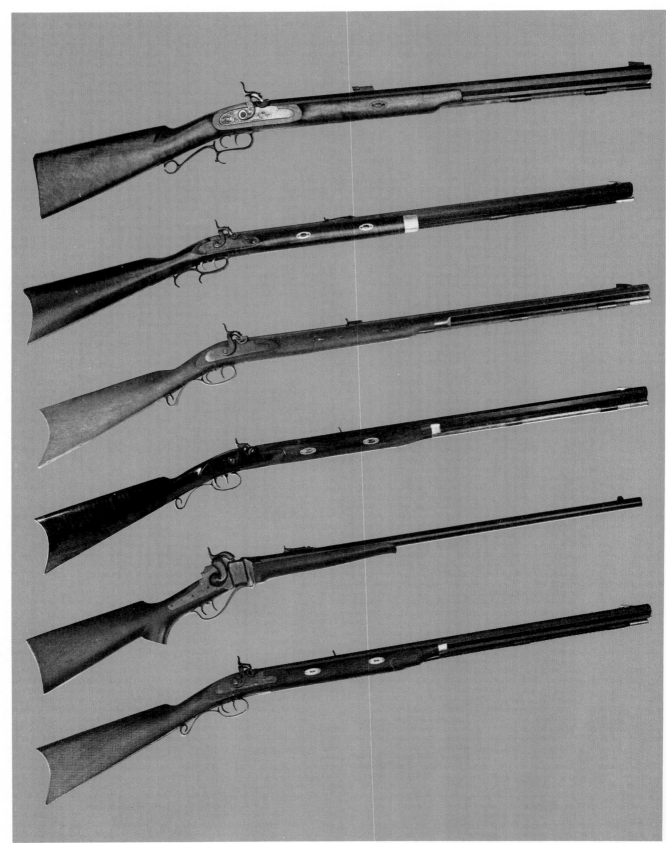

Some reliable and economical blackpowder rifles, (from top): Thompson/Center Renegade, Connecticut Valley Arms Big Bore Mountain Rifle, Lyman Great Plains Rifle, Itha-ca/Navy Arms Hawken, Shiloh Sharps Model 1863 Sporting Rifle (a breechloader), and Allen Fire Arms Sante Fe Hawken.

Many rifles, such as this CVA Big Bore, feature adjustable double set triggers.

Another factor to consider is that not all muzzleloading rifles have the same rate of twist. Some are rifled slower (such as one turn in 66 inches) for round ball, while others have a faster rate (one in 48 inches) for conicals. However, I have effectively hunted with conical bullets in a "round ball" barrel, managing to keep all of my shots within a three-inch area at 50 yards. It is simply a matter of spending time with your rifle on the range before you take it afield. The small investment of an afternoon spent "making smoke" can pay off handsomely in the confidence you'll have at the moment of truth on the hunt.

Another variable you will find on today's muzzleloading rifles are sights. All are of the open variety. In fact, game laws in most states prohibit the use of scopes or optical devices of any kind on blackpowder rifles. The sights come in two versions: fixed and adjustable. Many hunters feel more familiar with the adjustable variety, which makes it somewhat easier to get your rifle on target (realizing, of course, that the amount of powder you pour down your barrel can also affect bullet placement). Personally, I prefer fixed sights on my hunting rifles, not only because they are more traditional but also because they are harder to get out of whack. Once they are filed and drifted and peened into place, they stay put.

When considering a blackpowder rifle for hunting, shoulder the gun and sight it on a light switch or knothole, making sure you can quickly and easily line up the front and rear sights. There's nothing wrong with switching sights on your rifle to make sure that you have the best possible front-and-rear arrangement, especially when you realize that you will probably be shooting in the half-light of early dawn or twilight. In addition, older shooters with changing eyesight may wish to have a gunsmith move their rear sight forward on the barrel for clearer alignment.

Many rifles come from the factory dressed up with polished brass patch boxes, trigger guards, and buttplates, all of which help make an attractive package but also have the potential to shine in the sunlight and spook game. If such polished adornments grace your hunting rifle, let them age naturally or chemically tone them down to a dull brown before taking your frontloader afield.

Muzzleloading big-game rifles are available in either flintlock or percussion, and each form of ignition has its merits. In states such as Pennsylvania, however, the hunter does not have a choice, as the law dictates that only flintlocks may be used. (Check the game laws where you plan to hunt to make sure the rifle will be legal as to ignition system, caliber, rifled bore, and ammunition before making a purchase.) There is a great deal of flash and smoke when you're hunting with a flintlock, but there is also an added sense of pride for the hunter that's somewhat akin to the feeling of a pheasant hunter who switches from a 12-gauge to a 20. A caplock, however, is more reliable in inclement weather.

Although by no means complete, the following is a list of some of the muzzleloading rifles that I have personally used and hunted with over the years, sometimes under the most unfavorable conditions. The one thing they have in common is that they have all served me well. They encompass the total spectrum of blackpowder sporters currently available to the muzzleloading hunter, and each represents good value for the money.

CVA Big Bore Mountain Rifle

The Big Bore is available in .54 and .58-caliber, is rifled for round ball, and has a screw-adjustable rear

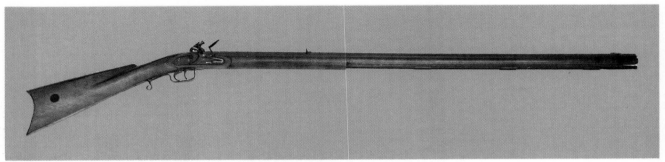

Barrel on Dixie Gun Works' Tennessee Mountain Rifle measures 41½ inches.

sight and a hooked breech for easy cleaning. Available in percussion only, it is one of the largest-caliber single-shot halfstocks on the market, and features browned furniture with pewter nosecap and twin wedge plates. The price is $309.95 finished, $220.95 for the kit. (Connecticut Valley Arms, 5988 Peachtree Corners E., Norcross, GA 30092.)

Tennessee Mountain Rifle

A classic example of the Appalachian .highlands "Poor Boy" long rifle, it is available in a .50-caliber and rifled for round ball (although I have successfully fired conicals in it). The TMR has a 41½-inch barrel, giving it the longest sighting plane of any mass-produced rifle available. It is available in either a right-hand or a left-hand version in flintlock or percussion. Sights are fixed, all metalwork is browned, and the stock is cherrywood. The price is $275 readymade; $225 in kit form. (Dixie Gun Works, Gunpowder Lane, Union City, TN 38261.)

Santa Fe Hawken

A classic example of the mountain man's workhorse is the Hawken rifle. Although listed as a .54, the bore actually measures a .526 and shoots better with a .520 round ball. Breech is hooked for easy removal and the sights are fixed. Lockplate is case hardened—as were some of the originals—and the rest of the metalwork is browned, with the exception of the pewter nosecap and polished wedge plates. Triggers are double set and the hefty stock is black walnut. It is available in percussion only. I have hunted with one of the first production models of the Santa Fe Hawken and found it to be a rugged and serviceable big-game rifle. It costs $325 readymade; $225 for the kit. (Allen Fire Arms, 2879 All Trades Rd., Santa Fe, NM 87501.)

Lyman Great Plains Rifle

Another version of the Hawken styling with twin wedge plates, scroll trigger guard, and browned furniture, it is available in either percussion or flintlock and in .50 or .54-caliber. The Lyman product is slightly modernized with coil mainspring, rather than the traditional flat spring, and comes with either fixed sights or an adjustable buckhorn rear sight that is one of the easiest to use on any production rifle. Although the rifle has not changed since it was first

introduced in 1979, the price is now $50 cheaper—$284.95 for percussion, $294.95 for flintlock, $199.95 for the kit (percussion only). (Lyman Products Corp., Rte. 147, Middlefield, CT 06455.)

Lyman Trade Rifle

The Trade Rifle, also made by Lyman, is one of the few hunting guns specifically rifled for the conical bullet. It comes with the same fixed or adjustable sight as the Great Plains Rifle and has a single unset trigger. Metalwork is blued and the single barrel wedge is of brass. Like the Great Plains Rifle, the Trade Rifle features a hooked breech and coil mainspring, and is available in .50 or .54-caliber in either flint or percussion versions. Its price has also been lowered, although the quality of the gun has not changed. It costs $199.95 for percussion, $209.95 for flintlock, $149.95 for the kit (percussion only).

Ithaca/Navy Arms Hawken

One of the finest Hawken-style rifles made, this piece is manufactured in the United States and features a stainless-steel liner in the breech and bolster area to help prevent blackpowder corrosion where it most often occurs. Available in .50 and .54-caliber and in either flintlock or percussion, the rifle features a very short-throw (fast) lock. It is rifled for round ball, and all furniture with the exception of the polished nose-cap and wedge plates, are browned. The rifle has double set triggers, hooked breech, and comes with a cleaning jag and a handy nipple wrench for field use. A great deal of hand assembly goes into this rifle. The price is $450 for percussion, $525 for flintlock, $320 for the percussion kit, $410 for the flintlock kit. (Navy Arms Co., 689 Bergen Blvd., Ridgefield, NJ 07657.)

Harper's Ferry Rifle

For states that only permit blackpowder hunting with a flintlock, the Harper's Ferry Rifle made by Navy Arms is an excellent choice because it is a replica of the "official" rifle that Lewis and Clark selected to arm their explorers' expedition in 1804. Unlike the original, though, this flintlock is .58-caliber and shoots best with round ball. It is a sturdy rifle with a metal ramrod, but its rear sights are not the easiest to see and should be replaced for shooting at distances of more than 50 yards. The price is $316.

Kodiak Mark II

One of the few mass-produced double rifles on the market today, the Kodiak is my optimum choice for hunting dangerous game. Its twin barrels and percussion locks provide a fast second shot when needed. (Not all states allow use of double-barreled rifles during the blackpowder season.) Available in .50 and .58-calibers, the Kodiak features two rear sights—one for each barrel—eliminating the expense of regulating both tubes and keeping the cost down to an affordable level for a double rifle. Although the .50-caliber shoots round ball and conical with equal ease, an oversized conical such as the Maxi-Ball is recommended for the .58. *Do not* use Minie balls in this rifle because recoil from one barrel could cause the loaded charge in the second barrel to move forward and create a dangerous air pocket. The gun comes with sling swivels, the barrels are blued, and the twin locks are polished in the "white" and etched with a big-game scene. As an option, a second set of barrels may be ordered for $294.25, which feature a 12-gauge and .58-caliber side-by-side arrangement for big-game seasons that overlap bird seasons or for when the opportunity unexpectedly provides itself for something small for the pot. Available in percussion only, the price is $525. (Trail Guns Armory, 1422 E. Main, League City, TX 77573.)

ESSENTIAL ITEMS

Aside from the basics that you would take on any hunt (license, knife, and so on), the blackpowder hunter requires certain accoutrements afield. Be sure you have these items before opening day rolls around.

• At least six pre-measured tubes of blackpowder or Pyrodex. (It is dangerous to load directly from a powder horn and pre-measured charges are both convenient and fast.) Excellent waterproof tubes are available from Butler Creek Corp. (Box GG, 1055 W. Broadway, Jackson Hole, WY 83001) or J&M Sales (Box 336, Richland, WA 99352).
• Soft lead round ball or conical bullets (the pre-measured tubes listed above have a space for carrying these).
• For round ball guns—pre-lubed, pre-cut patches of the proper caliber. Good ones are available from Ox-Yoke Originals, Inc. (130 Griffin Rd., West Suffield, CT 06093).
• For percussion rifles—brass capper with an ample supply of properly fitting caps. Take more than you'll need as these little bits of metal are easily lost. Two of my favorite cappers are the Straight Line from Uncle Mike's or the Tedd Cash capper from Dixie. Make sure these will work on your rifle before taking them on the hunt.
• For flintlock rifles—extra flint and leather, and a pan charger full of 4F priming powder (spring-loaded brass chargers are available from Uncle Mike's and Dixie).
• Short starter.
• Emergency kit—small screwdriver, piece of thin wire or paper clip to serve as a vent or nipple pick to unclog flashhole, screw-type "worm" that can be threaded to your ramrod tip in case you have to remove a stuck ball, nipple wrench (for percussion guns).

Sharps Model 1863 Sporting Rifle

An excellent replica of the original Sharps buffalo rifle, this .54-caliber rifle actually loads from the breech. (Check your state's laws concerning legality of breech loaders during the blackpowder deer season.) Using prerolled blackpowder paper cartridges (kits and instructions are available from the company) the Sharps is the fastest-loading blackpowder rifle available to the hunter. Its authentically shallow, fast-twist rifling dictates conical bullets be used, and I have found that tight-fitting, flat-based slugs work best. The chamber holds 90 to 100 grains of FFG, and I have found the gun capable of downing any game animal on the North American continent. The rifle is available with a variety of options (double set triggers, custom wood, and so on) but is not available in kit form due to the complexity of its design. It is manufactured and hand assembled in the United States and, unlike other percussion rifles listed here, uses musket caps (all others use No. 11 percussion caps). The price is $675. (Shiloh Sharps Products Co., 100 Centennial Dr., Box 885, Big Timber, MT 59011.)

Thompson-Center Renegade

Merely a stripped-down version of their popular Hawken Rifle, the Renegade is slightly less expensive than its best-selling counterpart and has no patch box or brass fittings. All parts are blued and the lock is case hardened. Available in flint or percussion and in either .50 or .54-caliber, the Renegade has excellent adjustable rear sights, double set triggers, coil mainspring, and hooked take-down breech. Its 26-inch barrel—the shortest of any currently produced blackpowder rifle—makes it easy to handle in thick cover. This very rugged and reliable hunting rifle handles conical bullets best. The price is $225 for percussion, $237.50 for flintlock. (Thompson/Center Arms, Farrington Rd., Rochester, NH 03867.)

Some states do not permit muzzleloading hunting with rifled guns. Contrary to popular belief, smoothbore muskets can be made to shoot accurately up to 50 yards, and six to 12-inch groups are acceptable for big-game hunting at that range. Obviously, the closer you can get with a smoothbore, the better. Without rifling, a round ball is the only logical choice (conicals would tumble) and a thick patch normally ensures the best groups. The Thompson/Center Renegade is available in a .56 smoothbore for $225. Dixie sells a Second Model Brown Bess Musket flintlock for $275. With its gaping .74 bore, the Musket is also capable of throwing a fair pattern of No. 6 shot at rabbits and grouse.

All muzzleloaders listed here are backed by the manufacturer's warranty. Better metallurgy makes them far superior to the 19th century arms they simulate.

Muzzleloaders have been effectively dropping big-game animals in this country since the 1600s. Given the practice and care you would bestow upon any hunting rifle, there is no reason why you can't go out with your frontloader this autumn and continue the tradition.

Loading Your Muzzleloader

By Rick Hacker

Unlike cartridge rifles, when hunting with a muzzleloader, *everybody* automatically becomes an in-the-field handloader, as each shot must be meticulously loaded by the hunter. This procedure can take as little as 30 seconds or as long as two minutes, depending on your skill, familiarization with the components, and the general speed and direction of the animal you are hunting.

In the hands of an unskilled shooter, loading a black powder rifle can be a cumbersome and time consuming experience in spilt powder, dropped balls, and flailing ramrods. However, the hunter who has practiced reloading at the range prior to opening day will find that his hands automatically grasp the right components in the right sequence and the reloading process actually becomes a fast, smooth, almost graceful ritual. The accompanying photos in this article show the step-by-step procedures, although there are a few "secrets" to remember.

First, it is important to always load with the same amount of powder each time (once you have worked up a proper hunting load, of course). Any variation will throw your shot off target. And always practice sighting in with the same lead projectile with which you will be hunting; even different brands of pre-cast lead balls may shoot differently in the same rifle! If your .54 caliber shoots well with a .530 projectile, don't take a .535 with you deer hunting, as it will not load or strike your point of aim in the same way.

One of the most common errors that both new and experienced muzzleloading hunters make during the excitement of a hunt is ramming home the ball before pouring in the powder. This practice has been the foundation of a great number of jokes, but it is no laughing matter on a big game hunt. No matter who is talking to you or what is rustling in the bushes, force yourself to concentrate on the loading procedure, pouring in your powder first, slapping the rifle stock to settle the grains into the breech, and then ramming the ball. When using round balls, I always opt for pre-cut, pre-greased patches as they are quicker to load. When shooting conicals, Mini's load easiest; R.E.A.L. (Rifling Engraved At Loading) Maxi-balls are quite accurate, but they are slower to load due to their thicker diameters which must be forced into the rifling upon loading. One of the best choices in conical bullets for hunting is the relatively new Buffalo Bullet (7352 Whittier Ave., Whittier, CA 90602). Available in .50 and .54 for big game hunting, these pre-greased bullets feature a tapered base for easy starting past the muzzle and serrated sides for engaging the rifling with a minimum of effort. They are extremely accurate. A variety of solid and hollow point versions are offered and they have become my optimum choice for hunting big or dangerous game. Whether loading round ball or conical, always ram your bullet down with the same amount of force each time to insure that your rifle will be shooting with consistency: to do otherwise might cost you a trophy.

Practice following each of the loading steps shown in the proper sequence. If your muzzleloader is new, read the manufacturer's specific directions for that gun. With the right load and the correct loading procedures, there is no reason why that big game animal won't be on the ground when the smoke clears.

about like the larger presses. You scoop in the powder and shot with Lee's dippers. It comes in 12-gauge only and loads both 2¾-inch and three-inch magnum shells.

Lee also manufactures some clever and inexpensive accessories such as a separate priming tool, primer-pocket cleaners, a case-neck chamfering tool, and case-length trimmers. The case trimmer can be operated by hand or, if you want to speed up the process, with an ordinary electric drill. The Lee primer seater, by the way, gives you such a sensitive feel for the primer-seating depth in the case pocket that it is widely used by benchrest shooters. I use a Lee primer seater for virtually all my rifle reloading, regardless of the other equipment used.

Mequon hand tools are basically the same as the Lee Loader set. Though the tools are used in a similar fashion, the Mequon loading kit is somewhat more complete. For a few dollars more than you pay for a Lee Loader, you also get a separate primer seater, case trimmer, and deburring tool. Both the Lee and Mequon sets are so inexpensive that you can recoup their cost in a single evening of reloading.

When Fred Huntington, founder of the RCBS reloading tool firm, sold his operations to Omark Industries (makers of Speer bullets and CCI primers and ammunition, among other things), we expected he would sit back to enjoy his collection of antique cars. But Fred didn't take to the easy life and found himself back in the loading-tool business. His latest product combines the compactness of hand tools with the leverage of a bench-mounted loading press. In fact, the Huntington Compact Press, as it's called, comes with a bracket for bench mounting but I think it is more useful as a portable hand tool.

The Huntington tool was formerly known as the Decker tool, and it is different from the other hand tools in that it uses standard, full-size (⅞ × 13) loading dies. This feature, combined with the tools two-handed leverage, means that full-length resizing of large rifle cases is possible. The only limiting factor is your muscle. I've found that .30/06 cases can be full-length resized with moderate effort and that little .223 cases are a snap.

The Huntington tool also uses industry-standard snap-in shell holders. The primer seater, which is built into the tool, couldn't be easier to use. The big advantage of the Huntington hand tool is also its biggest drawback. The full-length dies it uses are not expensive by any means but, by the same token, they can cost more than a complete Lee or Mequon loading set. That's why you have to give some thought to the type of reloading you want to do and select the best El Cheapo tool for the job. The debate is usually between cost and convenience.

Though the Lee and Mequon hand tools come with powder dippers, there will come a time when you'll want to flex your wings and try different powders and loads. This sort of experimentation to develop the best load for your rifle or handgun is one of the most enjoyable and educational reloading pursuits. Lee markets an inexpensive set of powder dippers that give you a wide range of possible powder charges for various calibers with a full range of powders. The set comes with a slide index to show which dipper to use for a given charge with any powder. With a little caution, nothing can go wrong. When you begin this sort of load experimentation, you'll definitely need a handloading manual such as those published by Lyman, Speer, Sierra, Hornady, and Nosler.

If you can spend a few extra dollars, you'll like the convenience of an adjustable powder measure or one that uses interchangeable measuring drums. A good example of the latter type is the RCBS Little Dandy measure. It is used primarily for charging handgun cartridges and is extremely fast, charging 100 cases in only a few minutes. Interchangeable measuring drums are available for just about every conceivable handgun load. Guide charts tell you which drum to use for which load and power.

The Quinetics powder measure is relatively small, and it is light in weight, inexpensive, and adjustable. It is also remarkably accurate through a wide range of powder charges, and it is very simple to use. But keep in mind that, if you use an adjustable powder measure, you should also use a powder scale to confirm the thrown weights of the measure. This means you'll have to spend more money for a scale, but you might get by with borrowing a friend's scale to confirm a few sample settings. Even when using adjustable measures that have a return setting index, I don't feel comfortable unless I double-check sample charge weights with a scale.

Did you know that it's possible to shoot a .357 Magnum handgun for about what it costs to shoot .22 Rimfire? In fact, you can shoot a wide variety of pistol and rifle calibers for less than 5¢ a round. The trick is to cast your own bullets from salvage lead alloys such as the weights used to balance auto tires.

When loading cast bullets in centerfire rifles, it is necessary to keep velocities below 1,800 to 2,000 fps (depending on the bullet lubricant) in order to avoid leading the barrel. These reduced loads are great for practice. In addition to being very cheap, they have a mild recoil and will never wear out your barrel.

Cast bullets in handguns are great because they can be loaded to duplicate jacketed bullet performance and often exceed their accuracy. Lyman, RCBS, Lee, and others make bullet molds in a tremendous variety of bullet shapes, calibers, and weights. In addition to their inexpensive line of bullet molds, Lee offers budget-priced sizing and bullet lubricating accessories that are fast and simple to use. An evening of casting bullets will more than pay for the equipment in money saved. After that, your bullets only cost what you pay for scrap lead, and you can often scrounge your lead supply.

Regardless of the equipment you use, handloading is always fascinating. In terms of fun and performance, the fellow who uses inexpensive hand tools doesn't have to take his hat off to anyone. In terms of getting the most shooting for his money, he is at the head of the line.

Reloading For Rifles

By Stanley W. Trzoniec

The reloading of centerfire ammunition has grown steadily in popularity over the last decade. With the price of factory ammunition always on the rise, it's not hard to see why men who shoot a lot are spending more time at the loading bench. To be a proficient shooter, you have to shoot a lot. To many, it's just a matter of economics. After the initial purchase of empty brass cartridge cases, which currently cost about 39¢ a case, subsequent loadings of the same .30/06 cartridge case cost approximately 19¢—12¢ for the bullet, 6¢ for the powder charge, and 1¢ for the primer. A factory load of the same type now costs 78¢. In other words, you can cut ammunition costs almost in half.

That's incredible, but handloaders benefit in other ways, too. They learn a great deal about ammunition—cases, bullets, primers, powders—and ballistics. Handloading also engenders real pride when home-grown ammunition groups in a very small circle downrange or a pet load takes a fine game animal.

Getting started is not difficult. The first thing you need is a place where you can load your ammunition in peace and quiet. Reloading is *not* dangerous, but distractions can cause you to make mistakes that could be dangerous. You must have the ability to concentrate on the work and you must employ common sense.

You can start out with low-priced hand tools such as the Lee Loader (see ''El Cheapo Reloading,'' for a description of the Lee Loader) and turn out top-

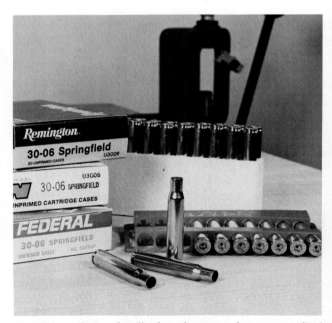

New Brass: Serious handloaders always purchase new, unfired cases instead of reloading fired cases. There are many reasons for this. Most important is the uniformity of interior dimensions within one brand name and one manufacturing lot. This alone gives you an advantage in achieving constant velocities and good tight groups. Stay away from bargain brands, foreign Berdan-primed cases (American cases are Boxer primed), and military surplus. Buy boxes of new brass with the same lot numbers and purchase enough cases to last through a long loading program.

quality fodder. These hand tools are great for use in confined areas and for field loading, but you will soon want to graduate to a bench press. Whether you load 20 cartridges at a time or 200, a bench press and related equipment soon pay for themselves in convenience and time saved. Today, you can purchase reloading equipment as separate units or in package deals. It's smart to buy the press and basic tools as a package and to buy a few additional items later as the need arises. It's best to purchase quality equipment sold under well-known and respected brand names. Reading about handloading and discussing it with experienced people will clue you in on which brands are best.

Let's go down my list of what I think you should buy on the first go-round. These items will enable you to start turning out good handloads as soon as the press is bolted down on your bench. The prime item is the bench press, and prices vary a great deal according to its quality and its capabilities. As you shop around, you will find that three distinct types of loading presses are available—the C-shaped press, the O-shaped press, and the turret press. The press in the photographs that accompany this article is of the O type. The C press is being phased out because it does not have the strength or the sheer ruggedness of the O type. Turret presses and progressive-type loaders came into being more recently but, for the first-timer, it's best to stay away from these complicated loaders until a need develops for faster loading.

The dies used in reloading presses bring fired cases back to the original factory dimensions. If you are into loading handgun ammunition, invest in tungsten carbide dies. They last longer and also eliminate the need to lubricate the cases. Rifle dies, for the most part, are available only in standard sets, and the cases must be lubricated so a case lube pad is needed.

A shellholder is necessary to hold the case in the press, and various sizes are available to fit the various cartridge cases. A case trimmer is a good idea because brass flows forward when fired, and trimming will be needed after five to six firings to bring the cartridges back to the right length. After trimming, you'll need a deburring tool to rid the case of burrs. A caliper is needed to determine the exact length of your cases and loaded rounds.

You'll need a scale to weigh powder charges, and a powder measure makes charging the cases easier and quicker by dispensing the same amount of propellant each time a lever is pulled. Some reloaders weigh every charge on a scale, but most use a powder measure and check its accuracy with a scale. You'll need a loading block and a funnel. A loading manual from one of the bullet manufacturing companies is very important. This "bible" should always be available when you are loading.

Though they are not essential, a primer "flipper," a primer-pocket cleaner, a case-neck brush, and a bullet puller (to correct mistakes) are convenient.

After setting up your press and arranging your tools, loading isn't difficult. The photographs that follow show the steps necessary to load one round of rifle ammunition. Of course, when you are in production, you'll deprime and resize a whole batch of shells before going on to the next step. In the photographs, I'm reloading a .30/06 cartridge case.

Lubing the Case

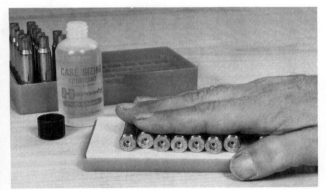

Lubing Cases: Rifle cases must be lubricated so that they will not stick to the walls of the sizing die. The lubricant is applied with a lube pad. You can roll seven or eight cases at a time on the impregnated pad. All die-making companies also market a case lubricant that works best with their dies. Go by their recommendations. Do not lubricate the shoulders of the cases. It is not necessary and to do so only invites shoulder collapse when the lube is forced down on this part of the case by the sizing die. While minor dents in the shoulder are blown out on firing, large dents often lead to early case failure or even case separation, which can damage your rifle or yourself.

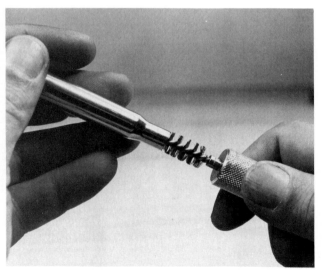

Case Neck Lubrication: After the outside body of the case is lubricated, the inside of the neck should be given a tingle of lube to help it slip over the neck-expander button incorporated in the sizing die. This plug expands the case mouth so that it has a uniform inside diameter and it achieves a tight fit on the bullet.

Sizing the Case

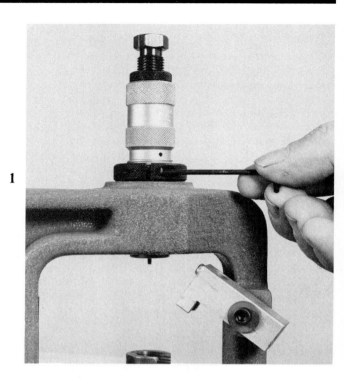

1

Inserting The Sizing Die: After snapping the correct shellholder onto the press ram, the sizing die is threaded into the top of the press. The first step in good handloading practice is to size all new factory cases in order to match the sizes machined into your particular die set. All die sets for a given caliber are made to the same standard dimensions, but most dies tend to have a personality of their own. By sizing all new cases as your first step, one variable is eliminated. To set up the sizing die, first move the ram to the top of the strike by pulling the operating handle. Screw the sizing die in until it touches the shellholder and then lock it in place by tightening the set screw in the locking ring. This is your setting for full-length sizing. With a two-die rifle set, in this single operation, the case is sized, it is decapped (if it has been fired), and the neck is expanded to take the bullet.

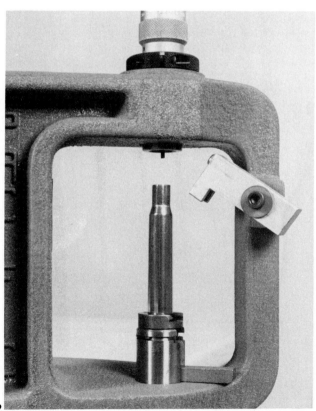

2

Preparation For Sizing: When the die is set up in accordance with the specifications for your press provided by the manufacturer, insert a case into the shellholder. Here, a quick visual check should be made to ensure that the case is all the way in the shellholder and is touching its rearward side. This will ensure a fully concentric case.

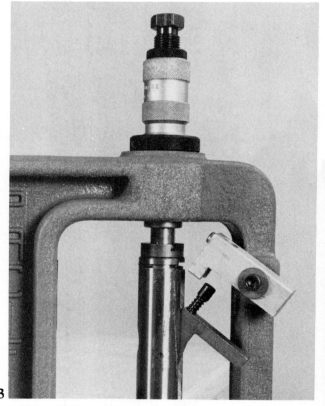

3

Full-Length Sizing: Now, grasp the press handle and pull it firmly. This runs the case up into the sizing die. A mild sensation of resistance will accompany this operation, especially if the case has been fired before. On the way down, during the return stroke, additional resistance will be felt. This is normal. It simply means the expander plug is doing a good job.

Cleaning and Trimming the Case

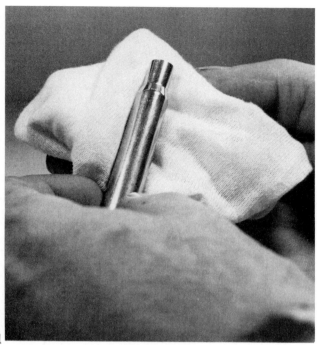

1

Cleaning The Cases: After you are through sizing, the exterior of your cases must be cleaned of lubricant. Leaving the lube on would contaminate the powder and primer later, making ignition impossible. It could also cause pressure problems in the rifle's chamber. Cleaning can be done with a soft cloth impregnated with a mild solvent.

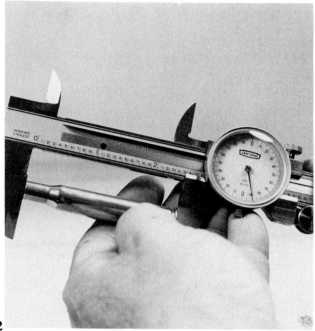

3

Case Trimming: Basically, there are two ways to trim a case back to the correct length. One is to use a trim die; the other is to use a horizontal tool called a case trimmer. With the former, you file the case down until it no longer protrudes through the top of the die. The latter is a small lathe-type tool based on pilots and collets. The pilot fits into the neck of the case, the collet holds the base, ensuring a true cut all around. Some manufacturers sell trimmers with a number of pilots or collets that can be used for most applications; others provide them for individual calibers. Check out both types and choose the one that suits your needs. In this photograph, a lathe-type case trimmer is being used.

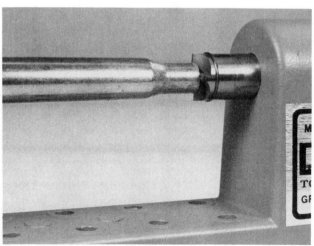

2

Measure All Cases: Depending on their age or usage, most cases will require a minor trimming after five to six loadings. After sizing and cleaning, measure all the empty cartridge cases. Our .30/06 case should be no longer than 2.494 inches to chamber smoothly. It can, however, be trimmed back to 2.484 inches to allow the case to grow in length as you fire. The overall lengths for all cartridges are listed in all good handloading books. Stay within all specifications set up in these manuals.

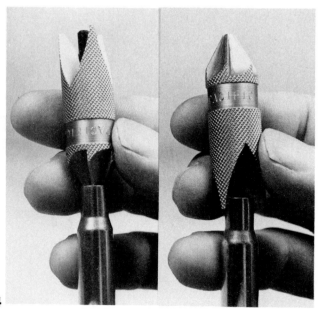

4

Deburring: After trimming, the neck of the cartridge case may have a burr or two. To remove them, use a deburring tool, which costs only a couple of dollars. This little tool chamfers the inside of the case mouth (left) or cleans up the outside of the neck (right) with one deft twist.

Priming the Case

1 *Priming Preparation:* Fill the primer magazine with primers and screw it into the press.

2 *Readying The Press:* With the case in the shellholder, raise the ram to clear the priming punch. Then, upward pressure on the handle will seat the primer in the base of the case.

Keeping Records: With all the cases loaded, they can be packed in the original cardboard box or in plastic cases designed specifically for this purpose. Labels should be used to list information about the load. In addition, a record book should be kept to record more detailed information. A sample page is shown in the photograph. Never, and I mean never, fail to record the components and charges you have used. It's foolhardy, and it can be dangerous. To do so would be akin to shooting in the dark.

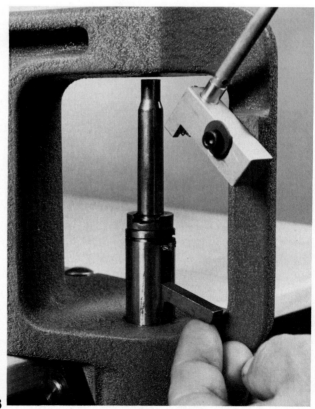

3 *Seating The Primer:* Do not touch the primer with your fingers. The photograph shows how the primer punch is moved into the slot in the ram. Primers are seated flush with, or a little below the flat head of the case. Use the primer specified in your manual for your caliber.

Loading the Powder

1

Loads And Bullets: For beginners, start at a point 5 to 6 percent below the maximum powder charge listed in your manual. In this case, 52.6 grains of IMR-4350 powder was chosen. As you gain experience, you can work up to more powerful loads. Watch for excess-pressure signs as you do so—cratered primers, sticky extraction, and so on. Bullet choice is tailored to the job at hand. In general terms, light bullets for small and medium game, heavier projectiles for larger game. Here, we are planning for an elk hunt so the 180-grain Hornady Spire Point bullet was loaded.

2

Setting The Powder Measure: With bullet weight and powder charge selected, set your powder measure to deliver a charge just short of the predetermined charge. We will later bring it up to the exact charge.

4

Charging The Cases: When you are satisfied that the powder weight is exact, simply pour the powder into the case. Do one case at a time, and move each charged case to the back of the loading block away from the empties. This avoids "double charging," which is possible when you are assembling some reduced loads. This is a very important step. Finish up by looking into each case to make sure the powder level is the same in all of them. If it is not, something is desperately wrong and you must find out what it is and correct it.

3

Weighing The Charges: The charge from the powder measure is poured into the pan of the scale. Because it is a few grains short, the little device to the right is used to fill out the charge. Turning the powder trickler's knurled knob dispenses very small quantities of powder into the pan to bring the charge to the true weight of the chosen load.

Seating the Bullet

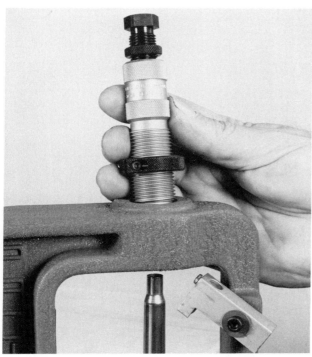

1

Bullet Seating: *This die seats the bullet at the proper depth in the case. It also crimps the case mouth tight against the bullet to hold it in place if that is required. Insert the seating die. After you have started a few turns into the threads, stop and remove the top part or bullet stem.*

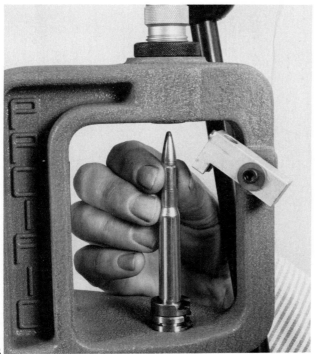

2

Adjusting The Seating Die: *With the ram in its highest position, screw the die in until you feel a slight resistance. This is the crimping part of the die coming in contact with the case neck. At this point, back off about half a turn to allow some working freedom between the two. Lock the die in place with the black locking ring. This is the no-crimp position used for most rifle cartridges.*

3

Starting The Bullet: *With the die set and locked, place a bullet in the case mouth. It should be straight and true. Only a small portion of the bullet will enter the case.*

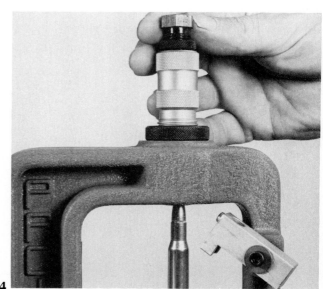

4

Adjusting The Bullet Stem: *Elevate the ram until the bullet enters the die. Carefully screw in the bullet stem until it comes in contact with the bullet. Then, tighten it down one or two more full turns. This will force the bullet into the case far enough to allow you to back off with the ram without the bullet falling out of the case. The next step is to raise and lower the ram while screwing the seating stem downward until the proper overall cartridge length, including the bullet, is reached. With this .30/06 case and bullet, the correct length is 3.245 inches. With the die stem properly adjusted, you can load bullets into all your cases with a single power stroke for each case.*

The Best Bow
And Arrow For You

By Rich LaRocco

"What kind of bow do you recommend for deer?"

"What's the best broadhead?"

"Are graphite or aluminum arrows best?"

"Should I buy a compound bow with programmed cams?"

If the mail I get as a field editor of OUTDOOR LIFE is any indication, thousands of sportsmen have such questions. It's simple to see why, when you stroll into a large, well-stocked archery shop nowadays and see the bewildering variety of bows, arrows, broadheads, bowsights, and other archery accessories on the market.

When you set out to buy your first bowhunting tackle or to upgrade your current gear, please realize that ideal archery equipment is just as elusive as the perfect tennis racquet, the all-purpose deer rifle, or the best car. A bow and arrow that's right for you might be wrong for me, and vice versa. To choose the gear that's right for you is a matter of weighing the shortcomings and strengths of each item in relation to your needs. Maybe you want a sleek, low-slung Corvette for its rocketlike acceleration and classy looks, while a blocky, plodding four-wheel-drive pickup suits me just fine. In the way of archery tackle, I often hunt elk, so I like to use a heavy bow, traditional broadheads, and heavy arrows capable of regularly penetrating a 600 to 900-pound animal. If you hunt nothing but deer, much lighter gear will do nicely.

Most of the questions I hear about bows deal with brand names. Here's an example: "My friends tell

me that bows made by——break a lot. Is that true?"

It is true that some bow makers have had trouble with limb breakage and other such problems. About five years ago, the public-relations directors of two big-name manufacturers admitted to me that they had major problems with limbs breaking. Yet I'd hesitate to condemn the products of either company today because the problems were solved and their products are now reliable. Both companies also replace or repair any defective bow free of charge.

It is difficult to assess how well a given bow holds up in comparison to others. Let's suppose that Company A makes 20,000 bows a year, while Company B makes 200 bows a year. If 10 percent of the bows made by Company A broke within one year, that would be a major problem. Every archery dealer in the entire country would scream bloody murder, especially if the company took months to provide replacement parts. Yet if 15 percent of the bows made by Company B caused similar problems, only 30 bows would be involved, and few people would know about it.

Virtually all bow manufacturers strive to make well-designed, high-quality products that are efficient and durable. Still, some bows are poorly made. One of my hunting partners bought a brand-name kit bow that was supposed to have a 55-pound maximum draw weight but actually pulled only a bit more than 40 pounds. Another buddy bought a horribly designed compound from one of the biggest makers. The cables often flipped off the wheels, a

Photographs by Rich LaRocco

The author shooting a recurve bow. A recurve has several disadvantages, which makes hunting with them a special challenge. Chief among the problems is that they shoot arrows more slowly, and don't work as well with sights.

This archer shoots a fast, hard-hitting two-wheel hunting bow. Notice the programmed cams, the string silencers, the peep sight, bowsight, bow quiver, stabilizer bar, and the wring sling.

problem I've since learned is common with that model. An outdoor-writer friend once received a compound bow from a top-name factory for field testing. The eccentric wheels were mounted crookedly, so my pal sent it back. The company sent off another bow. You guessed it—one of the wheels was as crooked as a card sharp's smile.

You can't entirely avoid such problems, but you can minimize chances of encountering them if you check with several archery dealers before you buy. Ask them which bow makers have good service departments and bows that seldom cause problems in the first place. No matter which brand you choose, I suggest buying a bow that's made by a well-established company and that sells for at least $100, even when discounted. Such a bow is more likely to be reliable and fast-shooting than a cheap model.

Other differences between bows are usually more important than brand names. First, you must decide between a longbow or recurve and a compound bow with all those funny-looking wheels and cables. Longbows and recurves—often called stick bows—are traditional, but usually shoot arrows more slowly than compounds of equal draw weight and do not lend themselves well to shooting with a bowsight. Shooting a stick bow also requires more practice. Because of these limitations, some archers who want a real challenge prefer to hunt with these traditional weapons. The trim lines of a traditional bow also appeal to the eye.

Unless you already shoot a stick bow accurately or you want the challenge of hunting with one, I strongly recommend a compound. My chief reason is that a compound lends itself well to sight shooting. Here's why. With a recurve or longbow, the amount of power needed to draw the bow (pull the bowstring) increases gradually until the bow is fully drawn. With a compound, the tension quickly reaches a peak at about the halfway point and then eases by as much as 50 percent or so at full draw. This reduction is known as let-off. Only a person built like Mr. America can hold a 50-pound recurve

bow at full draw for very long, so the tendency is to ignore the bowsight and rush the shot. Yet, Miss America could probably hold a 50-pound compound at full draw for several seconds. This gives an archer time to aim carefully by using a bowsight to the best advantage and concentrate on shooting form.

Equipped with a compound and bowsight, almost anybody can become reasonably accurate at close range in just six or seven shooting sessions of a half an hour each. You won't attain perfect scores at the local archery range in such a short time, but you should be able to keep almost all arrows inside a one-foot circle at 20 yards. To learn to shoot that well with a stick bow could take months.

I recommend bows with two wheels over those with four or more because there are fewer moving parts to break. In addition, two-wheelers shoot just as well as most four-wheelers and are generally quieter. Get a model with the wheels mounted in the notched ends of the limbs, not on metal or plastic holders cemented to the ends of the limbs. Because

Round eccentric wheel compared to a programmed eccentric wheel. Programmed eccentrics, though more efficient—translating into greater arrow speed—put more stress on limbs, bowstrings, and cables, and cause more breakage.

less weight is concentrated on the limbs to slow them down, split-limb compounds generally shoot faster than those with wheels in hangers.

I have mixed feelings about so-called "programmed" cams. On the one hand, they are more efficient and therefore shoot an arrow faster. On the other hand, they are harder for many hunters to draw and release, and they put additional stress on a bow's limbs, cables, and bowstrings. The cables and strings of programmed-cam bows often break. For these reasons, I have continued to rely on a round-wheel bow.

Short-draw attachments, which allow an archer to use a shorter-than-normal shaft, have the same advantages and disadvantages, with an additional shortcoming. Often, slender, low-profile broadheads must be used because wide heads won't clear the riser (handle section of your bow). That reduces the quick-killing power of your arrow. In addition, because short-draw arrows are shorter and lighter, they lose speed at a faster rate than long heavy arrows do. That could mean the difference between complete penetration and inadequate penetration. I like my arrow to zip completely through an animal, causing maximum damage and cutting a broadhead hole on both sides so that there is an easy-to-follow blood trail.

Many bowhunters today talk a great deal about arrow speeds, flat trajectories, overdraw attachments, the latest technological archery innovations, and so forth. I hate to hear this sort of talk for the same reason I cringe when rifle hunters rant and rave about ultrahot magnum loads and the bullet drop of bullets beyond a quarter of a mile. A flat-shooting bow tempts a hunter to try excessively long shots, yet it does nothing to improve his ability to shoot a tight group. If you sometimes miss a 12-inch circle at 20 yards, you'll miss a 7½-foot circle at 150 yards!

When I hunted with expert bowhunter Dave Snyder in Nevada a few years ago, he said something we should all remember. Keep in mind that, in 1981, Snyder killed the largest elk ever taken with bow

Bowhunter prepares to mount a short-draw attachment, which positions an arrow rest closer to the bowstring. Shorter, lighter arrows can be used, therefore, which results in greater arrow speed.

and arrow and, the following year, he took a mule deer that ranked No. 2 on the all-time list. He knows whereof he speaks. He said: "The secret to successful bowhunting is a 20-yard broadside shot."

Therefore, when you select your bowhunting gear, don't be so concerned with speed. Durability, quietness, and accuracy are very important. No matter what kind of archery tackle you have, you won't be consistently successful at filling big-game tags until you learn to get close to game before you shoot.

Choose a hunting bow with as much power as you can use accurately under hunting conditions. Some states set minimum requirements for hunting bows. Many states, such as Utah, my home state, require a big-game bow to have a draw weight of at least 40 pounds. Many deer have been killed with such light bows but, if you can handle it, a 50-pound draw weight is a more reasonable minimum. With bear, elk, or moose, I'd hesitate to hunt with a bow pulling less than 60 pounds and I prefer one closer to 70. Using a light bow on large game is akin to hunting polar bear with a .22 Rimfire rifle. It can be done. I read about one Eskimo who killed more than a dozen ice bears with a .22 Rimfire rifle, but it's not wise.

Buy a bow with an adjustable draw weight. My favorite can be cranked up from 50 to about 70 pounds. As you build up your strength, you can increase the poundage, but you also may need to change arrows. A shaft that flies well from a 50-pound bow is probably too flexible to fly well from a 70-pound bow, especially with a broadhead. Weight adjustment also enables you to tune your bow more accurately for perfect arrow flight. How to do that is too complicated to describe here, but suffice it to say that, by adjusting the limbs, you can match your bow to the arrow.

Before you select a bow, it's wise to shoot several models. One of my friends once laid out a couple hundred hard-earned greenbacks for a top-of-the-line bow, sight unseen, because it was a popular model in our area. But it didn't feel comfortable, so he shot poorly with it and soon sold it. He had learned his lesson, so he shot seven different bows at various archery shops before settling on another model. Now he feels confident when he draws down on an animal.

If you hunt in teeth-cracking cold, consider getting a bow with a wooden handle. Because metal conducts heat extremely well, a metal handle is cold to the touch, even if insulated by a rubber cover and your glove.

There's one last thing to look for. Get a bow with limbs that can be cranked down enough so that the bowstring and cables can be removed. This feature allows for quick field repairs. Try to get a bow with double-teardrop cable ends. These enable you to change bowstrings in just a few seconds.

The vast majority of bowhunters today use aluminum arrows. There are good reasons for this. Aluminum shafts are physically consistent, and that leads to fine accuracy. Unlike wood, aluminum does not warp when wet or exposed to humidity changes.

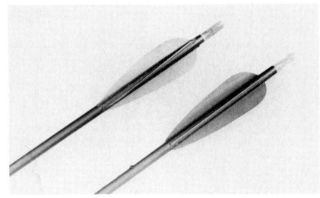

The size of an aluminum arrow is indicated on the shaft. The first two numbers refer to the diameter of the shaft, and the last two refer to the thickness of the walls of the shaft. The text explains the system more fully.

Aluminum arrows are more durable than wood, graphite, or fiberglass and, if they are bent, can be straightened at almost any good archery shop. Though good aluminum arrows usually cost more than other kinds, I have found them to be less expensive in the long run because they can be shot thousands of times. Buy the best shafts you can afford. You're better off with six good ones than you are with two dozen mismatched, poor-quality arrows. I use Easton XX75 shafts in the 2219 size. These feature an aluminum alloy that is especially resistant to bending and a tough, bright orange, anodized finish. Some hunters like to camouflage their shafts, but I have found no need to do so for big-game hunting. I like these bright-orange arrows because they're easy to find after a complete penetration or a miss.

Your arrows must match your bow, which means they must possess just the right degree of flexibility. An arrow that is just right for a 55-pound bow might be too flexible for a 65-pound bow and yet it would probably be too stiff for a 45-pound bow. The degree of flexibility is called spine. The spine of an aluminum arrow is determined by its diameter and the thickness of its walls. My arrows, for example, are of the 2219 size. This means that the shaft is 22/64 of an inch in diameter and that the walls of the hollow shaft are 19/100 of an inch thick.

Most bowhunters use an arrow selection chart to choose their shafts. You can consult such a chart in any archery shop and in most archery catalogs. However, it has been my experience that most charts recommend arrows that are spined too light for broadhead shooting and that they fishtail badly.

Before buying arrows, visit an archery shop with an indoor range and ask to shoot a variety of arrows before you select one. Buy half a dozen of the shafts that suit you and your bow best. Then, go home, screw in some broadheads, and try them. If your arrows fly well with hunting broadheads, you're lucky because you'll be able to use the same shaft for hunting that you use for target practice. In most cases, target shafts fly like mosquito-chasing bats when tipped with broadheads, so most of us have to buy stiffer shafts for hunting.

Have your arrows fletched in a bright, easy-to-see color such as fluorescent pink or fluorescent orange and use equally bright nocks. When you shoot, the fletching is as easy to see as a firefly, even in dim light or shadows. You can see what happens, hit or miss, and you can see where you hit your game. Despite published scientific evidence that some ant-

lered game animals do have color vision, I have never seen a deer or an elk show evidence that they saw fluorescent-orange vanes.

Plastic fletching or feathers will do the job. Because feathers fold down when they strike something solid such as an arrow rest, they are said to be more forgiving of shooting errors or a poorly tuned bow. In other words, it's easier to get them to fly straight. But I use plastic vanes because they have several important advantages. If you are persistent, you can make them fly perfectly, too.

Unlike feathers, vanes are waterproof and stabilize an arrow well, even in hot weather. I've tried various methods of waterproofing feather fletching, such as spraying with dry-fly dressing, but nothing worked for longer than half a day in wet brush. Feathers are noisy, too, not only in your quiver but in flight. That could prevent you from getting a shot or, worse still, it could cause an animal to move when it hears the arrow swishing through the air like an angry hawk. That could result in a miss or a bad hit. Plastic fletch-

When choosing an arrow for your bow, realize that most charts recommend too-flexible shafts for broadheads. Test different shafts to find the best one for you.

Use a strongly spiraled fletching for broadhead shooting. This photo compares two four-vane arrows: the arrow on the left has the helical (spiraled) fletch, while the arrow on the right has a straight fletch.

From left: three flattened-tip broadheads—a Zwickey Black Diamond Delta, a Ben Pearson Switchblade and a Shear Advantage (sold only together with arrow)—and three pencil-point, replaceable-blade broadheads—a Satellite, a Viper (whose blades pivot rearward upon penetration) and a three-blade Savora.

ing is also much more durable than feathers. I've shot plastic-vaned arrows through tin cans, hay bales, and cardboard boxes hundreds of times, and only a dozen vanes tore or came loose.

Fletching with three five-inch vanes or four four-inch vanes are the common choices. I don't like the three-fletch system because the bowhunter must look at the arrow or feel the index on the nock to make sure the fletches are aligned properly on the bow. When you put a four-vaned shaft on the bowstring, you know it's on right. The split second that you save could make the difference between getting a good shot and none at all.

Last year, I missed a buck at 20 yards when my arrow struck a willowy branch and whistled off course. The deer ran 20 yards and stopped to look for the source of the sound. By then, I'd already nocked another arrow and drawn my bow, so I could aim and shoot very quickly. The arrow pierced both lungs. I'm convinced that if I'd had a three-fletch arrow, I wouldn't have been able to nock a second shaft quickly enough and that the deer would have seen my movement.

Insist on getting helically fletched arrows. With this type, the fletches spiral around the shaft, forcing the arrow to spin in flight. This is especially important when shooting broadheads, which tend to plane to one side if the fletching is straight.

Most broadheads are precision made and are capable of cleanly killing any North American big-game animal. Yet differences among them do exist, and some are important. A few heads are too narrow for my liking, while some have poorly made blades of thin, brittle steel. Others are too heavy to be shot, except on the end of an extra-stiff arrow and with a very heavy bow. Also, I do not favor broadheads with only two cutting edges, even though I took an elk and a deer last year with that kind of head. A three-bladed or four-bladed head makes a much

larger wound, resulting in quicker kills and better tracking sign. Multibladed heads also penetrate just as well, if not better than a two-edged model, probably because there is less pinch on the shaft as it follows the head into solid material.

For hunting larger game, such as elk, I strongly recommend a head with a flattened, knifelike point. My tests have shown that such a head penetrates much better than one with a pencil point. This was proven to me a few years ago by Chuck Adams during a wild-boar hunt in California. To prove his point, Chuck had me shoot into the tough, gristle-armored chest of a freshly killed wild boar. I was using a popular head with four replaceable, razorlike blades, and my arrows barely penetrated six inches. Then he screwed a broadhead with a flattened tip onto one of my shafts. The head sliced completely through the pig. I could hardly believe the difference, so I shot several times with the same result. Since then, I've used these broadheads, except when experimenting with new models. The chief disadvantage is that you must learn to sharpen them. It took me five hours to sharpen my first multibladed head correctly. Even now, I need at least 15 minutes to do a really good job on each one.

An elk hunting friend of mine has shot nine elk with bow and arrow, but he has had complete penetration only once. His broadhead is one of the popular models and employs replaceable razor blades. By contrast, I've shot only three elk, but the broadhead has penetrated entirely through the chest cavity every time.

No matter what kind of head you use, make sure it is sharp enough to shave with.

I don't have enough space to permit a detailed discussion of all the other pieces of gear you need, but I can at least mention them. To hold your arrows, I recommend a bow quiver. You'll also need a shooting glove or tab. Mechanical release aids are good for target shooting, but they have disadvantages when hunting. For an arrow rest, I recommend a simple, rubber or plastic version coupled with a Berger button or cushion plunger. You'll need an arm guard to protect your bow arm from the bowstring. I believe that a bowsight is the most important piece of equipment other than bow, arrows, and broadheads. Buy a simple, sturdy model with two pin slots. Don't bother with a bow stabilizer rod. Again, they're great for paper punching but a bother when hunting. If you hunt in swampy terrain where tracks on a blood trail would be soon lost, consider buying a string tracker, which attaches a long monofilament to your arrow so you can find your game after a shot. Don't bother with camouflage bow tape or bow socks. Camouflage your bow with dull spray paint made for the purpose.

Having all the right gear won't make you a successful bowhunter overnight, but it certainly can't hurt. Many experienced bowhunters have learned through hard experience that the proper gear can make the difference between saying to your friends, "I blew it" and "I got him!"

Why You Haven't Scored With A Bow

By Rich LaRocco

I was filling the gas tank of Ron Wilson's pickup when a four-wheel-drive pulled into the service station and stopped behind us. The two men who stepped out were dressed in camouflage, and I noticed a compound bow hanging on a gun rack in the rear window.

"Coming or going?" I asked the bowhunters.

"Going back home," one of the men replied. "We've been hunting for a week, and now we have to get back to work."

"Have any luck?" I asked.

"Well, we didn't get anything," he said, "But we did see some."

"How many?" I asked.

"Let's see. Five, I guess."

"One was a real nice one, too," his partner added. "They were all way out of range, though. We've been bowhunting for five seasons now, and that's the way it always happens."

A few minutes later, Ron and I were back on the road, excited at the prospect of driving the last few miles to our favorite deer area. We were planning to hunt the final week of the bow season, and we were confident we'd score.

"You know, I feel bad about those guys back there," Ron said. "I'll be disappointed if we don't see five bucks this afternoon!"

As it turned out, we saw more bucks than that before darkness fell on central Utah. By week's end, Ron and I both had filled deer tags, and we'd both passed up opportunities at small bucks.

Could our success be attributed entirely to luck? We don't think so, though we're quick to admit that an element of luck is present in every big-game hunt. The point is that neither of us has ever spent a bow season afield without getting at least one good close-range opportunity, mainly because we try to avoid committing the kinds of mistakes most bowhunters make. If those two "unlucky" bowhunters we'd met would change their ways, I'm certain they'd occasionally experience some luck, too.

So what did they do wrong? Why do most bowhunters fail to score while others consistently fill their deer tags?

One of the most common errors, in my opinion, is hunting where there are very few deer. One fellow I met complained that he'd taken only one shot at a deer in three years of waiting near game trails. I questioned him further and learned that he was hunting in a mountain range where deer herds had been reduced drastically be severe winters and by building developments that destroyed winter range. His stands also were near paved highways and, although tracks on the game trails he watched were abundant, most were probably made at night by fawns and does. I was feeling sorry for the man, so I invited him to spend the next weekend at my hunting camp. By 4 p.m. Friday, he was waiting near a housesize rock where I'd seen deer pass almost every day the previous week.

In less than an hour, a buck strolled by and stopped broadside at a range of about 20 yards. I'm

159

Photograph by Tom Huggler

sorry to report that my friend missed. But, of course, he'd had very little experience shooting at game. The same afternoon, a three-by-three mule deer bedded in some high sagebrush near my tree stand. I climbed as quietly as a two-toed sloth out of my tree and stalked within easy bow range of the buck before ending its career with a broadhead arrow through the chest.

A hunter is wise to keep track of game surveys made by state wildlife departments and to switch hunting areas if statistics indicate a sharp drop in deer numbers. Pre-season scouting also is extremely helpful. My hunting partners and I spend several days every year scouting for deer shortly before the bow season. Last year, I located a new hotspot this

way. One morning in July, two companions and I glassed a rugged canyon carefully and saw 20 bucks, including one monster with an antler spread of at least 40 inches. After bow season opened, I never ventured into that canyon without seeing at least one four-point mule deer. I passed up 15 and 20-yard shots at two four-pointers just so I could save my tag for that gigantic buck. On the last day of the bow season, I saw 12 different mature bucks, including a herd of seven four-pointers and the old master himself, but I couldn't stalk close enough for a good shot.

Even if you're hunting in an area known to hold many deer, you still might not see any of them at close range unless you pay close attention to sign.

A few years ago, I moved to New York and set about learning the ways of whitetails. It wasn't long before I learned not to put a tree stand along the edge of a field. Does and fawns often feed in fields until well after daybreak, and they frequently return before sunset, but bucks hardly ever venture into the open except under cover of darkness. At least this was the case in the heavily hunted places I visited. Bucks, especially mature ones, also avoided entering open woods with very little underbrush. The key to getting a buck seemed obvious: Put my stand in the worst tangle of briers, vines, and undergrowth I could find. The first time I tried this theory, I slipped a Treesling and some tree steps into my daypack, crawled on a narrow game trail into the worst kind of thicket, found a tree beside a deer path, and climbed it to wait for my chance. I'd been in the tree for no more than an hour when a fat whitetail buck angled toward the base of my tree, smashing dry leaves and cracking twigs as he came. I drew my bow immediately and waited as he walked closer and finally turned broadside just three paces from my tree. By then, I was struggling just to keep my bow drawn. My shot was horrible. The bowstring ripped off my armguard, the lower bow limb struck a tree branch with a loud *whack,* and my arrow fluttered away like a wounded bat. It was a miracle that I even hit the deer. The broadhead smacked into the buck's hindquarter and, though it didn't sever the main femoral blood vessels, the deer managed to run less than 70 yards before falling dead.

Being in the right place is important, but it's not all there is to bowhunting success. Thousands of archers spend day after day in North America's best deer habitat, yet most go home with no venison or antlers. After bowhunting from New York to California and from Canada to Alabama, I've concluded that the most common mistake bowhunters make is moving too fast or too much. Over the years, I've

noticed several dozen bowhunters who were sitting in tree stands, stillhunting, glassing, and so on. Almost invariably, it was movement that caught my eye.

Some tree stand sitters seem to be as nervous as kindergartners in Sunday school. And very few stalkers and stillhunters are deliberate enough to avoid being seen by a sharp-eyed deer. For some reason, a deer has great difficulty seeing a human who is still or is moving slowly (unless the person is silhouetted against a contrasting background), yet whitetails and muleys both have an almost supernatural ability to detect quick movements, even at long distances.

Several years ago, I guided a fellow who had never had a good bow shot at a deer, though he'd killed several trophies with a rifle. Late in the afternoon, we saw three does and a beautiful buck with five long points on each antler. The herd was feeding near the edge of some oaks about 150 yards away. Stalking within 30 to 40 yards would have been easy because the wind was in our favor and some car-size boulders offered good cover. I had already taken my buck, so I was carrying only a camera, hoping to get a good photograph of the action. Almost immediately, my pal began scurrying like a scorpion toward the deer, his bow held high like the scorpion's poisonous tail.

"Slow down!" I hissed.

But my warning went unheeded, and my friend continued down the hill at much too fast a pace. He did not bother to stay behind the rocks. Naturally, the deer saw him and bounded into the woods.

"Must have smelled us," my companion said.

Bowhunters have no choice but to move while drawing the bow when the quarry is very close. Experienced hunters lift and shoot their bows only when the game's vision is obscured by tree trunks, brush, and other cover, or when the animal is look-

A surprising yet common malady of unsuccessful bowhunters is hunting where there are very few deer.

ing away. Waiting for the right time to take a shot requires patience, which is a quality all too lacking among many bowhunters.

You can actually be too patient, however. I heard of one Pennsylvania hunter who spent at least a week a year in the same tree stand and never saw a single buck in eight seasons. I was guilty of this kind of inflexibility two years ago when I hunted a high mountain range in Nevada. My hunting party and I suffered through a week of rain and cold wind, and saw very little game. Later, we learned that the deer had migrated several miles to lower elevations where mountain mahogany offered cover from the rain. I suppose we should have explored more when we didn't see as many deer as we'd found during a pre-season scouting trip.

I think many bowmen are unsuccessful because they do very little serious hunting in prime periods. I like to be in my tree stand or in position for glassing a hillside even before the first light of dawn arrives, and I rarely head back to camp until after legal shooting hours are over. Most bowhunters I've met, however, seem to be afraid to travel in the dark. Usually, dawn finds them sleeping, hiking, eating, or driving on the road. You might not be able to stalk a buck you see just before sunset, but you can learn something about his movement pattern.

Deer in some areas travel a great deal during daylight. Two years ago, my friends and I saw many bucks still feeding at 10 and 11 a.m. One member of our party left his tree stand about 9 a.m. one day but, before he could reach his car, which was parked on a nearby dirt road, he met a friend who said it was too early to quit. So my pal returned to his stand and waited a few more minutes. He was sipping from a canteen when a yearling buck walked out of heavy brush and tiptoed directly beneath his tree stand. My friend grabbed his bow and sent an arrow through the buck's back, through its chest, and into the ground. I helped trail the deer to where it lay dead not 40 yards from my friend's car.

One big difference between bowhunters who get their game and those who do not is that most successful archers have a good knowledge of game habits. They usually spend time afield before hunting season to familiarize themselves with game movement patterns, prevailing winds, water sources, feeding areas, and bedding grounds.

A couple of years ago, my friend Chuck Jorgensen arrived just after dawn on opening day at a water hole where he had erected a portable tree stand several weeks earlier. During pre-season scouting trips, he had learned that several bucks drank at the water hole amost every day at mid-morning. Another hunter was already at the water hole, noisily trying to put a climbing-type tree stand in a tree across the pond. The other hunter had started the bow season by hiking about the woods, looking for a good place to put his stand when he stumbled across the water hole.

"Sorry, pal, I've had my stand set up for a long time here," Chuck said.

"Well, it's public land," the other fellow replied.

Fortunately, the man was wrong. It was private property and, after a few more heated words, Chuck persuaded the man to find another place to hunt. Half an hour later, despite all the noise, a buck walked within easy bow range, and my friend had a fresh supply of venison.

There are many reasons bowhunters fail to score. Check this list and see whether you find any of your own mistakes:

- Wearing noisy clothing.
- Spending most of your time in a pickup, hoping to see deer near a road.
- Snapping twigs and crunching leaves as you still-hunt.
- Ignoring the wind direction.
- Failing to change hunting tactics when conditions change (continuing to wait near water holes in wet weather, for instance).
- Failing to practice shooting your bow under realistic hunting conditions.
- Skimming terrain too quickly with binoculars.
- Succumbing to buck fever.

Entire articles could be written about each of these common bowhunting mistakes, but the last one listed deserves more consideration here. Buck fever! If you're a normal, healthy human being, I'm sure you've been afflicted by this psychological problem at least once.

I define buck fever as overexcitement that's so strong it adversely affects hunting ability. It affects each person differently. The only cure I know of is experience, and even that is not foolproof. I used to have a horrible time guessing range accurately until I succeeded in taking several big-game animals with a bow. Then I gained the confidence I needed to settle down and think straight before taking aim.

Some bowhunters get so excited when a buck is nearby that they can't even summon up the strength to draw their bow. I know a fellow who watched in awe as a huge bull elk walked within 14 yards before vanishing into the timber, and *then* he realized that he'd been holding his bow.

Most bowmen seem to have a hard time shooting accurately at a live animal. They might be able to punch tiny bull's-eyes in paper targets all day long but, when a large animal is standing there, buck fever takes hold, and many bowhunters forget all the fine points of shooting.

If buck fever is to blame for your lack of success, I'd suggest making several pre-season scouting trips. Try to get within easy bow range of as many deer as possible. Soon you'll find that you can continue to function when a wary animal is at close range. You'll be able to breathe without gasping and stand without having your kneecaps attack each other. Subject yourself to the close-range presence of game often enough, and soon you'll be more likely to keep your calm during bow season the next time an old buck strolls up to you and looks you in the eye.

Well . . . maybe!

PART 5

THE VENISON

Ground Rules For Great Venison

By Dwight Schuh

A popular advertising slogan could easily be paraphrased to apply to hunting: "Only your butcher knows for sure."

He's the one who sees the results of meat care in the field. Most butchers who handle deer, elk, and other big game can tell meat-care horror stories.

The time-worn advice is to get your animal to a cooler on the day of the kill, which is fine if you're camped next to a road near town. But what if you're five miles back in the boonies with nothing but a packframe and two legs for transportation? To complicate things further, many bow and special rifle seasons take place in August and September during warm, meat-spoiling weather. Under those conditions, you'll need special knowledge to save your game.

Meat spoils in two ways: from the inside out and from the outside in. Of most immediate concern is internal spoilage or "bone sour." Bob Dixon, a butcher at the Oregon State University Meat Science Laboratory, explained that, when an animal dies, its organs stop working but its muscle cells don't. They go right on doing their jobs and, in the process, they create heat. In a live animal, circulating blood performs the same function as water in a car's cooling system: It carries away excess heat to maintain a constant body temperature, about 101° in the case of most big game animals. After an animal dies, the cells keep producing heat but, with a defunct cooling system, body temperature rises to 110° or higher.

Photograph by Bill McRae

After cutting venison into stew-size cubes, dust meat with flour. Brown the chunks in a skillet containing bacon fat.

Photographs by John Weiss

steaks. Slide the dinner platter into an oven pre-heated to 400° until the cheese is melted and just barely beginning to reveal a trace of browning. Serves four.

SAVORY VENISON STEW

2 lbs. venison, cubed
¼ cup bacon drippings
2 onions, cut into chunks
2 carrots, cut into chunks
2 stalks celery, cut into chunks
2 10-oz. cans beef broth
2 cups dry red wine
2 bay leaves, crumbled
salt and pepper to taste

Dust the meat with flour and brown in a skillet containing the bacon fat, then transfer both the meat and remaining bacon drippings to a stew pot. Add the remaining ingredients, cover the pot, and slowly simmer for at least two hours. Serves four.

MEXICALI ROSE

1 lb. deerburger
2 4-oz. cans whole green chilies
2 eggs
½ cup flour
1 tsp. salt
1⅓ cups milk
1 lb. cheddar cheese, grated

In a skillet, brown the deerburger, then pour off any grease. In the bottom of a casserole dish, place a layer of chilies. Place a thin layer of deerburger on top, then a thin layer of the cheese. Now place another layer of chilies, deerburger, and cheese on top of the first. In a bowl, thoroughly blend the eggs, flour, salt, and milk, then pour the mixture over the top

of the layers in the casserole dish. Bake uncovered at 350° for 30 minutes or until a custard-like topping forms. This is a mildly hot dish. Serves four.

STUFFED DEER HEART

1 heart
1½ cups prepared stuffing mix
¼ tsp. thyme
¼ tsp. poultry seasoning
¼ tsp. black pepper
4 tbsps. tomato sauce
1 cup beef bouillon
1 bay leaf, crumbled
½ tsp. garlic powder

Core the inside of the heart, removing the walls forming the chambers, to create a large pocket. Prepare the stuffing mix according to the package instructions. Then knead into the stuffing the thyme, poultry seasoning, and pepper. Pack the cavity of the heart with the stuffing. Place the heart in a deep saucepan. Blend the tomato sauce with the beef bouillon, then stir in the crumbled bay leaf and garlic. Pour this into the saucepan with the heart, cover, and simmer over low heat for two to three hours or until the heart is tender. Serves two.

GEORGIA-STYLE STEAKS

2 lbs. tenderloin steaks or chops, cut thick
1 cup catsup
1 tbsp. salt
1 tbsp. chili powder
2 tbsps. tarragon
1 onion, chopped
⅓ cup A-1 Steak Sauce

In a skillet, sear the steaks in just a bit of cooking oil on medium-high heat. Meanwhile, place the remaining ingredients in a saucepan and over low heat bring the mixture to a boil, stirring continuously. Transfer the steaks to a shallow roasting pan, pour the sauce over the top and bake for 1½ hours at 350°. Serves four.

INDIAN SUMMER ROAST

    1 3-lb. shoulder roast
    ½ tsp. nutmeg
    ¼ cup flour
    1 medium-sized oven cooking bag
    1 cup apple cider
    salt and pepper

Sprinkle the venison roast with a bit of salt and pepper and then rub it into the meat with your fingers. Now sprinkle the nutmeg on top of the roast. Shake the flour inside the oven bag, carefully set the roast inside, then pour the apple cider into the bottom of the bag. Close the bag with a twist-tie and make six inch-long slits on the top, then roast in a 325° oven for two hours. Transfer the roast to a hot plate, slice, then pour the cider gravy over the top. Serves four to six.

STUFFED HOLIDAY VENISON

    2 large round steaks, ¾-inch thick
    ½ tsp. salt
    ¼ tsp. black pepper
    ¼ cup flour
    3 cups bread crumbs
    1 medium onion, chopped
    1 stalk celery, chopped
    1 green pepper, chopped
    ½ cup butter
    ½ tsp. paprika
    bacon strips

Shape the steaks with your meat mallet until they are only one-quarter of an inch thick and rectangular, using a knife to trim them as necessary. Blend the salt, pepper, and flour and very gently pound it into the steaks with your hammer. In a bowl, mix all the remaining ingredients to form a stuffing, using as much water as necessary to make it moist and thoroughly kneading the stuffing with your hands. Lay the steaks end to end on a flat surface. Lay your stuffing in the center of one of the steaks, then spread it out somewhat to the edges. Next, roll the meat from one end to the other. What you'll have is a barrel-shaped affair with the meat on the outside, wrapped around the stuffing on the inside. Tie in several places with cotton string to hold everything together. Set the rolled, stuffed roast in a lightly greased roasting pan and completely cover it with bacon strips. Bake for one hour in an oven preheated to 325°. Serves four.

HUNGARIAN POT ROAST

    1 3-lb. shoulder or neck roast
    1 large clove garlic
    1 onion, chopped
    2 carrots, sliced thick
    ½ tsp. oregano
    ½ tsp. parsley flakes
    1 stalk celery, chopped
    1 cup beef broth or bouillon
    1 tsp. Hungarian paprika
    ½ cup sour cream
    salt and pepper

Slice the garlic clove into thin slivers, then insert them into thin slits made in the roast with a knife. Rub the roast with salt and pepper, then brown the roast in a skillet using a bit of oil (preferably olive oil). Place the roast in a pot and add all the remaining ingredients except the sour cream. Cover the pot and with the burner on low heat slowly simmer the roast for 1½ hours or until it is tender. Transfer the roast to a hot platter and slice, then ladle the vegetables over the meat, using a slotted spoon. Add the sour cream to the broth in the pot, turn the heat up, and

Tie the stuffed venison steaks with cotton string to hold in the delicious filling. Bake for one hour at 325°.

cook until the sauce is steaming, then pour over the slices of pot roast. Serves four.

LIVER WITH ONIONS AND MUSHROOMS

1½ lbs. liver
2 onions, sliced
1 cup mushroom slices
3 tbsps. butter
3 tbsps. cooking oil
¼ cup vermouth
flour

In a skillet, blend the cooking oil and butter, then sauté the onions and mushrooms. Slice the liver, dredge it with flour, then push the onions and mushrooms around the rim of the pan and begin cooking the liver in the middle. When the liver is cooked, transfer it to a hot platter where it will stay warm. Now stir the vermouth into the pan juices and stir with the onions and mushrooms until everything is piping hot. Ladle the sauce over the liver slices and serve. Serves four.

VENISON BOURGUIGNON

2 lbs. venison, cubed
3 onions, cut into chunks
½ cup bacon drippings
2 cups Burgundy
1 large can beef broth
¼ tsp. thyme
¼ tsp. marjoram
1 tsp. salt
½ tsp. black pepper
1 lb. fresh mushrooms

Sauté the onions in a skillet containing the bacon drippings until the onion chunks are brown around the edges, then transfer to your stew pot. In the same skillet, now brown the meat after dusting it with flour. Add the remaining ingredients (except the mushrooms) to the stew pot, cover and simmer on low heat for three hours. Add the mushrooms during the final one-half hour of cooking. Serves four.

STEAKS IN PORT WINE

4 large tenderloin or sirloin tip steaks
6 tbsp. butter
1 tsp. salt
½ tsp. black pepper
1 8-ounce can mushrooms
2 tsps. lemon juice
¼ cup water
¼ cup port wine
4 thick slices French bread

In a high-sided skillet, melt the butter and stir in the salt and pepper. Now, sauté the mushrooms, then transfer them to a platter in your oven to keep them warm. Next, cook the steaks in the butter until they are browned on the outside and pink on the inside, turning them frequently and dribbling just a bit of lemon juice on each. Now transfer the steaks to the platter in your oven to keep them warm. To the drippings in the skillet, add the water and the wine and stir continuously until the mixture comes to a boil, then quickly reduce the heat. Meanwhile, toast the French bread. To serve, arrange the toasts on a hot platter, set a steak on top of each, pour the wine sauce over the tops of the steaks, then sprinkle on the mushrooms. Serves four.

VENISON SAUERBRATEN

1 2-lb. shoulder or neck roast
½ tsp. black pepper
5 whole cloves
2 bay leaves, crushed
1 cup vinegar (or dry red wine)
6 carrots, cut into thick chunks
6 small white onions
2 stalks celery, cut into thick chunks
1 tbsp. sugar
10 gingersnap cookies, crushed

Place the roast in a glass or plastic bowl. Add to the bowl the pepper, cloves, bay leaves, and vinegar (or wine). Then add to the bowl as much cold water as necessary to completely cover the meat. Allow the meat to marinate in your refrigerator for two days, turning it frequently. Remove the meat, pat dry, and brown on all sides in a skillet with a bit of olive oil. Transfer the pot roast to a deep pot, add the vegetables, and two cups of the marinade. Cover and simmer on low heat for 1½ hours. Transfer the meat and vegetables to a hot platter. Then stir the sugar and crushed gingersnaps into the marinade in the pot to make a sauce. After slicing the meat, ladle the sauce over the top and surround with the vegetables. Serves four.

CHICAGO!

1 lb. deerburger
2 tsps. butter
2 8-oz. cans tomato sauce
½ tsp. salt
½ tsp. Worcestershire sauce
1 8-oz. package cream cheese
1 8-oz. carton small-curd cottage cheese
¼ cup sour cream
1 small green pepper, chopped
¼ cup scallions, minced
1 6-oz. package wide noodles

In a skillet, brown the deerburger, then pour off any grease that forms. Stir in the tomato sauce, salt, and Worcestershire sauce, and allow to simmer on very low heat. In a separate bowl, blend the cream cheese, cottage cheese, and sour cream, then stir in the green pepper and just a bit of the scallions. Prepare the noodles according to the package instructions, drain thoroughly, then stir the noodles into the cheese blend. Butter the inside of a casserole dish, then spread the noodle-cheese mixture in the bottom. Spoon the meat and tomato sauce on top of the noodles and sprinkle with the remaining scallions. Bake at 350° for 45 minutes. Serves four generously.

VENISON CIDER STEW

2 lbs. venison, cubed
1 tsp. dried onion flakes
2 tsps. salt
¼ tsp. thyme
¼ tsp. nutmeg
3 potatoes, cut into chunks
4 carrots, cut into chunks
1 apple, chopped
1 cup tart apple cider

Brown the venison in a skillet, sprinkling on the onion, salt, thyme, and nutmeg while stirring continually. Transfer the seasoned meat to a crockpot or stew pot, add the vegetables and apple, then pour the cider over the top. Slow-cook on very low heat for at least three hours. If too much of the liquid begins to evaporate, replenish it with a mixture of one-half cup water blended with one-half cup cider. Serves four.

DEUTSCHSTU

2 lbs. venison, cubed
¼ cup bacon drippings
2 tsps lemon juice
½ tsp. Worcestershire sauce
1 tsp. garlic powder
2 bay leaves, crumbled
¼ tsp. paprika
¼ tsp. allspice
12 small white onions, whole
4 carrots, cut into chunks
3 potatoes, cut into chunks

Flour the venison cubes, then brown in the bacon drippings. Transfer the meat and remaining drippings to your stew pot, sprinkle on the seasonings, then cover with hot water. Slowly simmer for two hours. Then add the vegetables, cover the pot, and simmer one hour longer. Serves four.

VENISON TERIYAKI WITH RICE

2 lbs. tenderloin steak sliced into thin strips
3 tbsps. olive oil
3 tbsps. soy sauce
½ tsp. garlic powder
1 tbsp. lemon juice
1 tbsp. brown sugar
2 cups uncooked Minute Rice
1 4-oz. can mushrooms
1 cup green peppers, sliced into strips
1 cup beef broth or beef bouillon

Add the olive oil and soy sauce to a wok or high-sided skillet, then stir in the garlic, lemon juice, and brown sugar. Heat the wok or skillet on medium-high heat until the liquid begins to steam. Add the tenderloin strips and stir-fry them until they are almost cooked. Meanwhile, prepare the Minute Rice according to the instructions on the package. Now add to the wok or skillet the mushrooms (drained), green peppers, and beef broth. Turn the heat down to medium, cover, and slowly cook until everything is steaming hot. Then ladle over a bed of rice on a preheated platter. Serves four.

The pièce de résistance! This easy-to-make venison teriyaki recipe serves four.

Index